# ZERO TRUST SECURITY

## *BUILDING CYBER RESILIENCE & ROBUST SECURITY POSTURES*

# *4 BOOKS IN 1*

### BOOK 1
*ZERO TRUST SECURITY: A BEGINNER'S GUIDE TO BUILDING CYBER RESILIENCE*

### BOOK 2
*ZERO TRUST SECURITY IN PRACTICE: STRATEGIES FOR BUILDING ROBUST SECURITY POSTURES*

### BOOK 3
*ADVANCED ZERO TRUST ARCHITECTURES: CYBER RESILIENCE AND EXPERT STRATEGIES*

### BOOK 4
*MASTERING ZERO TRUST SECURITY: CYBER RESILIENCE IN A CHANGING LANDSCAPE*

# ROB BOTWRIGHT

*Published by Rob Botwright*
*Library of Congress Cataloging-in-Publication Data*
*ISBN 978-1-83938-528-5*
*Cover design by Rizzo*

*Disclaimer*

*The contents of this book are based on extensive research and the best available historical sources. However, the author and publisher make no claims, promises, or guarantees about the accuracy, completeness, or adequacy of the information contained herein. The information in this book is provided on an "as is" basis, and the author and publisher disclaim any and all liability for any errors, omissions, or inaccuracies in the information or for any actions taken in reliance on such information.*

*The opinions and views expressed in this book are those of the author and do not necessarily reflect the official policy or position of any organization or individual mentioned in this book. Any reference to specific people, places, or events is intended only to provide historical context and is not intended to defame or malign any group, individual, or entity.*

*The information in this book is intended for educational and entertainment purposes only. It is not intended to be a substitute for professional advice or judgment. Readers are encouraged to conduct their own research and to seek professional advice where appropriate.*

*Every effort has been made to obtain necessary permissions and acknowledgments for all images and other copyrighted material used in this book. Any errors or omissions in this regard are unintentional, and the author and publisher will correct them in future editions.*

# TABLE OF CONTENTS – BOOK 1 - ZERO TRUST SECURITY: A BEGINNER'S GUIDE TO BUILDING CYBER RESILIENCE

# TABLE OF CONTENTS – BOOK 2 - ZERO TRUST SECURITY IN PRACTICE: STRATEGIES FOR BUILDING ROBUST SECURITY POSTURES

# TABLE OF CONTENTS – BOOK 3 - ADVANCED ZERO TRUST ARCHITECTURES: CYBER RESILIENCE AND EXPERT STRATEGIES

# TABLE OF CONTENTS – BOOK 4 - MASTERING ZERO TRUST SECURITY: CYBER RESILIENCE IN A CHANGING LANDSCAPE

## Introduction

In an era where digital transformation has reshaped the very fabric of our lives, cybersecurity has become paramount. The interconnected world we live in has opened up unprecedented opportunities, but it has also exposed us to ever-evolving and sophisticated cyber threats. In response to these challenges, a revolutionary approach has emerged— one that has transformed the cybersecurity landscape and set a new standard for safeguarding our digital existence. This approach is known as Zero Trust Security.

Welcome to the world of "Zero Trust Security: Building Cyber Resilience & Robust Security Postures." This comprehensive book bundle delves into the principles, strategies, and advanced architectures that collectively form the foundation of Zero Trust—an approach that challenges conventional notions of cybersecurity and empowers organizations to take control of their digital destiny.

In this four-book collection, we embark on a journey that spans from the fundamentals of Zero Trust to its most advanced and innovative applications. Whether you are new to the concept or a seasoned cybersecurity professional seeking to master the intricacies of Zero Trust, this bundle offers a wealth of knowledge and practical guidance.

**Book 1 - Zero Trust Security: A Beginner's Guide to Building Cyber Resilience**: Our journey begins with the basics, as we introduce the core principles of Zero Trust. We lay the groundwork by questioning the traditional perimeter-based security model and advocating for a "never trust, always verify" approach. Beginners and enthusiasts alike will find

5

this book to be an essential primer for building a solid foundation in cybersecurity.

**Book 2 - Zero Trust Security in Practice: Strategies for Building Robust Security Postures**: Moving beyond theory, our second book brings the concept of Zero Trust to life. Through real-world scenarios and case studies, we demonstrate how organizations can practically implement Zero Trust principles. From network segmentation to identity management, readers will gain insights into the strategies that drive robust security postures.

**Book 3 - Advanced Zero Trust Architectures: Cyber Resilience and Expert Strategies**: As our understanding of Zero Trust deepens, we explore advanced architectures and expert strategies. In this book, we unveil cutting-edge concepts such as micro-segmentation, immutable infrastructure, and decentralized identity. Advanced practitioners will discover innovative approaches to fortifying their cybersecurity defenses against the most formidable threats.

**Book 4 - Mastering Zero Trust Security: Cyber Resilience in a Changing Landscape**: The cybersecurity landscape is in a perpetual state of flux, with new challenges and threats constantly emerging. In our final book, we address the evolving nature of cybersecurity and equip readers with the knowledge and strategies needed to adapt and thrive. By mastering Zero Trust, organizations can navigate this dynamic landscape with confidence and resilience.

This book bundle is not just a compilation of knowledge—it's a roadmap for building cyber resilience and creating robust security postures. Whether you are an individual looking to enhance your cybersecurity expertise or an organization seeking to fortify its defenses, the insights contained within these pages will serve as your guiding light.

We invite you to embark on this transformative journey through the world of Zero Trust Security. As you delve into these books, may you gain the wisdom and tools needed to safeguard your digital assets and embrace the future of cybersecurity with confidence and resilience.

# BOOK 1
## ZERO TRUST SECURITY
## A BEGINNER'S GUIDE TO BUILDING CYBER RESILIENCE

## ROB BOTWRIGHT

## Chapter 1: Understanding the Zero Trust Paradigm

Zero Trust Security is a revolutionary approach to cybersecurity that challenges traditional network security paradigms. It operates on the fundamental principle of "never trust, always verify." In other words, it assumes that threats can come from both inside and outside the network, and trust is never granted by default. Instead, every user, device, and application must continuously authenticate and validate their identity and permissions.

This shift in mindset is crucial in today's ever-evolving threat landscape, where traditional perimeter-based security models are no longer sufficient. With Zero Trust, the focus shifts from securing the perimeter to securing individual assets and resources within the network. This approach recognizes that threats can breach the perimeter, and therefore, security must extend to the data and systems themselves.

Zero Trust encompasses several core concepts that are essential to its implementation. One of the key principles is "least privilege access," which means granting the minimum level of access necessary for a user or device to perform its tasks. This reduces the potential attack surface and limits the damage that can be done if a breach occurs.

Another core concept is "micro-segmentation," which involves dividing the network into smaller, isolated segments or zones. Each segment has its own security policies and controls, making it more difficult for attackers to move laterally within the network if they manage to breach one segment.

Continuous monitoring is also integral to Zero Trust. Rather than relying solely on perimeter defenses, organizations implement real-time monitoring and analysis of network traffic and user behavior. Suspicious activities can be detected and responded to promptly, minimizing the dwell time of threats within the network.

Zero Trust Security also emphasizes the importance of "user and device authentication." This means that all users and devices, whether they are inside or outside the network, must prove their identity and meet security requirements before they are granted access to resources. This verification occurs continuously throughout a user's session, ensuring that trust is never assumed.

Furthermore, "encryption" plays a critical role in Zero Trust. Data should be encrypted both in transit and at rest to protect it from unauthorized access or interception. This ensures that even if an attacker gains access to data, it remains unintelligible without the proper decryption keys.

Adaptive access control is another important concept in Zero Trust. It involves dynamically adjusting access permissions based on changing factors such as user behavior, location, and the security posture of the device. This ensures that access remains appropriate and secure as conditions evolve.

Zero Trust is not a one-size-fits-all approach; it can be tailored to an organization's specific needs and risk profile. Implementation may involve a phased approach, starting with critical assets and gradually expanding to cover the entire network.

In summary, Zero Trust Security challenges traditional security models by assuming that trust should never be granted by default. It encompasses core concepts such as least privilege access, micro-segmentation, continuous monitoring, user and device authentication, encryption, and adaptive access control. This approach is designed to address the dynamic and evolving nature of modern cybersecurity threats, providing a more robust and resilient defense strategy.

The Evolution of Cyber Threats and the Need for Zero Trust

The evolution of cyber threats over the years has been nothing short of remarkable. From early computer viruses and worms to sophisticated nation-state-sponsored attacks, the threat landscape has grown in complexity and scale. This evolution has necessitated a corresponding evolution in cybersecurity strategies, leading to the emergence of Zero Trust Security as a crucial paradigm shift.

In the early days of computing, cybersecurity was primarily concerned with defending against simple viruses and malware. The focus was on perimeter security, with firewalls and antivirus software being the primary defense mechanisms. However, as technology advanced, so did the capabilities of cyber attackers.

The rise of the internet brought about new attack vectors, such as phishing and distributed denial-of-service (DDoS) attacks. Cybercriminals began targeting valuable data and financial assets, leading to data breaches and financial losses on a massive scale.

As organizations moved to the cloud and embraced mobile devices, the attack surface expanded further. Traditional security models struggled to keep pace with the dynamic nature of these environments. Attackers exploited vulnerabilities in software, hardware, and human behavior, highlighting the limitations of perimeter-based defenses.

Nation-state actors and organized cybercrime groups added another layer of complexity to the threat landscape. Their motivations ranged from espionage and political agendas to financial gain and disruption. Advanced persistent threats (APTs) became a significant concern, as they demonstrated the ability to infiltrate and persist within targeted networks for extended periods.

The need for a new approach to cybersecurity became evident. Zero Trust Security emerged as a response to these evolving threats. It recognized that the traditional perimeter-based security model was no longer sufficient, as threats could come from within and outside the network.

Zero Trust advocates for the continuous verification of trust, regardless of a user or device's location. It challenges the assumption that once inside the network, everything is safe. Instead, it enforces the principle of "never trust, always verify."

By adopting Zero Trust principles, organizations can address the challenges posed by modern cyber threats. It requires them to rethink their security architecture, implementing controls such as micro-segmentation, least privilege access, and continuous monitoring. These measures help organizations detect and respond to threats more effectively, reducing the risk of data breaches and cyberattacks.

In a world where cyber threats continue to evolve and grow in sophistication, Zero Trust Security provides a proactive and adaptive approach to cybersecurity. It acknowledges that the need for security goes beyond the perimeter and recognizes that trust should never be assumed. Instead, it must be continuously verified to ensure the protection of critical assets and data.

Advanced Principles of Zero Trust Security

Building on the foundational principles of Zero Trust Security, advanced concepts and strategies are essential for organizations looking to implement a robust and effective Zero Trust model. These advanced principles go beyond the basics and require a deeper understanding of the threat landscape and the intricacies of modern cybersecurity.

One of the advanced principles of Zero Trust is the concept of "threat intelligence integration." Organizations must not only focus on verifying the trustworthiness of users and devices but also stay informed about the latest threats and vulnerabilities. Threat intelligence feeds provide valuable information about emerging threats, enabling organizations to proactively adjust their security policies and controls.

Advanced Zero Trust models also emphasize the importance of "dynamic access controls." In addition to static access policies, dynamic controls consider factors such as user behavior, device health, and real-time threat intelligence. Access permissions can be adjusted in real-time based on changing conditions, ensuring that users have the appropriate level of access at all times.

Furthermore, "zero trust analytics" plays a critical role in advanced Zero Trust Security. This involves the use of machine learning and behavioral analytics to identify anomalous user behavior and potential security threats. By continuously monitoring user activities and network traffic, organizations can detect suspicious activities and respond promptly.

Another advanced concept is "application-level security." In addition to securing the network, Zero Trust extends its focus to securing individual applications and services. This includes implementing strong authentication, encryption, and access controls at the application level to protect critical data and services.

"DevSecOps integration" is also a crucial aspect of advanced Zero Trust. By integrating security practices into the DevOps process, organizations can ensure that security is a priority throughout the development and deployment of applications and services. This reduces the risk of vulnerabilities being introduced during the development lifecycle.

Additionally, "zero trust visibility" is essential in advanced Zero Trust Security. Organizations must have complete visibility into their network, users, and devices to effectively monitor and enforce security policies. Advanced visibility tools provide insights into network traffic, user behavior, and potential threats.

In summary, advanced principles of Zero Trust Security expand on the foundational concepts by incorporating threat intelligence integration, dynamic access controls, zero trust analytics, application-level security, DevSecOps integration, and zero trust visibility. These advanced strategies empower organizations to enhance their cybersecurity posture and respond effectively to the evolving threat landscape.

Zero Trust as a Cornerstone of Cyber Resilience

Cyber resilience is a critical aspect of modern cybersecurity. It refers to an organization's ability to withstand and recover from cyberattacks while maintaining its essential functions and data integrity. In an era of persistent and sophisticated cyber threats, cyber resilience is not just a desirable goal; it is a necessity.

One of the cornerstones of cyber resilience is the adoption of Zero Trust Security principles. Zero Trust aligns closely with the goals of cyber resilience by emphasizing continuous verification of trust, even within the network. It operates on the assumption that threats can breach the perimeter, and trust should never be granted by default.

In a cyber-resilient organization, the implementation of Zero Trust principles is fundamental. The organization recognizes that cyber threats are not a matter of "if" but "when," and it prepares accordingly. It employs advanced authentication mechanisms, such as multi-factor authentication (MFA), to ensure that only authorized users and devices gain access to critical resources.

Micro-segmentation, a key component of Zero Trust, also contributes to cyber resilience. It divides the network into smaller, isolated segments, limiting the lateral movement of attackers. Even if a breach occurs, the attacker's ability to traverse the network is restricted, minimizing the potential damage.

Continuous monitoring is another crucial aspect of both cyber resilience and Zero Trust. By constantly analyzing network traffic and user behavior, organizations can detect and respond to threats in real-time. This proactive approach reduces the time it takes to identify and mitigate cyberattacks, minimizing their impact.

The integration of threat intelligence into the Zero Trust framework enhances cyber resilience further. Threat intelligence feeds provide information about emerging threats and vulnerabilities, enabling organizations to adjust their security posture accordingly. This proactive stance helps prevent attacks and reduces the likelihood of successful breaches.

Furthermore, encryption is a vital component of both cyber resilience and Zero Trust. Encrypting data both in transit and at rest ensures that even if attackers gain access to it, they cannot use it without the encryption keys. This protects sensitive information and maintains data integrity during and after a cyber incident.

In summary, Zero Trust Security serves as a cornerstone of cyber resilience by aligning with its core principles. It emphasizes continuous verification of trust, employs advanced authentication mechanisms, implements micro-segmentation, embraces continuous monitoring, integrates threat intelligence, and utilizes encryption to protect critical assets and data. Together, these elements contribute to an organization's ability to withstand and recover from cyberattacks while maintaining essential functions and data integrity.

Advanced Identity and Device Authentication Techniques

Identity and device authentication are fundamental components of Zero Trust Security, and advanced techniques in these areas are crucial for strengthening security in a Zero Trust environment.

One advanced authentication technique is "biometric authentication," which uses unique physical or behavioral traits, such as fingerprints, facial recognition, or voice patterns, to verify a user's identity. Biometrics provide a high level of security as they are difficult to replicate or steal.

"Behavioral authentication" is another advanced approach that assesses user behavior patterns, such as typing speed and mouse movements, to verify identity. Deviations from the established behavior can trigger alerts, indicating potential unauthorized access.

"Continuous authentication" is a key concept in Zero Trust Security. Instead of a one-time login, continuous authentication monitors the user's activities throughout their session. This technique ensures that trust is continuously verified, and access is revoked if suspicious behavior is detected.

"Device fingerprinting" is a method used to uniquely identify and authenticate devices accessing the network. It creates a profile of each device based on characteristics like hardware, software, and configuration, making it more difficult for unauthorized devices to gain access.

"Smart card authentication" involves the use of physical or virtual smart cards that store cryptographic keys and certificates. Users must present the smart card, along with a PIN or biometric authentication, to access resources, adding an extra layer of security.

In addition to advanced authentication techniques, device authentication is equally crucial in a Zero Trust environment. "Device attestation" verifies the integrity and security posture of a device before granting access. It ensures that devices meet security standards before being allowed onto the network.

"Device trust scores" assign a numerical score to each device based on its security posture. Devices with lower trust scores may have limited access or additional authentication requirements, while trusted devices enjoy broader access.

Advanced identity and device authentication techniques enhance the security posture of a Zero Trust environment, ensuring that only authorized users and devices gain access to critical resources while continuously monitoring for suspicious behavior.

Cutting-edge Network Segmentation Strategies

Network segmentation is a foundational component of Zero Trust Security, and advanced segmentation strategies are essential for creating robust security postures.

One cutting-edge strategy is "application-aware segmentation." Instead of segmenting the network solely based on IP addresses or subnets, this approach takes into account the specific applications and services being accessed. Access policies are defined based on the application's role and importance.

"Software-defined segmentation" leverages software-defined networking (SDN) to dynamically adjust network segments based on changing conditions. It allows for greater flexibility and adaptability in response to evolving threats and requirements.

"User-centric segmentation" focuses on segmenting the network based on user roles and permissions. Users are granted access only to the resources necessary for their tasks, reducing the attack surface and minimizing lateral movement in the network.

"Adaptive segmentation" uses real-time threat intelligence and behavioral analytics to adjust segmentation policies dynamically. If suspicious activity is detected, the segmentation policies can be tightened to isolate potentially compromised areas.

Additionally, "zero trust segmentation" aligns closely with the core principles of Zero Trust Security. It assumes that trust should never be granted by default and enforces strict segmentation policies even within the network. This approach reduces the risk of lateral movement by attackers who manage to breach one segment.

"Micro-segmentation" is a key concept in advanced network segmentation. It involves dividing the network into small, isolated segments, each with its own security policies. This granularity ensures that even if an attacker gains access to one segment, their ability to move laterally is severely restricted.

"Segmentation orchestration" uses automation to manage and enforce segmentation policies dynamically. Policies can be adjusted in real-time based on user behavior, device health, and threat intelligence, ensuring that access remains appropriate and secure.

Advanced network segmentation strategies are crucial for implementing Zero Trust Security effectively. They reduce the attack surface, limit lateral movement, and provide granular control over access to critical resources, strengthening the overall security posture.

Endpoint Security in Advanced Zero Trust Environments

Endpoint security is a critical component of Zero Trust Security, and advanced strategies in this area are essential for protecting organizations in today's dynamic threat landscape.

One advanced approach is "endpoint detection and response (EDR)." EDR solutions continuously monitor endpoints for suspicious activity, providing real-time threat detection and response capabilities. They collect and analyze endpoint data to identify and mitigate threats quickly.

"Next-generation antivirus (NGAV)" represents an evolution beyond traditional antivirus solutions. NGAV solutions use advanced techniques such as behavioral analysis and machine learning to detect and prevent known and unknown threats.

"Zero Trust endpoint security" aligns with the core principles of Zero Trust Security. It ensures that endpoints are never trusted by default and continuously verifies their security posture. Even within the network, trust is never assumed, and access is granted based on strict policies.

To truly understand the principles and significance of Zero Trust Security, it's helpful to explore its historical context. While the term "Zero Trust" itself may be relatively recent, its foundational ideas can be traced back to the early days of computer networking and cybersecurity.

In the early years of computing, security was a relatively simple concept. Networks were often closed, isolated, and largely based on trust. The prevailing belief was that if you could secure the perimeter and keep unauthorized users out, your network and data would be safe. This led to the development of perimeter-based security models, where the network boundary was fortified with firewalls, access controls, and other security measures.

However, as technology evolved and the internet became a ubiquitous part of our lives, this traditional security model faced significant challenges. The emergence of remote work, mobile devices, and cloud computing expanded the attack surface beyond the traditional network perimeter. Attackers began to target vulnerabilities not only in the network but also in applications, devices, and human behavior.

The shift from closed, on-premises networks to open, interconnected ecosystems brought about a paradigm shift in cybersecurity. Traditional perimeter-based defenses struggled to adapt to this new reality. Cyber threats were becoming more sophisticated, often bypassing perimeter security and targeting vulnerabilities within the network.

One pivotal moment in cybersecurity history was the rise of "Advanced Persistent Threats" (APTs). APTs are long-term, targeted cyberattacks carried out by skilled adversaries with specific objectives, such as espionage or data theft. These attacks often involve multiple stages and can persist undetected within a network for extended periods. The traditional perimeter-based security model proved inadequate in defending against APTs, as attackers found ways to infiltrate networks and evade detection.

Around the same time, a series of high-profile data breaches and cyberattacks garnered significant attention. Organizations across various industries fell victim to cybercriminals who exploited vulnerabilities in their security defenses. The costs of these breaches, both in terms of financial losses and damage to reputation, were staggering.

In response to these evolving threats and challenges, a group of cybersecurity experts and thought leaders began to advocate for a new approach to security. This approach rejected the traditional notion of trust and advocated for a paradigm shift. It challenged the assumption that once inside the network, everything could be trusted. Instead, it promoted the idea that trust should never be granted by default and should be continuously verified.

This new approach became known as "Zero Trust Security." The term was coined by John Kindervag, a cybersecurity analyst at Forrester Research, in a 2010 research paper. Zero Trust challenged organizations to reevaluate their security postures and adopt a more proactive and dynamic mindset.

The core tenets of Zero Trust Security are rooted in the belief that threats can come from both inside and outside the network. It advocates for the principle of "never trust, always verify." In practice, this means that every user, device, and application, whether inside or outside the network, must continuously authenticate and validate their identity and permissions.

The shift to Zero Trust requires a departure from the traditional perimeter-centric model of security. Instead, the focus shifts to securing individual assets and resources within the network. Security is applied at the granular level, with strict access controls and policies governing every interaction.

To implement Zero Trust Security effectively, organizations must embrace several key principles. These include "least privilege access," which means granting the minimum level of access necessary for a user or device to perform its tasks. By reducing the attack surface, this principle limits the damage that can be done if a breach occurs.

Micro-segmentation is another fundamental concept in Zero Trust. It involves dividing the network into smaller, isolated segments or zones, each with its own security policies. This approach makes it more difficult for attackers to move laterally within the network if they manage to breach one segment.

Continuous monitoring is integral to Zero Trust. Instead of relying solely on perimeter defenses, organizations implement real-time monitoring and analysis of network traffic and user behavior. Suspicious activities can be detected and responded to promptly, minimizing the dwell time of threats within the network.

Zero Trust Security also emphasizes the importance of "user and device authentication." This means that all users and devices, whether they are inside or outside the network, must prove their identity and meet security requirements before they are granted access to resources. This verification occurs continuously throughout a user's session, ensuring that trust is never assumed.

Furthermore, "encryption" plays a critical role in Zero Trust. Data should be encrypted both in transit and at rest to protect it from unauthorized access or interception. This ensures that even if an attacker gains access to data, it remains unintelligible without the proper decryption keys.

Adaptive access control is another important concept in Zero Trust. It involves dynamically adjusting access permissions based on changing factors such as user behavior, location, and the security posture of the device. This ensures that access remains appropriate and secure as conditions evolve.

Zero Trust is not a one-size-fits-all approach; it can be tailored to an organization's specific needs and risk profile. Implementation may involve a phased approach, starting with critical assets and gradually expanding to cover the entire network.

In summary, the historical context of Zero Trust Security is a story of evolution in response to a changing threat landscape. It acknowledges the limitations of traditional perimeter-based security models and advocates for a paradigm shift that prioritizes continuous verification of trust. Zero Trust Security challenges organizations to rethink their security postures, adopt granular access controls, and embrace a proactive and dynamic approach to cybersecurity.

## Chapter 2: The Evolution of Cybersecurity

Before delving deeper into the principles and practices of Zero Trust Security, it's essential to explore the landscape of cybersecurity that existed before the emergence of the Zero Trust paradigm. These pre-Zero Trust cybersecurity models, while foundational in their own right, laid the groundwork for the evolution of security practices and the need for a more proactive and dynamic approach.

In the early days of computer networking, cybersecurity was a relatively nascent field, and the threats faced by organizations were vastly different from those encountered today. Traditional security models were grounded in the belief that a well-fortified network perimeter could keep adversaries at bay. This approach came to be known as "perimeter-based security."

Perimeter-based security operated on the premise that once an organization's network perimeter was secure, the internal environment could be trusted. Access controls and security measures were primarily focused on defending the perimeter from external threats. Firewalls, intrusion detection systems, and access controls were the primary tools of the trade.

One of the fundamental concepts within perimeter-based security was the notion of a "trusted network." Organizations considered their internal networks as safe zones where trust was implicitly granted to all devices and users inside the perimeter. While this model worked reasonably well in simpler and less interconnected environments, it had inherent limitations.

As the internet expanded, remote work became more common, and organizations embraced cloud computing, the concept of a well-defined network perimeter began to erode. Remote employees needed access to corporate resources, and cloud services extended beyond the traditional boundaries of an organization's data center. This shift introduced new challenges to the established security model.

Cyber adversaries were quick to exploit these evolving trends. They realized that rather than attempting to breach the fortified perimeter, they could target vulnerabilities within the network itself. Spear-phishing attacks, zero-day exploits, and targeted malware became prevalent tools in the attacker's arsenal. These threats often bypassed perimeter defenses, compromising internal systems and data.

The rise of Advanced Persistent Threats (APTs) represented a significant turning point in the cybersecurity landscape. APTs are sophisticated and well-funded attacks carried out by nation-state actors or organized cybercrime groups. They operate stealthily, often infiltrating networks and maintaining a persistent presence for extended periods, evading detection by traditional security measures.

The limitations of perimeter-based security became evident as organizations faced increasingly sophisticated and persistent threats. Cybersecurity incidents, data breaches, and the associated financial and reputational costs highlighted the need for a new security paradigm. It was in this evolving landscape that the concept of Zero Trust Security began to take root.

Zero Trust challenged the traditional assumption of trust within the network and advocated for a proactive and continuous verification of trust, regardless of the user's location or the device they were using. This marked a significant departure from the traditional model, which granted implicit trust to devices and users within the network perimeter.

As organizations recognized the limitations of the existing security paradigm, they started to embrace the principles of Zero Trust Security. They understood that trust could no longer be assumed, and security measures needed to adapt to the evolving threat landscape. Zero Trust became a guiding philosophy, emphasizing the importance of continuous authentication, strict access controls, and real-time monitoring.

The journey from perimeter-based security to Zero Trust was not without challenges. It required a shift in mindset, a reevaluation of existing security practices, and a willingness to adopt new technologies and strategies. However, the benefits of enhanced security, reduced attack surface, and improved threat detection made the transition worthwhile.

In summary, the landscape of cybersecurity before the emergence of Zero Trust Security was characterized by perimeter-based models that assumed trust within the network. These models faced significant challenges as technology evolved, threats became more sophisticated, and the network perimeter eroded. The rise of Advanced Persistent Threats (APTs) highlighted the shortcomings of traditional security paradigms. Zero Trust Security emerged as a response to these challenges, advocating for continuous verification of trust, adaptive access controls, and a proactive approach to cybersecurity. It marked a fundamental shift in how organizations approached security in an ever-changing threat landscape.

In the dynamic and interconnected world of today, the landscape of cybersecurity has become increasingly complex and challenging. As we navigate this digital age, it's essential to understand the modern cybersecurity challenges that individuals, organizations, and society as a whole are facing.

One of the foremost challenges in modern cybersecurity is the rapid evolution of cyber threats. Cybercriminals and malicious actors continually adapt and refine their tactics, techniques, and procedures. They exploit vulnerabilities in software, hardware, and human behavior, making it challenging for cybersecurity professionals to keep pace.

The sophistication of cyber threats has reached unprecedented levels. Advanced Persistent Threats (APTs), which are typically state-sponsored or organized cybercrime group attacks, can remain undetected within a network for extended periods, conducting espionage, data theft, and sabotage. These APTs are often well-funded and possess advanced capabilities, posing a severe risk to organizations and nations.

Another critical challenge is the expanding attack surface. The proliferation of internet-connected devices and the adoption of emerging technologies like the Internet of Things (IoT) have significantly increased the attack surface. Each connected device represents a potential entry point for cyber attackers, demanding robust security measures.

Cloud computing, while offering numerous benefits, introduces its own set of cybersecurity challenges. Organizations store sensitive data and run critical applications in the cloud, raising concerns about data security, compliance, and access control. Misconfigurations and inadequate security practices can lead to data breaches and service interruptions.

The trend toward remote work, accelerated by global events, has further complicated cybersecurity. Remote employees connect to corporate networks from various locations and devices, making it challenging to enforce consistent security policies and monitor network traffic effectively. Cyber attackers exploit these remote work scenarios, targeting remote access solutions and vulnerable endpoints.

Phishing attacks have evolved from simple email scams to highly targeted and convincing campaigns. Cybercriminals use social engineering tactics to deceive individuals and gain access to sensitive information. Phishing attacks are often the initial entry point for more extensive cyberattacks, emphasizing the importance of user awareness and education.

Ransomware attacks have become a pervasive and lucrative threat. Attackers encrypt an organization's data and demand a ransom for its release. The financial incentives behind ransomware attacks have led to the development of increasingly sophisticated ransomware strains, posing a severe financial and operational threat to businesses.

Data privacy and regulatory compliance have also become significant concerns. Governments worldwide have enacted stringent data protection regulations, such as the European Union's General Data Protection Regulation (GDPR) and the California Consumer Privacy Act (CCPA). Organizations must navigate complex compliance requirements while safeguarding sensitive customer and employee data.

Supply chain attacks have gained prominence as attackers target the software and hardware supply chain. Malicious actors compromise trusted vendors or insert malware into software updates, potentially impacting a wide range of organizations. Such attacks underscore the importance of vetting and securing the entire supply chain.

Cybersecurity skills shortages pose a persistent challenge. The demand for cybersecurity professionals has outpaced the supply of skilled experts. Organizations struggle to find and retain cybersecurity talent, leading to resource constraints in managing and mitigating cyber risks.

The inherent vulnerabilities in emerging technologies like artificial intelligence (AI) and the lack of comprehensive cybersecurity frameworks for these technologies present novel challenges. Adversarial machine learning techniques, for example, can undermine the reliability of AI systems, impacting critical decision-making processes.

The sheer volume of security alerts and data generated by modern cybersecurity tools has overwhelmed security teams. Security Information and Event Management (SIEM) systems, threat intelligence feeds, and automated detection tools produce massive amounts of data, often resulting in alert fatigue and the potential for critical alerts to be overlooked.

In summary, modern cybersecurity faces a myriad of challenges driven by the rapid evolution of cyber threats, the expanding attack surface, the adoption of cloud computing and remote work, the sophistication of phishing and ransomware attacks, data privacy concerns, supply chain vulnerabilities, and a shortage of cybersecurity skills. Addressing these challenges requires a multifaceted approach that combines technological solutions, user education, regulatory compliance, and a proactive cybersecurity mindset.

**Chapter 3: Key Principles of Zero Trust Security**

The first principle of Zero Trust Security is "Verify Explicitly," and it serves as the foundation for the entire Zero Trust model. In traditional security models, there was often an implicit assumption that once a user or device gained access to the network, they could be trusted. This implicit trust extended to internal users and devices, creating a vulnerable environment where threats could go undetected.

The "Verify Explicitly" principle challenges this assumption and introduces a critical mindset shift. It advocates for the idea that trust should never be assumed, and access to resources should be granted only after thorough verification. This verification process occurs continuously and is based on multiple factors, including user identity, device health, location, and the security posture of the application or resource being accessed.

In a Zero Trust environment, users and devices are required to prove their identity and meet specific security criteria before they are granted access. This verification happens not only when initially logging in but continuously throughout the user's session. This means that trust is never taken for granted, and access permissions are constantly reevaluated.

User authentication plays a central role in the "Verify Explicitly" principle. Organizations implement strong authentication mechanisms, such as multi-factor authentication (MFA), to ensure that users are who they claim to be. MFA requires users to provide multiple forms of verification, such as a password and a one-time code sent to their mobile device, adding an extra layer of security.

Device authentication is equally important. Devices seeking access to the network or resources must be verified to ensure they meet security standards. This verification process involves checking the device's security configurations, software updates, and compliance with organizational security policies.

Location-based verification is another aspect of "Verify Explicitly." By tracking the physical location of users and devices, organizations can make access decisions based on geographic context. For example, if a user typically accesses resources from a corporate office but suddenly attempts access from a foreign country, this change in location may trigger additional security checks.

Furthermore, the security posture of the application or resource being accessed is considered in the verification process. If an application has known vulnerabilities or is experiencing a security incident, access may be restricted until the issues are resolved. This ensures that only secure and trusted resources are accessible.

Continuous monitoring is a crucial component of "Verify Explicitly." Organizations continuously monitor user behavior and network traffic for anomalies and suspicious activities. Any deviations from normal behavior can trigger alerts, prompting further investigation and potential access revocation.

The "Verify Explicitly" principle is about maintaining a proactive and vigilant approach to security. It eliminates the assumption of trust and replaces it with a continuous verification process that adapts to changing conditions. This approach significantly reduces the attack surface by ensuring that only authorized users and devices gain access to critical resources.

By implementing "Verify Explicitly," organizations can enhance their security posture, minimize the risk of unauthorized access, and detect and respond to security threats more effectively. This principle lays the groundwork for the other Zero Trust principles, reinforcing the notion that trust should be earned and verified at every step of the user's journey within the network.

The second core principle of Zero Trust Security is "Least Privilege Access," which builds upon the foundation of "Verify Explicitly." In traditional security models, users often had broad access privileges within a network or system, granting them unnecessary permissions to sensitive resources. This practice created a larger attack surface and increased the potential impact of security breaches.

The "Least Privilege Access" principle advocates for a more restrictive approach to access control. It posits that users and devices should be granted the minimum level of access required to perform their tasks, and no more. This concept aligns closely with the idea of limiting trust and minimizing potential exposure to threats. Implementing "Least Privilege Access" begins with a thorough assessment of users' and devices' roles and responsibilities within the organization. Understanding what specific tasks and functions each user or device requires is essential for determining the appropriate level of access.

Access controls are then implemented to enforce the principle. Access control policies specify who is allowed to access specific resources and what actions they can perform once they gain access. These policies are enforced consistently across the network and are based on the principle of "need to know" and "need to do."

User roles and permissions play a critical role in "Least Privilege Access." Users are assigned roles that align with their job functions, and these roles are associated with specific access permissions. For example, a human resources manager may have access to employee records but not financial data, while a financial analyst may have access to financial data but not HR records.

Device-level access controls are equally important. Devices are categorized based on their security posture and compliance with organizational policies. Devices that meet security standards are granted access, while those that do not are restricted until they meet the criteria.

Regular access reviews and audits are essential for maintaining the "Least Privilege Access" principle. Organizations periodically review and validate user and device access permissions to ensure they remain aligned with roles and responsibilities. This process helps identify and correct any overprivileged accounts.

Privileged access management (PAM) is a critical component of "Least Privilege Access." Privileged accounts, such as administrator accounts, have the potential to cause significant damage if compromised. PAM solutions are used to manage, monitor, and secure privileged access, ensuring that only authorized individuals can use these accounts and only when necessary.

"Least Privilege Access" extends to applications and services as well. Access to applications and data should be granted based on the user's role and the specific requirements of their job. Unnecessary access to sensitive data should be restricted, reducing the risk of data breaches.

One of the key benefits of "Least Privilege Access" is its ability to limit the potential damage caused by security incidents. If a user account is compromised, the attacker's access is restricted to the minimum privileges associated with that account, minimizing the harm they can inflict.

Furthermore, "Least Privilege Access" supports the principle of "Zero Trust Micro-Segmentation." Micro-segmentation involves dividing the network into small, isolated segments, each with its own access controls. By enforcing the principle of least privilege within each segment, lateral movement by attackers is significantly restricted.

User education and awareness are essential for the successful implementation of "Least Privilege Access." Users need to understand the importance of restricted access and why it is crucial for security. Training programs can help users recognize the risks associated with overprivileged accounts and the benefits of adhering to the principle.

In summary, "Least Privilege Access" is a fundamental principle of Zero Trust Security that focuses on granting users and devices the minimum level of access required to perform their tasks. Access controls, user roles, device categorization, access reviews, and privileged access management are key components of this principle. By implementing "Least Privilege Access," organizations can reduce their attack surface, limit the potential impact of security incidents, and enhance overall security posture. This principle reinforces the idea that trust should be earned and access should be restricted to what is necessary, aligning with the core principles of Zero Trust Security.

## Chapter 4: Identifying and Authenticating Users and Devices

Multi-Factor Authentication (MFA) is a vital component of modern cybersecurity, and it aligns closely with the principles of Zero Trust Security we've been exploring. MFA is a security practice that goes beyond traditional username and password authentication. Instead, it requires users to provide multiple forms of verification before granting access to a system or resource. This approach significantly enhances security by adding layers of protection and ensuring that users are who they claim to be.

The core idea behind MFA is to ensure that access is granted only to individuals who can prove their identity through multiple means. In a typical MFA scenario, users are required to provide something they know (such as a password), something they have (such as a mobile device or smart card), and something they are (such as a fingerprint or facial recognition).

By requiring users to provide multiple forms of verification, MFA adds a significant barrier to unauthorized access. Even if an attacker obtains a user's password, they would still need the additional factors, which are typically more challenging to compromise.

One of the most common forms of MFA is the use of one-time codes sent to a user's mobile device. After entering their password, the user receives a code on their mobile device that they must enter to complete the authentication process. This ensures that the user possesses something they have (their mobile device) in addition to something they know (their password).

Smart cards and hardware tokens are another form of MFA. Users insert a smart card into a card reader or use a hardware token to generate a time-based code. This adds a layer of physical security to the authentication process, as the user must possess the physical card or token.

Biometric authentication is becoming increasingly prevalent in MFA. This involves using unique biological traits, such as fingerprints, facial recognition, or retinal scans, to verify a user's identity. Biometrics provide a strong "something you are" factor, as these traits are difficult to replicate.

MFA can be applied in various contexts, from accessing corporate networks and applications to online banking and email accounts. It plays a crucial role in protecting sensitive data and resources.

For example, consider a scenario where an employee is attempting to access their company's cloud-based file storage system from a remote location. To log in, the employee enters their username and password. However, the MFA system is also set up to send a one-time code to the employee's mobile device. The employee must enter this code to complete the login process.

Even if an attacker somehow acquires the employee's password, they would still need access to the employee's mobile device to receive the one-time code. Without the second factor (the mobile device), the authentication process remains incomplete, thwarting the attacker's attempts.

MFA is not only about enhancing security but also about adapting to the dynamic nature of the modern workforce. With the rise of remote work and the use of various devices to access corporate resources, traditional password-based authentication has become increasingly vulnerable. Users may access systems from unsecured networks or devices, making them susceptible to password theft or interception.

MFA provides an extra layer of security in these scenarios. Even if a user logs in from an unfamiliar location or device, MFA ensures that they must still provide the additional factors for verification. This mitigates the risks associated with remote and mobile access.

The adoption of MFA has been driven by the realization that passwords alone are no longer sufficient to protect sensitive data and systems. Passwords can be weak, easily forgotten, or stolen through various means. Cybercriminals frequently employ techniques like phishing and credential stuffing to compromise accounts protected by passwords alone.

MFA adds a level of complexity that makes it significantly harder for attackers to gain unauthorized access. Even if an attacker manages to steal a user's password through phishing or other means, they would still need the second or third factor of authentication to succeed.

MFA is also crucial for safeguarding critical infrastructure and systems. In industries such as healthcare, finance, and utilities, where the consequences of a security breach can be severe, MFA is often mandated to protect access to sensitive systems and data.

To implement MFA effectively, organizations must consider user experience and usability. While the additional security is paramount, it's essential to strike a balance between security and convenience. Users should be able to complete the authentication process with relative ease, and the MFA methods chosen should be user-friendly.

In summary, Multi-Factor Authentication (MFA) is a pivotal cybersecurity practice that aligns with the principles of Zero Trust Security. MFA requires users to provide multiple forms of verification before granting access, significantly enhancing security. It adds layers of protection beyond traditional passwords and addresses the vulnerabilities associated with password-based authentication. MFA is adaptable to various contexts, from remote work scenarios to critical infrastructure protection, and plays a vital role in safeguarding sensitive data and resources in the modern cybersecurity landscape.

Device identity verification is a critical aspect of modern cybersecurity, aligning closely with the principles of Zero Trust Security. In a connected world where devices play a central role in our personal and professional lives, ensuring the trustworthiness of these devices is paramount. Device identity verification is the process of confirming that a device attempting to access a network or resource is legitimate and meets the security standards set by an organization.

The concept of device identity verification revolves around the principle that trust should never be assumed, even for devices within an organization's network. Traditionally, network security often relied on trust boundaries, where devices within the network perimeter were assumed to be safe, and those outside were considered untrusted. However, this trust model no longer aligns with the dynamic and interconnected nature of modern networks.

Device identity verification begins with the process of onboarding a device into the network. This process involves registering the device and establishing its identity within the organization's infrastructure. During onboarding, the device's attributes, such as hardware characteristics, unique identifiers, and security configurations, are recorded.

One common approach to device identity verification is the use of digital certificates. Each device is issued a unique digital certificate that serves as a form of digital identification. These certificates are signed by a trusted Certificate Authority (CA) and include information about the device, its owner, and the CA that issued the certificate.

When the device attempts to connect to the network, its certificate is presented for verification.

Another method is the use of hardware-based identifiers, such as MAC (Media Access Control) addresses or unique hardware tokens. These identifiers are associated with specific devices and can be used to verify a device's identity. However, it's important to note that MAC addresses can be spoofed, so additional security measures are often necessary.

Device identity verification also encompasses the concept of device health and compliance. It ensures that devices meet security standards and policies set by the organization. This includes verifying that devices have up-to-date operating systems, security patches, and antivirus software.

Continuous monitoring plays a crucial role in device identity verification. Organizations employ tools and solutions that continuously assess the security posture of devices connected to the network. Any deviations from security standards or suspicious behavior can trigger alerts and actions to remediate the issue.

In a Zero Trust Security model, device identity verification is integrated into the overall security posture. Trust is never assumed based on the device's location within the network. Instead, devices are required to prove their identity and security compliance every time they access network resources.

For example, consider an employee who brings their laptop to the office. In a traditional trust-based model, once the laptop is inside the corporate network, it is often granted broad access to resources. However, in a Zero Trust model, the laptop must undergo device identity verification each time it connects to the network, regardless of its physical location.

Device identity verification is particularly critical in scenarios where remote and mobile access is prevalent. As employees use various devices to connect to corporate networks from different locations, verifying the identity and security of these devices becomes paramount. Any compromised or untrusted device could potentially serve as an entry point for attackers.

Additionally, device identity verification supports the principle of "Least Privilege Access." Even if a device is deemed trustworthy, it should only be granted access to the specific resources and data required for its legitimate purpose. This principle minimizes the potential damage that a compromised device can inflict.

Furthermore, device identity verification aligns with the concept of "Zero Trust Micro-Segmentation." By verifying the identity and security of devices within isolated network segments, organizations can limit lateral movement by attackers if one segment is compromised.

In summary, device identity verification is a fundamental component of modern cybersecurity, particularly in a Zero Trust Security model. It ensures that devices attempting to access network resources are legitimate, meet security standards, and are continuously monitored for compliance. This approach eliminates the assumption of trust based on location within the network and supports the principles of least privilege access and micro-segmentation. In an increasingly interconnected and dynamic digital landscape, device identity verification is essential for safeguarding sensitive data and resources.

## Chapter 5: Micro-Segmentation: Securing the Perimeter and Beyond

Micro-segmentation is a powerful cybersecurity strategy that goes hand in hand with the principles of Zero Trust Security we've been exploring. At its core, micro-segmentation is a network security technique that divides an organization's network into small, isolated segments, or "micro-segments," with the goal of enhancing security, limiting lateral movement by attackers, and minimizing the attack surface. To truly understand micro-segmentation, let's break down its key components and how it fits into the broader cybersecurity landscape.

The term "segmentation" itself implies the act of dividing something into parts, and in the context of network security, this division has a specific purpose: to improve the security posture of the network. Traditionally, network segmentation was more coarse-grained, with networks typically divided into a few broad segments based on factors like department or physical location. This approach did provide some level of isolation, but it often relied on the assumption that trust could be granted within these broader segments.

Micro-segmentation takes segmentation to a granular level, breaking down the network into much smaller and more specific segments. Instead of having a single large segment for a department, an organization might have multiple micro-segments for individual teams or even applications. This fine-grained approach means that trust is never assumed within these segments, aligning perfectly with the core tenets of Zero Trust Security.

To implement micro-segmentation effectively, organizations typically use network security tools and technologies. These tools allow them to define specific policies and rules that govern communication within and between micro-segments. These rules are often based on factors such as user identity, device health, and the sensitivity of the data or applications being accessed.

Imagine a scenario where an organization's IT infrastructure consists of multiple departments, each with its own set of applications and data. In a traditional network, these departments might be separated into broad segments. However, in a micro-segmentation model, each application or data repository could have its own micro-segment, isolated from the others. Access to these micro-segments is controlled by strict policies that require verification, even within the network.

This level of isolation provides several benefits. First and foremost, it limits the lateral movement of attackers. In a traditional network, if an attacker gains access to one segment, they often have a pathway to move laterally to other parts of the network. With micro-segmentation, the attacker's movement is restricted to the specific micro-segment they've compromised, reducing the potential impact of a breach.

Micro-segmentation also enhances overall network security by minimizing the attack surface. Each micro-segment has its own set of access controls and policies, ensuring that only authorized users and devices can communicate with the resources within that segment. This limits the exposure of sensitive data and applications to potential threats.

Furthermore, micro-segmentation aligns well with the "Least Privilege Access" principle we discussed earlier. Within each micro-segment, access is granted only to what is necessary for the specific task or function associated with that segment. This principle helps organizations reduce the risk of overprivileged accounts and restricts access to the bare minimum required.

In the context of Zero Trust Security, micro-segmentation reinforces the idea that trust should be earned and verified at every step. Even if a user or device is within the network, it must adhere to the policies and controls of the micro-segment it's attempting to access. This approach eliminates the assumption of trust based on network location and ensures a proactive and vigilant security posture.

Implementing micro-segmentation does require careful planning and ongoing management. Organizations must define clear policies for each micro-segment, specifying who can access what and under what conditions. These policies should be regularly reviewed and updated to align with changing security requirements.

Additionally, organizations should invest in network security solutions that support micro-segmentation, such as Next-Generation Firewalls (NGFWs) and Software-Defined Networking (SDN) technologies. These tools provide the necessary controls to enforce the policies and rules defined for each micro-segment.

In summary, micro-segmentation is a network security strategy that divides an organization's network into small, isolated segments to enhance security, limit lateral movement by attackers, and minimize the attack surface. It aligns perfectly with the principles of Zero Trust Security by ensuring that trust is never assumed based on network location. Micro-segmentation provides numerous benefits, including improved security posture, reduced attack surface, and alignment with the principle of least privilege access. While it requires careful planning and management, it is a powerful tool for safeguarding sensitive data and resources in today's dynamic cybersecurity landscape.

Now that we have a solid understanding of what micro-segmentation is and its alignment with Zero Trust Security principles, let's delve into the practical aspects of implementing micro-segmentation and the tangible benefits it brings to organizations.

The implementation of micro-segmentation begins with careful planning and a deep understanding of an organization's network architecture. To start, an organization needs to identify its critical assets, sensitive data, and the applications that support its business processes. These assets and applications serve as the building blocks for creating micro-segments.

Once the assets and applications are identified, the next step is to define the policies and rules that govern communication within and between micro-segments. These policies are the heart of micro-segmentation, specifying who can access what resources and under what conditions. Policies are typically based on factors such as user identity, device health, and the sensitivity of the data or applications being accessed.

A key consideration during the implementation phase is how micro-segmentation integrates with existing network infrastructure. Organizations may need to make adjustments to their network architecture to accommodate micro-segmentation effectively. This may involve deploying next-generation firewalls (NGFWs), software-defined networking (SDN) technologies, or micro-segmentation-specific solutions.

To illustrate the implementation process, let's consider a hypothetical scenario. Imagine a healthcare organization that wants to implement micro-segmentation to enhance the security of its patient data. The first step is to identify the patient data repository as a critical asset. This asset becomes the focus of a micro-segment.

Next, policies are defined for the patient data micro-segment. Access to this segment is restricted to authorized healthcare providers who have undergone identity verification. Additionally, devices accessing this segment must meet specific security criteria, such as having up-to-date antivirus software.

Communication between the patient data micro-segment and other parts of the network is governed by strict rules. Only necessary communication paths are allowed, and all traffic is monitored and logged for security purposes. Any deviation from the established policies triggers alerts for further investigation.

The benefits of implementing micro-segmentation are numerous and far-reaching. One of the most significant advantages is enhanced security. By dividing the network into isolated micro-segments, organizations limit the lateral movement of attackers. Even if an attacker gains access to one micro-segment, they are unable to move freely throughout the network, reducing the potential impact of a breach.

Micro-segmentation also helps organizations minimize their attack surface. Each micro-segment has its own set of access controls, ensuring that only authorized users and devices can communicate with the resources within that segment. This isolation reduces the exposure of sensitive data and applications to potential threats.

Moreover, micro-segmentation aligns perfectly with the "Least Privilege Access" principle we discussed earlier. Within each micro-segment, access is granted only to what is necessary for the specific task or function associated with that segment. This approach helps organizations reduce the risk of overprivileged accounts and restricts access to the bare minimum required.

In a Zero Trust Security model, micro-segmentation reinforces the idea that trust should be earned and verified at every step. Even if a user or device is within the network, it must adhere to the policies and controls of the micro-segment it's attempting to access. This proactive approach ensures that trust is never assumed based on network location.

Another notable benefit of micro-segmentation is its support for compliance requirements. Many industries, such as healthcare and finance, have stringent data protection regulations that demand robust security measures. Micro-segmentation provides a structured and demonstrable approach to securing sensitive data and achieving compliance.

To continue with our healthcare example, implementing micro-segmentation for patient data not only enhances security but also helps the organization meet regulatory requirements, such as the Health Insurance Portability and Accountability Act (HIPAA). The isolation and strict access controls of the patient data micro-segment align with HIPAA's data protection standards.

Moreover, micro-segmentation can aid in threat detection and response. Because it enforces strict communication rules and monitors all traffic, any suspicious activity or deviation from established policies is quickly detected. This early detection enables organizations to respond to security incidents promptly and effectively.

The benefits of micro-segmentation extend to operational efficiency. While it may seem counterintuitive, micro-segmentation can simplify network management by providing a clear structure for access controls and policies. It reduces the complexity of traditional firewall rules that attempt to manage access at a broader level.

Additionally, the isolation provided by micro-segmentation can improve network performance. By segmenting traffic and restricting communication paths, organizations can reduce network congestion and ensure that critical applications have the bandwidth they need.

In summary, the implementation of micro-segmentation involves careful planning, policy definition, and integration with existing network infrastructure. The benefits of micro-segmentation include enhanced security, reduced attack surface, alignment with the principle of least privilege access, support for compliance requirements, improved threat detection and response, and potential operational efficiency gains. Micro-segmentation is a powerful strategy that enhances an organization's cybersecurity posture while aligning seamlessly with the principles of Zero Trust Security.

## Chapter 6: Monitoring and Analytics in a Zero Trust Environment

Real-time monitoring tools are essential components of modern cybersecurity, providing organizations with the capability to detect and respond to security threats as they happen. These tools are designed to continuously analyze network traffic, system activity, and user behavior in real-time, allowing security teams to identify anomalies, suspicious activities, and potential security incidents promptly.

One of the key features of real-time monitoring tools is their ability to provide instant visibility into an organization's network and systems. They collect and analyze data from various sources, such as network logs, endpoint devices, firewalls, and intrusion detection systems, and present this information in a centralized dashboard. This dashboard offers security teams a real-time view of the organization's security posture.

The primary goal of real-time monitoring is to identify and respond to security incidents as they occur. Security Incidents can range from unauthorized access attempts and malware infections to data breaches and denial-of-service attacks. By continuously monitoring network and system activity, real-time monitoring tools can detect these incidents in their early stages, enabling rapid response and mitigation.

For example, if a real-time monitoring tool detects repeated failed login attempts on a user's account, it can trigger an alert to the security team. This alert prompts the team to investigate the potential security breach, take corrective actions, and prevent further unauthorized access.

Real-time monitoring tools employ a variety of detection methods and algorithms to identify security threats. These methods include signature-based detection, anomaly detection, and behavior analysis. Signature-based detection involves comparing incoming data and traffic patterns to known attack signatures, while anomaly detection focuses on identifying deviations from normal behavior. Behavior analysis assesses user and device behavior over time to detect suspicious activities.

Machine learning and artificial intelligence (AI) are increasingly being integrated into real-time monitoring tools to enhance their detection capabilities. These technologies enable the tools to identify complex and evolving threats that may go unnoticed by traditional methods.

One of the key advantages of real-time monitoring tools is their ability to provide immediate alerts and notifications to security teams. When a potential security incident is detected, the tool generates an alert, which can be sent via email, SMS, or other communication channels to notify security personnel. This rapid notification allows security teams to respond promptly and minimize the impact of security incidents.

Furthermore, real-time monitoring tools often include automated response capabilities. In addition to alerting security teams, these tools can take predefined actions to mitigate security threats. For example, if a real-time monitoring tool detects a distributed denial-of-service (DDoS) attack, it can automatically initiate traffic filtering to block malicious traffic and keep network services operational.

Continuous monitoring is essential for organizations to stay ahead of emerging threats. Cyberattackers are constantly evolving their tactics, techniques, and procedures, making it crucial for security teams to have real-time visibility into their network and systems. Continuous monitoring allows organizations to detect and respond to zero-day vulnerabilities and previously unknown threats quickly.

Real-time monitoring tools are versatile and can be applied to various areas of cybersecurity, including network security, endpoint security, and cloud security. In network security, these tools monitor network traffic for signs of intrusion, malware, or data exfiltration. In endpoint security, they track the behavior of individual devices, ensuring that they are not compromised or exhibiting malicious activity. In cloud security, real-time monitoring tools help organizations detect unauthorized access and data exposure in cloud environments.

Moreover, real-time monitoring tools contribute to compliance efforts. Many regulatory frameworks and industry standards require organizations to have monitoring and alerting mechanisms in place to detect and respond to security incidents. Real-time monitoring tools provide organizations with the means to meet these compliance requirements and demonstrate their commitment to security.

To illustrate the significance of real-time monitoring, consider a financial institution that relies on real-time monitoring tools to protect its customers' financial data. These tools continuously analyze network traffic, looking for any signs of suspicious activity or attempts to access sensitive customer information. If a tool detects a potential breach, it immediately alerts the institution's security team, allowing them to take immediate action to safeguard customer data and investigate the incident.

In summary, real-time monitoring tools are indispensable components of modern cybersecurity, offering organizations real-time visibility into network and system activity. These tools detect security threats as they happen, enabling rapid response and mitigation. They employ various detection methods, including signature-based detection, anomaly detection, and behavior analysis, often enhanced by machine learning and AI. Real-time monitoring tools provide immediate alerts and automated response capabilities, contributing to a proactive cybersecurity posture. They are versatile and applicable to network, endpoint, and cloud security, making them essential for organizations looking to protect their sensitive data and systems in an ever-evolving threat landscape.

Behavioral analytics is a cutting-edge approach to threat detection in the realm of cybersecurity, and it plays a crucial role in the continuous battle against evolving cyber threats. This innovative technique goes beyond traditional signature-based methods by focusing on the behavior and activity patterns of users and entities within an organization's network and systems.

In a world where cyber threats are becoming increasingly sophisticated and elusive, relying solely on known attack signatures is no longer sufficient. Behavioral analytics steps in to fill this gap by continuously monitoring and analyzing the behavior of users, devices, and applications to identify anomalies and potential security threats.

At its core, behavioral analytics is based on the understanding that every user, device, and entity within a network has a unique behavioral footprint. This footprint encompasses the typical patterns of activity, such as login times, data access, communication patterns, and application usage. By establishing a baseline of normal behavior for each entity, behavioral analytics can quickly identify deviations from these patterns, signaling potential security incidents.

To implement behavioral analytics effectively, organizations deploy specialized tools and solutions that collect and analyze vast amounts of data from various sources. These sources include network logs, endpoint data, system logs, and user activity logs. The collected data is then processed in real-time, using machine learning and advanced algorithms to identify patterns and anomalies.

Imagine a scenario where an employee typically accesses sensitive customer data during regular business hours. If the behavioral analytics tool detects that the same employee is attempting to access this data at 2:00 AM from an unusual location, it raises an alert. This alert prompts the organization's security team to investigate the potentially unauthorized access.

One of the key advantages of behavioral analytics is its ability to identify insider threats, where malicious or negligent actions originate from within the organization. Insiders have a unique advantage in that they often know the network's structure and can potentially evade traditional security measures. Behavioral analytics helps mitigate this risk by flagging unusual behavior, such as an employee attempting to access data they have no legitimate reason to access.

Moreover, behavioral analytics aids in the detection of advanced persistent threats (APTs), which are stealthy and prolonged cyberattacks that often go undetected for extended periods. APTs are designed to evade traditional security measures, making them exceptionally challenging to identify. Behavioral analytics excels in this area by monitoring for subtle anomalies in behavior that might be indicative of an ongoing APT.

Another valuable application of behavioral analytics is in the identification of account compromise and credential theft. Cybercriminals frequently use stolen credentials to gain unauthorized access to systems and resources. Behavioral analytics can spot unusual login patterns or authentication attempts that may indicate compromised accounts, prompting organizations to take swift action.

To illustrate this, consider a scenario where an employee's credentials are stolen and used by an attacker to access sensitive data. Traditional security measures might not detect this unauthorized access, as the attacker is using valid credentials. However, behavioral analytics can detect the abnormal behavior associated with the stolen credentials, such as login times and access patterns, and issue an alert.

Behavioral analytics tools often employ machine learning algorithms to adapt to the evolving nature of threats. These algorithms continuously learn from historical data, allowing the system to improve its accuracy in identifying anomalies and security threats over time. This adaptive capability is particularly valuable in today's fast-paced and dynamic threat landscape.

Moreover, behavioral analytics can provide valuable insights for incident response. When a potential security incident is detected, the tool can offer detailed information about the behavior leading up to the incident, enabling security teams to investigate and respond effectively.

In a Zero Trust Security model, behavioral analytics aligns perfectly with the principle of "Never Trust, Always Verify." Instead of relying on assumed trust, organizations continuously verify the behavior of users and entities within their network. Trust is established and maintained based on ongoing behavioral analysis.

The benefits of behavioral analytics extend beyond threat detection. They include the ability to reduce false positives, enhance incident response, and provide valuable insights into user behavior and system performance. Additionally, by identifying and addressing security threats early, organizations can minimize the potential impact of breaches and reduce the associated costs.

To put it into perspective, imagine a financial institution that relies on behavioral analytics to protect its customers' financial data. The institution's behavioral analytics tool continuously monitors user activity, device behavior, and application usage. If it detects anomalous behavior, such as an employee accessing customer data outside of their regular patterns, it immediately alerts the security team. This prompt detection allows the institution to investigate and mitigate potential security threats swiftly, safeguarding customer data and maintaining trust.

In summary, behavioral analytics is a powerful approach to threat detection in cybersecurity, focusing on the behavior and activity patterns of users and entities within a network. It goes beyond traditional signature-based methods by continuously monitoring and analyzing behavior to identify anomalies and potential security threats. Behavioral analytics is effective in detecting insider threats, advanced persistent threats (APTs), account compromise, and credential theft. It aligns seamlessly with the principles of Zero Trust Security, providing organizations with continuous verification of behavior. Its adaptive nature, machine learning capabilities, and ability to reduce false positives make it a valuable tool in the fight against evolving cyber threats.

**Chapter 7: Implementing Zero Trust in the Cloud**

Cloud-native security controls are vital components in safeguarding modern cloud environments, where organizations host their applications, data, and infrastructure in cloud service providers like AWS, Azure, and Google Cloud. As organizations increasingly migrate their workloads to the cloud, they face unique security challenges, and cloud-native security controls offer tailored solutions to address these issues effectively.

The term "cloud-native" signifies that these security controls are purpose-built for cloud environments, embracing the dynamic and scalable nature of cloud computing. Unlike traditional security tools, which may struggle to adapt to the cloud, cloud-native security controls seamlessly integrate with cloud platforms and services, providing organizations with robust protection tailored to their cloud workloads.

One of the fundamental aspects of cloud-native security controls is their ability to provide visibility into cloud resources and activities. In a cloud environment, resources are provisioned and deprovisioned dynamically, making it challenging to keep track of what's happening. Cloud-native security tools continuously monitor cloud resources, allowing organizations to have real-time visibility into the state of their cloud infrastructure.

Consider a scenario where an organization uses a cloud-native security control to monitor its virtual machines, databases, and containers in a public cloud environment. If a new virtual machine is spun up or an unauthorized user attempts to access a database, the cloud-native security control detects these activities and generates alerts. This immediate visibility enables organizations to respond promptly to potential security incidents.

Furthermore, cloud-native security controls are designed to enforce security policies specific to cloud environments. These policies can encompass various aspects, such as access controls, encryption, identity and access management, and compliance requirements. Cloud-native tools allow organizations to define and enforce these policies consistently across their cloud resources.

One critical security aspect that cloud-native controls address is identity and access management (IAM). In a cloud environment, effective IAM is crucial for ensuring that the right users and entities have the appropriate level of access to cloud resources. Cloud-native IAM solutions allow organizations to define granular access controls and permissions, aligning with the principle of "Least Privilege Access."

For instance, an organization can use a cloud-native IAM tool to grant specific permissions to users or roles based on their job responsibilities. This ensures that users have access only to the resources and actions necessary for their tasks, reducing the risk of unauthorized access or privilege escalation.

Cloud-native security controls also offer robust encryption capabilities, ensuring the confidentiality and integrity of data in transit and at rest. These controls enable organizations to encrypt data, such as customer information or sensitive business data, to protect it from potential breaches or data leaks.

Additionally, cloud-native security controls are designed to support compliance requirements specific to the cloud environment. Various industries and regions have stringent regulations governing data protection and privacy. Cloud-native controls provide the mechanisms and features needed to help organizations achieve compliance with these regulations.

To illustrate the importance of cloud-native security controls, let's consider a scenario involving a healthcare organization that stores patient medical records in a cloud-based database. The organization relies on cloud-native security controls to ensure the confidentiality and integrity of this sensitive patient data. These controls continuously monitor access to the database, enforce strict access controls based on roles and permissions, and encrypt the data both in transit and at rest. In doing so, the organization complies with healthcare regulations and safeguards patient information.

Cloud-native security controls also embrace automation, allowing organizations to implement security at scale. In a cloud environment where resources can rapidly scale up or down based on demand, automation becomes essential. Cloud-native security controls can automatically detect new resources, apply security policies, and respond to security incidents, reducing the manual effort required to maintain security.

Another critical aspect is the integration of cloud-native security controls with cloud service provider APIs and services. These controls leverage the capabilities and features offered by cloud providers to enhance security. For example, they can integrate with AWS Identity and Access Management (IAM) or Azure Active Directory for centralized user authentication and access control.

In a Zero Trust Security model, cloud-native security controls play a pivotal role in ensuring that trust is never assumed, even within the cloud environment. They continuously verify the security posture of cloud resources and enforce security policies consistently. This approach aligns seamlessly with the Zero Trust principle of continuous verification.

Furthermore, cloud-native security controls contribute to the principle of "Micro-Segmentation" within cloud environments. By enforcing granular access controls and policies, they limit lateral movement by attackers, ensuring that resources are accessed only by authorized users and entities.

In summary, cloud-native security controls are essential for protecting modern cloud environments. They provide real-time visibility, enforce security policies, manage access controls, support encryption, ensure compliance, embrace automation, and integrate with cloud service provider services. Cloud-native controls are tailored to the dynamic and scalable nature of cloud computing, aligning perfectly with the principles of Zero Trust Security. Organizations that leverage these controls can confidently secure their cloud workloads while embracing the agility and scalability that the cloud offers.

Cloud service provider integration is a critical aspect of modern cloud security, as it enables organizations to leverage the capabilities and features offered by leading cloud service providers such as Amazon Web Services (AWS), Microsoft Azure, and Google Cloud Platform (GCP) to enhance their security posture within the cloud environment. In today's interconnected and dynamic cloud landscapes, seamless integration with cloud service providers is essential for achieving robust and effective security.

These cloud service providers offer a wide range of services, including infrastructure-as-a-service (IaaS), platform-as-a-service (PaaS), and software-as-a-service (SaaS), each catering to different aspects of an organization's IT needs. While cloud providers are responsible for the security of the cloud infrastructure itself, organizations share responsibility for securing their data, applications, and workloads running in the cloud. To fulfill this shared responsibility model, cloud service provider integration becomes imperative.

One of the primary benefits of cloud service provider integration is the ability to leverage native cloud security features and services. Cloud providers offer a suite of security tools and services that are purpose-built for their respective cloud environments. These tools cover various aspects of cloud security, including identity and access management (IAM), network security, data encryption, and threat detection.

For example, AWS provides services like AWS Identity and Access Management (IAM), which allows organizations to define and manage user roles and permissions within their AWS accounts. Azure offers Azure Active Directory (AD) for user authentication and access control, while GCP provides Google Cloud Identity and Access Management for similar purposes. Integrating these native IAM services ensures consistent and secure access management across the cloud environment.

Another essential aspect of cloud service provider integration is the ability to manage and secure cloud-native resources. In a cloud environment, organizations use a wide range of resources, such as virtual machines, databases, containers, and serverless functions. Cloud providers offer dedicated security services to manage and secure these resources.

For instance, AWS offers Amazon GuardDuty, a threat detection service that continuously monitors for malicious activity and unauthorized access within AWS environments. Azure Security Center provides centralized security management and advanced threat protection for Azure resources, while Google Cloud Security Command Center offers security analytics and threat detection across GCP services. Integrating these native security services enhances threat detection and response capabilities.

Moreover, cloud service provider integration facilitates network security within the cloud environment. Organizations can leverage cloud-native security groups, network access control lists (NACLs), and virtual private clouds (VPCs) to define and enforce network security policies. These native network security features enable organizations to control traffic flow, isolate resources, and restrict access based on specific criteria.

In addition to network security, cloud providers offer data encryption services to protect data at rest and in transit. For instance, AWS provides Amazon S3 Server-Side Encryption to automatically encrypt data stored in Amazon S3 buckets. Azure offers Azure Disk Encryption to protect virtual machine disks, and GCP provides Google Cloud Key Management Service for data encryption and key management. Integrating these encryption services ensures data confidentiality and integrity within the cloud.

Cloud service provider integration also extends to threat detection and incident response. Cloud providers offer security information and event management (SIEM) solutions that aggregate and analyze security telemetry data from various cloud services. These SIEM solutions enable organizations to detect and respond to security incidents in real-time.

For example, AWS offers Amazon GuardDuty for threat detection and AWS CloudTrail for auditing and compliance monitoring. Azure provides Azure Monitor and Azure Sentinel for threat detection, while GCP offers Google Cloud Security Command Center for security analytics. Integrating these native SIEM solutions streamlines threat detection and response efforts.

In a Zero Trust Security model, cloud service provider integration is instrumental in implementing and enforcing Zero Trust principles within the cloud environment. Zero Trust requires continuous verification of identity and device trustworthiness, and cloud providers offer native IAM and authentication services that align with these principles. By integrating these services, organizations can ensure that trust is never assumed, even within their cloud environments.

Furthermore, cloud service provider integration supports the principle of "Least Privilege Access" by allowing organizations to define granular access controls and permissions for cloud resources. This ensures that users and entities have the minimum level of access required to perform their tasks, reducing the attack surface and potential risks.

To illustrate the significance of cloud service provider integration, consider an e-commerce company that relies on AWS to host its online store. By integrating AWS Identity and Access Management (IAM) and Amazon GuardDuty, the company ensures that only authorized users and entities can access its AWS resources. Any suspicious activity or potential security threats are detected and responded to promptly, safeguarding customer data and maintaining trust.

In summary, cloud service provider integration is a cornerstone of modern cloud security, enabling organizations to leverage native cloud security features and services. Integrating with cloud providers allows organizations to enhance their security posture by utilizing purpose-built tools for identity and access management, network security, data encryption, and threat detection. This integration aligns seamlessly with Zero Trust Security principles, ensuring continuous verification and the principle of least privilege access within the cloud environment.

Organizations that embrace cloud service provider integration can confidently secure their cloud workloads while harnessing the scalability and flexibility of the cloud.

## Chapter 8: Zero Trust and Mobile Security

Secure Mobile Device Management (MDM) is a critical aspect of modern cybersecurity, as the proliferation of mobile devices in the workplace presents both opportunities and challenges when it comes to securing sensitive data and maintaining a robust security posture. Mobile devices, including smartphones and tablets, have become integral to business operations, enabling employees to work remotely, access corporate resources, and stay connected on the go. However, these devices also introduce new vectors for security threats, making secure MDM essential.

MDM solutions provide organizations with a centralized platform to manage and secure mobile devices across their network. These solutions offer a range of capabilities, including device provisioning, application management, data encryption, remote wipe and lock, and compliance enforcement. Secure MDM is designed to balance the benefits of mobile productivity with the need for robust security.

One of the core functions of secure MDM is device provisioning and management. Organizations can use MDM solutions to enroll and configure mobile devices, ensuring they adhere to security policies from the moment they are connected to the network. This includes setting up password requirements, configuring device settings, and applying security patches and updates.

Imagine a scenario where an employee receives a new company-issued smartphone. With secure MDM, the IT department can remotely enroll the device, apply necessary security configurations, and ensure it complies with corporate security policies. This streamlined process reduces the risk of misconfigured devices and enhances security from the start.

Application management is another critical aspect of secure MDM. Organizations can use MDM solutions to distribute, update, and manage mobile applications on employee devices. This capability allows IT teams to ensure that employees have access to the necessary business apps while also enforcing security measures.

For example, a healthcare organization may use secure MDM to distribute a secure messaging app to its medical staff. IT administrators can control app access, permissions, and updates, ensuring that sensitive patient information is communicated securely and that only authorized personnel have access to the app.

Data security is a top priority in secure MDM. MDM solutions provide data encryption options to protect data both at rest and in transit on mobile devices. This encryption helps safeguard sensitive information, such as customer data, intellectual property, and proprietary business data, from unauthorized access in case a device is lost or stolen.

In a scenario where a company executive's tablet is stolen, the secure MDM solution can remotely wipe the device, erasing all data to prevent unauthorized access. Additionally, data encryption ensures that even if someone attempts to bypass device security, the encrypted data remains protected.

Secure MDM solutions also offer compliance enforcement capabilities. Organizations can define and enforce security policies to ensure that mobile devices comply with industry regulations and internal security standards. This includes measures such as password complexity requirements, device encryption, and application whitelisting.

Consider a financial institution that must comply with industry regulations like the Payment Card Industry Data

Security Standard (PCI DSS). Secure MDM helps the institution enforce compliance by ensuring that all mobile devices used by employees adhere to PCI DSS requirements, such as encryption and access controls.

Furthermore, secure MDM solutions enable organizations to implement remote monitoring and threat detection. IT teams can track the security status of mobile devices, identify potential security threats, and take action to mitigate risks. This proactive approach helps organizations detect and respond to security incidents before they escalate.

In a Zero Trust Security model, secure MDM aligns seamlessly with the principle of "Never Trust, Always Verify." It continuously verifies the security status of mobile devices and enforces access controls based on the device's compliance with security policies. Trust is not assumed; it is verified at every interaction.

Secure MDM also supports the principle of "Least Privilege Access." Organizations can define granular access controls based on user roles and device compliance. This ensures that employees have access only to the resources and data required for their specific roles, reducing the risk of data exposure and unauthorized access.

To illustrate the importance of secure MDM, consider a large multinational corporation with a mobile workforce spread across the globe. By implementing secure MDM, the organization can centrally manage and secure thousands of mobile devices used by employees in different locations. This ensures consistent security policies, compliance with international regulations, and rapid response to security incidents.

In summary, secure Mobile Device Management (MDM) is a vital component of modern cybersecurity, allowing organizations to manage and secure mobile devices while balancing productivity and security. MDM solutions provide capabilities for device provisioning, application management, data encryption, remote wipe, and compliance enforcement. Secure MDM aligns with the principles of Zero Trust Security, continuously verifying device trustworthiness and enforcing least privilege access. Organizations that embrace secure MDM can harness the benefits of mobile productivity while maintaining a robust security posture in an increasingly mobile-centric world.

Mobile app security is a pivotal element in the overarching framework of a Zero Trust Security model, as the ubiquity of mobile applications in our daily lives brings with it a multitude of security challenges and considerations. In a world where mobile devices are ubiquitous and serve as conduits to critical data and services, ensuring the security of mobile applications is paramount.

To comprehend the significance of mobile app security within a Zero Trust framework, one must first grasp the fundamental principles of Zero Trust Security. Zero Trust operates on the premise that trust should never be assumed, regardless of the location of the user or the device. Instead, it emphasizes continuous verification of identity, device integrity, and security posture throughout every interaction.

Mobile applications are integral to our personal and professional lives, granting us access to an array of services, from email and social media to corporate resources and sensitive data. However, this convenience comes with inherent security risks, as mobile apps can be vulnerable to a spectrum of threats, including data breaches, malware, and unauthorized access.

In a Zero Trust Security model, the traditional security perimeter, which relied on perimeter defenses such as firewalls, is rendered obsolete. Instead, security is applied directly to the assets themselves, including mobile apps. This shift necessitates a holistic approach to mobile app security that aligns seamlessly with the principles of Zero Trust.

One of the foundational aspects of mobile app security in a Zero Trust model is the continuous verification of device trustworthiness. Mobile devices come in various forms, including smartphones and tablets, running on diverse platforms such as iOS and Android. Each device presents its unique security posture, which can change dynamically.

To address this challenge, organizations employ Mobile Device Management (MDM) solutions to ensure that devices meet security requirements. MDM solutions continuously monitor devices, checking for compliance with security policies, patch levels, and the presence of security features like encryption. Devices that fail to meet these requirements are flagged, and their access to mobile apps and corporate resources may be restricted until they regain compliance.

Imagine an employee who uses a company-issued smartphone to access sensitive corporate data via a mobile app. In a Zero Trust model, the device's security posture is continuously verified. If the employee's device falls out of compliance, perhaps due to a missing security patch, the MDM system detects this and prompts the employee to update their device. Until the device is brought back into compliance, access to sensitive data is restricted.

Another crucial aspect of mobile app security is the continuous verification of user identity. In a Zero Trust model, user authentication is a cornerstone of security. Mobile apps must ensure that the person using the app is indeed the authorized user, and this verification should persist throughout the user's interaction with the app.

To achieve this, organizations implement robust authentication mechanisms within mobile apps. These mechanisms may include multi-factor authentication (MFA), biometric authentication (such as fingerprint or facial recognition), and single sign-on (SSO) solutions. By requiring users to continually authenticate themselves, mobile apps align with the Zero Trust principle of never assuming trust.

Consider a banking app that allows users to access their accounts and perform transactions. In a Zero Trust model, the app employs MFA to verify the user's identity continuously. Even after the initial login, the app may require additional authentication steps for high-risk transactions, such as transferring a large sum of money. This vigilant approach ensures that the app remains secure and trustworthy.

Furthermore, mobile app security encompasses the principle of least privilege access. In a Zero Trust model, access to resources and data is granted based on the user's specific needs and role. Mobile apps should adhere to this principle by implementing granular access controls and permissions.

For instance, a healthcare app that stores patient medical records must ensure that only authorized medical professionals have access to sensitive patient data. The app should grant access according to user roles and permissions, ensuring that non-medical staff or unauthorized users cannot view or modify patient records.

Data encryption is another critical component of mobile app security within a Zero Trust model. Mobile apps often handle sensitive information, such as personal data, financial records, and proprietary business data. To protect this data from unauthorized access or interception, encryption is essential.

Mobile apps can implement encryption techniques to secure data both at rest and in transit. At rest, data is encrypted when stored on the device, rendering it unreadable without the proper decryption key. In transit, data is encrypted as it travels between the device and servers, safeguarding it from interception by malicious actors.

For instance, a messaging app may use end-to-end encryption to ensure that messages sent between users are encrypted on the sender's device and only decrypted on the recipient's device. This means that even if intercepted during transmission, the messages remain indecipherable.

Threat detection and incident response are integral elements of mobile app security within a Zero Trust model. Mobile apps should be equipped with mechanisms to detect and respond to security threats and incidents promptly. Continuous monitoring for anomalies and suspicious activities is crucial.

In a Zero Trust model, threat detection within mobile apps involves scrutinizing user behavior, device behavior, and network traffic for signs of potential security breaches. For example, an e-commerce app may employ anomaly detection algorithms to identify unusual purchase patterns that could indicate fraudulent activity.

In the event of a security incident, mobile apps should have the capability to respond swiftly. This may include locking user accounts, notifying users of suspicious activities, or triggering additional authentication steps to verify the user's identity.

To illustrate the importance of mobile app security within a Zero Trust framework, consider a financial institution that offers a mobile banking app. This app enables customers to access their accounts, transfer funds, and pay bills. In a Zero Trust model, the app continuously verifies the user's identity, monitors the device's security posture, encrypts sensitive data, and employs threat detection mechanisms to protect against fraudulent activities. By adhering to these principles, the app ensures a high level of security, instilling trust and confidence in its users.

In summary, mobile app security is a vital component of a Zero Trust Security model, as mobile applications play a central role in our digital lives. Security in mobile apps aligns with the principles of continuous verification, robust authentication, least privilege access, data encryption, threat detection, and incident response. By implementing these principles, organizations can ensure the security and trustworthiness of their mobile apps, even in an environment where trust is never assumed.

## Chapter 9: Zero Trust in Practice: Case Studies

Imagine a large multinational enterprise with thousands of employees, numerous offices worldwide, and a vast digital infrastructure connecting its teams, partners, and customers across the globe; this enterprise recognized the need to bolster its cybersecurity posture and transitioned to a Zero Trust Security model to enhance its defenses.

The journey towards implementing Zero Trust Security began with a thorough assessment of the organization's existing security measures, policies, and infrastructure. The enterprise needed to understand its current vulnerabilities and identify areas that required improvement. This initial step is crucial in shaping the direction and scope of a Zero Trust implementation.

In this case, the organization's assessment revealed several weaknesses, including outdated access controls, inconsistent authentication mechanisms, and inadequate monitoring of network traffic. These findings underscored the urgency of adopting a Zero Trust approach, as the traditional perimeter-based security model was no longer sufficient to protect against evolving threats.

The first phase of Zero Trust implementation involved defining clear and granular access controls. The enterprise recognized that access should be based on the principle of "Least Privilege." This means that employees and systems should only have access to the resources and data necessary for their specific roles and responsibilities.

To achieve this, the organization revamped its identity and access management (IAM) system. User roles and permissions were meticulously defined, and multi-factor authentication (MFA) became mandatory for accessing critical systems and applications. These changes aimed to reduce the attack surface and minimize the risk of unauthorized access.

A significant part of the Zero Trust journey involved the deployment of advanced network segmentation strategies. The enterprise recognized the importance of isolating critical assets and data from the broader network, thereby limiting lateral movement in case of a breach. This approach aligned with the principle of "Micro-Segmentation."

In practice, the organization divided its network into distinct segments, each with its unique security policies and controls. Access between segments was strictly controlled and monitored. For example, only authorized personnel with specific roles could access the segment containing sensitive financial data. This segmentation enhanced security by containing potential threats and limiting their impact.

Continuous monitoring and analytics became central to the organization's Zero Trust implementation. The enterprise understood that real-time visibility into network activities was essential for identifying anomalies and potential security incidents promptly. This aligned with the Zero Trust principle of continuous verification.

To achieve this, the organization invested in advanced security information and event management (SIEM) solutions, which aggregated and analyzed security telemetry data from across the network. These solutions provided real-time alerts and insights into unusual network behavior, enabling rapid response to potential threats.

Additionally, the enterprise adopted a proactive approach to threat detection and response. It established an incident response team responsible for investigating and mitigating security incidents. This team worked closely with the SIEM system to identify and respond to threats promptly. This aligns with the Zero Trust principle of "Never Trust, Always Verify."

The enterprise also implemented Zero Trust in its cloud environments. With the increasing adoption of cloud services, it recognized the need to extend its security model to the cloud. This involved integrating cloud-native security controls and policies to ensure consistent security across on-premises and cloud-based resources.

The organization leveraged cloud providers' native security features, such as identity and access management (IAM) and encryption, to secure its cloud workloads. It also implemented network segmentation in its cloud environments to isolate different applications and services, further reducing the attack surface.

Real-world case studies played a pivotal role in shaping the organization's Zero Trust journey. The enterprise studied examples of successful Zero Trust implementations in similar industries and learned valuable lessons from their experiences. These case studies provided insights into best practices, potential challenges, and effective strategies for Zero Trust adoption.

One of the critical success factors in this Zero Trust implementation was the commitment of leadership to the security transformation. The organization's senior leadership recognized that cybersecurity was not just an IT concern but a strategic imperative. They provided the necessary resources, support, and sponsorship for the Zero Trust initiative.

Training and awareness programs were essential components of the implementation. The organization invested in cybersecurity training for employees at all levels, emphasizing the importance of security awareness and compliance with Zero Trust policies. This human element was critical in ensuring that the Zero Trust principles were embraced throughout the organization.

Over time, the enterprise observed significant improvements in its cybersecurity posture. The Zero Trust model had reduced the risk of data breaches and unauthorized access, providing greater confidence in the security of sensitive information. Security incidents were detected and mitigated more swiftly, minimizing potential damage.

Furthermore, the organization's Zero Trust implementation had positioned it to adapt to evolving cybersecurity threats and challenges. The continuous verification of identity, device trustworthiness, and network activities aligned perfectly with the dynamic and unpredictable nature of modern cyber threats.

In summary, this case study illustrates how a large multinational enterprise successfully implemented Zero Trust Security to enhance its cybersecurity posture. The journey involved a thorough assessment of existing security measures, the adoption of principles such as least privilege access and network segmentation, the integration of cloud-native security controls, continuous monitoring, and proactive threat detection and response. Leadership commitment, employee training, and real-world case studies were instrumental in the organization's success. Zero Trust transformed the enterprise's security approach, providing robust protection against evolving threats in an interconnected digital world.

Picture a small, family-owned business that has been serving its community for decades, offering everything from hardware supplies to gardening tools. In an increasingly digital age, this business recognized the need to protect its customer data and maintain trust in the face of emerging cyber threats. What follows is a case study of how this small business achieved Zero Trust Security success, proving that the principles of Zero Trust can be applied effectively regardless of an organization's size.

The journey toward Zero Trust began with the small business assessing its existing security measures. While it did not have the vast digital infrastructure of a large corporation, it relied on technology for essential operations, including point-of-sale systems and inventory management. The assessment revealed that its cybersecurity practices needed improvement to safeguard customer data and business continuity.

One of the first steps in adopting Zero Trust principles was to rethink the business's approach to identity and access management. Even though it had a small staff, the business recognized the importance of ensuring that the right people had access to the right systems and data. This aligned with the principle of "Verify Explicitly."

The business implemented user authentication measures to verify the identity of its employees. While traditional usernames and passwords sufficed for some systems, the business also adopted multi-factor authentication (MFA) for more sensitive applications and data. This simple yet effective step added an extra layer of security, ensuring that access was granted only to verified individuals.

Furthermore, the small business embraced the principle of "Least Privilege Access." It recognized that not all employees needed access to every system or piece of data. For example, the cashier at the front counter did not require access to financial records. By limiting access based on job roles, the business reduced the risk of unauthorized access and potential data breaches.

Segmentation played a pivotal role in the Zero Trust journey. While the business did not have an extensive network like large enterprises, it recognized that dividing its network into segments with distinct security controls could enhance security. For instance, it created separate network segments for its point-of-sale systems, administrative systems, and guest Wi-Fi.

Access controls were tightened within these segments. Only authorized employees could access the point-of-sale segment, while administrative systems were accessible only to management. This segmentation limited the lateral movement of potential threats and ensured that a breach in one area did not compromise the entire network.

Continuous monitoring was another integral part of the Zero Trust implementation. The small business understood that real-time visibility into network activities was essential for identifying anomalies and potential security incidents promptly. This aligned with the Zero Trust principle of continuous verification.

To achieve this, the business invested in security monitoring tools that tracked network traffic and user activities. While it did not have a dedicated security team, the tools provided automated alerts and notifications that alerted staff to suspicious activities. This proactive approach to threat detection helped the business respond swiftly to potential security incidents.

Cloud adoption was another consideration in the Zero Trust journey. Like many small businesses, it began using cloud services to streamline operations and reduce costs. However, it recognized that securing cloud resources was just as crucial as securing on-premises systems.

The business integrated cloud-native security controls into its cloud environment. This included identity and access management for cloud services and data encryption for sensitive information stored in the cloud. These measures ensured that the principles of Zero Trust extended seamlessly to the cloud, aligning with the evolving nature of modern business operations.

Training and awareness were key elements of the Zero Trust implementation. The small business educated its employees about the importance of cybersecurity and their role in maintaining a secure environment. While it had a smaller workforce, every team member understood the significance of following security protocols and reporting any potential threats.

Over time, the small business saw notable improvements in its cybersecurity posture. The adoption of Zero Trust principles had reduced the risk of data breaches and unauthorized access to customer information. The implementation of MFA and access controls added layers of security that deterred potential attackers.

Furthermore, the business's proactive approach to monitoring and threat detection helped it identify and respond to security incidents promptly. Even though it had limited resources, it demonstrated that a small organization could effectively implement Zero Trust Security principles to protect its digital assets and customer trust.

In summary, this case study exemplifies how a small, family-owned business successfully implemented Zero Trust Security to enhance its cybersecurity posture. By adopting principles such as continuous verification, least privilege access, segmentation, and cloud-native security, the business demonstrated that Zero Trust can be adapted to suit the needs and resources of organizations of all sizes. Training and awareness were vital components, highlighting the importance of a security-conscious culture. Ultimately, this small business showed that the principles of Zero Trust are scalable and applicable to businesses aiming to protect customer data and maintain trust in an increasingly digital world.

**Chapter 10: Future Trends in Zero Trust Security**

In the ever-evolving landscape of cybersecurity, staying ahead of emerging threats is a constant challenge, and as the digital realm expands, so do the technologies that aim to safeguard it. Zero Trust Security, with its fundamental principle of "Never Trust, Always Verify," continues to adapt and incorporate emerging technologies to bolster its defenses and meet the demands of a dynamic and interconnected world.

One of the most significant and transformative technologies in the realm of Zero Trust is artificial intelligence (AI) and machine learning. These technologies are at the forefront of the battle against increasingly sophisticated cyber threats. AI and machine learning enable organizations to analyze vast amounts of data in real-time, identifying patterns and anomalies that may indicate security incidents or breaches.

Imagine an AI-powered security system continuously monitoring network traffic. As it processes data, it learns what constitutes normal behavior and can quickly detect deviations from that norm. If a user suddenly attempts to access a sensitive database they've never accessed before, the system raises an alert. AI and machine learning enhance the continuous verification aspect of Zero Trust, providing a proactive defense against emerging threats.

Zero Trust also incorporates the concept of "Behavioral Analytics" as an emerging technology. This involves profiling user and device behavior over time to establish a baseline of typical activity. Any deviations from this baseline can trigger alerts for potential security incidents.

For instance, if an employee typically accesses their work applications from within the company's physical office but suddenly attempts to log in from a different country, behavioral analytics would detect this as an anomaly. The system can then prompt additional verification steps, such as multi-factor authentication, to ensure the user's identity and protect against unauthorized access.

The Internet of Things (IoT) is another area where Zero Trust must adapt to emerging technologies. As IoT devices become more prevalent in homes and workplaces, they introduce new potential vulnerabilities. Zero Trust principles can be extended to IoT by requiring continuous verification of device identity and behavior.

Consider a smart thermostat in an office building connected to the corporate network. In a Zero Trust model, the thermostat's identity and behavior are continuously monitored. If the device suddenly starts transmitting unusual data patterns, it could signal a potential security breach. Zero Trust principles applied to IoT can help protect against unauthorized access or exploitation of these devices.

Zero Trust also embraces "Zero Trust Network Access" (ZTNA) as an emerging technology. ZTNA focuses on providing secure access to applications and resources without granting access to the entire network. This approach is particularly relevant in an era where remote work and cloud services are prevalent.

With ZTNA, users are authenticated and authorized on a per-application basis. This means that even if a user gains access to one application, they do not automatically gain access to other network resources. ZTNA ensures that access is granted only to the specific applications and data required for a user's role, adhering to the principle of least privilege access.

Additionally, "Software-Defined Perimeters" (SDP) are gaining traction as an emerging technology within the Zero Trust framework. SDP solutions create micro-segments within a network, allowing organizations to isolate critical assets and reduce the attack surface. Users and devices must authenticate and be authorized to access these micro-segments.

In practice, SDP solutions grant access based on user identity, device posture, and contextual factors such as location and time. This technology enhances network segmentation and access controls, providing a robust defense against lateral movement by potential threats.

As cloud computing continues to be a fundamental part of modern business operations, "Secure Access Service Edge" (SASE) is emerging as an essential technology in the Zero Trust toolkit. SASE combines network security and wide-area networking (WAN) capabilities into a unified cloud-based service.

With SASE, organizations can securely connect users to applications and resources, regardless of their location. It applies Zero Trust principles to network access, ensuring that users and devices are continuously verified before granting access to cloud-based applications. SASE aligns seamlessly with the Zero Trust approach of verifying trust at every interaction.

Furthermore, "Blockchain" technology has been explored as an emerging technology in the context of Zero Trust. Blockchain offers a decentralized and tamper-resistant ledger that can be used to verify the authenticity of data and transactions. It has the potential to enhance the trustworthiness of identity and access management systems, ensuring the integrity of user identities and permissions.

Imagine a Zero Trust authentication system that uses blockchain to store and verify user identities. Each user's identity and access permissions are recorded on the blockchain, making it nearly impossible for malicious actors to manipulate or forge identity information. Blockchain-based identity verification enhances the trustworthiness of the Zero Trust model.

In summary, as the cybersecurity landscape continues to evolve, Zero Trust Security adapts by incorporating emerging technologies to bolster its defenses. Artificial intelligence and machine learning enhance threat detection, while behavioral analytics identify anomalies. The Internet of Things and IoT devices require continuous verification of identity and behavior. Zero Trust Network Access (ZTNA) and Software-Defined Perimeters (SDP) provide secure and segmented access to resources. Secure Access Service Edge (SASE) enables secure connections to cloud-based applications. Blockchain technology enhances trust in identity and access management systems. By embracing these emerging technologies, Zero Trust Security continues to provide a resilient and proactive defense against evolving cyber threats in an interconnected world.

In the ever-shifting landscape of cybersecurity, staying one step ahead of threats is a never-ending challenge, and as technology advances, so do the strategies and tactics of cybercriminals. It's in this context that the concept of Zero Trust Security continues to evolve and adapt, remaining a robust defense against an ever-evolving threat landscape.

Picture the traditional cybersecurity approach, with its reliance on perimeter defenses and the assumption of trust within the network. This model, while effective in its time, became increasingly vulnerable as threats evolved. Attackers found new ways to breach perimeters, exploit vulnerabilities, and move laterally within networks, all while remaining undetected.

Zero Trust emerged as a response to these challenges, emphasizing the fundamental principle of "Never Trust, Always Verify." It recognized that trust should never be assumed, whether it's a user, a device, or an application, and that verification should occur continuously throughout every interaction.

As the threat landscape continues to evolve, Zero Trust Security has adapted and incorporated new strategies to stay ahead of emerging threats. One of these adaptations involves a shift from static to dynamic trust models. Traditional security models often used static trust, where once a user or device was authenticated, they were trusted until the end of the session.

Imagine a user logging into their corporate network in the morning. In a static trust model, once they're authenticated, they enjoy unfettered access to network resources for the entire day. However, this presents a significant risk if the user's credentials are compromised later in the day. Dynamic trust models, which Zero Trust embraces, re-verify trust continuously throughout the user's session, reducing the window of vulnerability.

Continuous authentication is a key component of dynamic trust models. Users are prompted for additional authentication, such as multi-factor authentication (MFA), at various points during their session, especially when attempting to access sensitive resources or performing high-risk actions. This approach aligns with the Zero Trust principle of continuous verification.

In the face of increasingly sophisticated threats, Zero Trust Security has also adopted more advanced threat detection techniques. Behavioral analytics, powered by artificial intelligence and machine learning, have become invaluable tools for identifying anomalies and potential security incidents.

Imagine an employee's behavior patterns within an organization's network. Behavioral analytics build a profile of normal behavior, allowing the system to quickly detect deviations. If, for instance, an employee who typically accesses a specific set of resources suddenly attempts to access highly sensitive data, the system flags this as an anomaly and can prompt additional verification steps.

Zero Trust's continuous monitoring and real-time alerting capabilities further enhance its resilience against emerging threats. The system constantly tracks network traffic, user activities, and device behavior, providing immediate visibility into potential security incidents.

In this dynamic environment, imagine a malicious actor gaining access to a network. Zero Trust's continuous monitoring detects unusual behavior almost immediately. The system can then initiate an automated response, such as isolating the compromised device from the network or prompting additional authentication from the user.

The Internet of Things (IoT) introduces new complexities to the threat landscape, and Zero Trust has adapted to secure these interconnected devices. IoT devices, ranging from smart thermostats to industrial sensors, often lack robust security features and can serve as entry points for attackers.

Consider a scenario where an attacker gains access to a corporate network through a vulnerable IoT device. Zero Trust principles require continuous verification of the device's identity and behavior. If the device behaves anomalously, the system can respond by restricting its access or isolating it from critical resources.

Zero Trust Network Access (ZTNA) is another adaptation that addresses the changing landscape of remote work and cloud services. With the traditional network perimeter dissipating, ZTNA focuses on providing secure access to specific applications and resources rather than granting access to the entire network.

Imagine an employee working remotely, accessing corporate applications through a Zero Trust Network Access solution. Instead of connecting to the entire corporate network, they access only the necessary applications, and their access is continuously verified. This approach aligns with the Zero Trust principle of least privilege access, ensuring that users and devices have access only to what they need.

Cloud adoption has also led to the integration of Secure Access Service Edge (SASE) within the Zero Trust framework. SASE combines network security and wide-area networking capabilities into a unified cloud-based service. This approach aligns with the Zero Trust model by applying security policies based on user identity, device posture, and context, regardless of the user's location.

Imagine a company with employees scattered across different locations, all connecting to cloud-based applications. SASE ensures that each user's access is continuously verified and secured, protecting against potential threats and vulnerabilities.

The emergence of "Zero Trust Containers" is yet another adaptation in response to the evolving threat landscape. Containerization technology has become increasingly popular for deploying applications, but it brings new security challenges.

Containers are lightweight, isolated environments that can run applications. Zero Trust Containers extend Zero Trust principles to containerized applications, ensuring that trust is never assumed. Each container is continuously verified and monitored for potential security issues.

In summary, the ever-evolving threat landscape necessitates ongoing adaptations in the realm of cybersecurity, and Zero Trust Security continues to evolve to meet these challenges head-on. Dynamic trust models, continuous authentication, advanced threat detection, behavioral analytics, IoT security, Zero Trust Network Access (ZTNA), Secure Access Service Edge (SASE), and Zero Trust Containers are all part of Zero Trust's arsenal to stay resilient in an ever-changing digital world. By continuously verifying trust and proactively addressing emerging threats, Zero Trust remains a formidable defense against cyber adversaries, ensuring that trust is never assumed, and security is always a top priority.

# BOOK 2
# ZERO TRUST SECURITY IN PRACTICE
# STRATEGIES FOR BUILDING ROBUST
# SECURITY POSTURES

# ROB BOTWRIGHT

## Chapter 1: The Foundations of Zero Trust Security

Imagine a world where cybersecurity is not just about building walls and gates, but about ensuring trust and security in every digital interaction—this is the world of Zero Trust, a paradigm shift that has transformed the way organizations approach cybersecurity. At the heart of Zero Trust are a set of principles and concepts that challenge traditional security models and provide a new, more robust framework for protecting digital assets and data.

Let's start with the foundational principle of Zero Trust: "Never Trust, Always Verify." This principle questions the very notion of trust within a network. Traditionally, once a user or device gained access to a network, they were often given a high level of trust throughout their session. However, in the dynamic and ever-changing landscape of modern cybersecurity, this assumption of trust is no longer tenable.

Consider a scenario where an employee logs into their corporate network from a remote location. In a traditional model, once they are authenticated, they are trusted to access various resources throughout their session. Zero Trust challenges this by continuously verifying the user's identity, device posture, and other contextual factors, ensuring that trust is never assumed.

Zero Trust also embraces the concept of "Least Privilege Access." This principle stipulates that users and devices should have the minimum level of access necessary to perform their job functions. In other words, access should be granted based on the principle of least privilege, which means that employees only have access to the resources and data essential for their specific roles and responsibilities.

Imagine an employee within an organization. In a Zero Trust model, this employee is granted access only to the resources and data they need to perform their job tasks, and nothing more. This approach reduces the attack surface and limits the potential damage that can be caused if their credentials are compromised. Network segmentation is another key concept in Zero Trust. Traditional networks often have a flat structure, where once an attacker breaches the perimeter, they have unfettered access to the entire network. Zero Trust introduces the idea of segmentation, dividing the network into distinct segments or zones, each with its unique security controls and policies. Picture an organization's network divided into segments—one for sensitive financial data, another for customer information, and yet another for general office resources. Access between these segments is tightly controlled, and users or devices must be continuously verified before they can access resources within a segment. This segmentation limits the lateral movement of threats and reduces the potential impact of a breach. Continuous monitoring is a cornerstone of Zero Trust. Traditional security models often rely on periodic assessments and occasional security audits. Zero Trust, on the other hand, mandates continuous monitoring and real-time analysis of network activities.

Imagine a security system that tracks network traffic, user behaviors, and device activities in real time. Any anomalies or deviations from established baselines are detected immediately, triggering alerts and potential security responses. This continuous monitoring aligns with the Zero Trust principle of "Never Trust, Always Verify."

Another essential concept within Zero Trust is the idea of "Micro-Segmentation." Micro-segmentation takes network segmentation to a granular level by creating tiny segments within a network, each with its own security controls and policies. This approach enhances security by isolating specific applications or assets. Consider an organization that uses micro-segmentation to create individual segments for each critical application. Access to these segments is tightly controlled, and users or devices must be continuously verified before they can access a specific application. This granular approach minimizes the potential for lateral movement within the network and provides enhanced protection. Identity and access management (IAM) play a crucial role in Zero Trust. The principle here is to ensure that only authorized individuals or devices gain access to resources. IAM solutions verify and manage user identities, enforce access policies, and provide the necessary authentication mechanisms, such as multi-factor authentication (MFA). Imagine a scenario where an employee attempts to access a sensitive database. IAM solutions verify the user's identity, check their permissions, and may require additional authentication steps, such as a fingerprint scan or a one-time code from a mobile app. IAM aligns perfectly with the Zero Trust principle of continuous verification. In summary, Zero Trust principles and concepts represent a fundamental shift in cybersecurity philosophy. "Never Trust, Always Verify" challenges the traditional assumption of trust within networks. "Least Privilege Access" restricts access to the minimum necessary for job functions. Network segmentation, micro-segmentation, and continuous monitoring enhance security. Identity and access management ensure that only authorized entities gain access. These principles and concepts collectively create a robust cybersecurity framework that adapts to the dynamic and ever-evolving digital landscape, where trust is never assumed, and security is a continuous process.

To truly understand the significance of Zero Trust in today's cybersecurity landscape, it's essential to delve into its historical background and the events that led to its emergence as a transformative paradigm. Zero Trust didn't appear in a vacuum; it evolved as a response to a rapidly changing digital world and the shortcomings of traditional security models. Imagine a time when corporate networks were like fortified castles with thick walls and a single, guarded entrance. These networks were designed with a "perimeter-based" security model in mind, which assumed that everything inside the network was trusted, and threats only existed outside the walls. Users within the network enjoyed access to various resources without undergoing frequent verification. As technology advanced and the digital landscape expanded, this perimeter-based model began to show its weaknesses. One of the defining moments in the historical background of Zero Trust was the rise of remote work and mobile devices. Suddenly, employees were accessing corporate networks from various locations, often using personal devices. The once-clear perimeter became blurred, and the assumption of trust within the network was no longer tenable.

Consider an employee working from home, accessing company servers from their personal laptop. In this scenario, the perimeter was no longer the physical office; it extended to wherever the employee happened to be. The traditional security model struggled to adapt, leading to vulnerabilities and potential breaches.

Another significant shift in the historical context of Zero Trust was the increasing sophistication of cyber threats. Attackers evolved from script kiddies to highly skilled hackers, capable of bypassing traditional defenses and exploiting vulnerabilities within networks. The historical model's reliance on static trust and the absence of continuous verification became glaring weaknesses.

Imagine a cybercriminal infiltrating a corporate network by exploiting a single vulnerability. Once inside, they moved laterally, gaining access to sensitive data without encountering any additional security checks. This lateral movement went unnoticed until it was too late, highlighting the shortcomings of traditional security models.

Around the same time, data breaches and high-profile cyberattacks made headlines, shaking public confidence in the security of digital systems. Organizations realized that they needed a new approach—one that focused on protecting assets and data, rather than relying solely on perimeter defenses.

Enter the concept of "Zero Trust," which began to take shape in the early 2000s. While the term was coined by Forrester Research in 2010, the foundational ideas had been circulating for years. Zero Trust challenged the traditional notion of trust within a network, advocating for continuous verification of users, devices, and applications, regardless of their location.

Picture the Zero Trust model in action. Every user, device, or application attempting to access network resources must undergo verification, ensuring that trust is never assumed. Users are continuously authenticated, and their access is limited based on the principle of least privilege—granting access only to what is necessary for their specific roles.

In this new paradigm, the network perimeter no longer held the same significance. The historical background of Zero Trust was marked by a shift from perimeter-based security to data-centric security. Instead of relying on the walls of the castle, Zero Trust focused on safeguarding the treasures within, making it significantly more adaptable to the dynamic digital landscape.

Over time, as cloud computing and remote work became integral parts of modern business operations, Zero Trust continued to evolve. Concepts like "Zero Trust Network Access" (ZTNA) and "Secure Access Service Edge" (SASE) emerged, reflecting the changing needs of organizations in a world where traditional network boundaries were becoming increasingly porous.

Imagine a scenario where an employee, working from a coffee shop, connects to cloud-based applications through a Zero Trust Network Access solution. Their access is continuously verified, regardless of their physical location, aligning perfectly with the principles of Zero Trust.

In recent years, the historical background of Zero Trust has been further shaped by the proliferation of Internet of Things (IoT) devices and the need to secure these endpoints. Zero Trust principles have extended to IoT, ensuring that even devices like smart thermostats or industrial sensors are continuously verified before gaining access to network resources.

Consider a world where IoT devices are securely integrated into corporate networks, each undergoing rigorous verification to ensure they don't pose a security risk. This extension of Zero Trust principles to IoT demonstrates its adaptability and relevance in the face of evolving technologies.

In summary, the historical background of Zero Trust is a story of evolution and adaptation in response to the changing digital landscape and the shortcomings of traditional security models. Zero Trust emerged as a paradigm that challenged the assumption of trust, focusing on continuous verification, least privilege access, and data-centric security. As technology continues to advance and cyber threats evolve, Zero Trust remains a resilient and forward-thinking approach to cybersecurity, safeguarding digital assets in an ever-changing world.

## Chapter 2: Planning Your Zero Trust Journey

In the realm of cybersecurity, the journey towards strengthening your defenses often begins with a clear understanding of where you currently stand. Imagine embarking on a quest to fortify a castle; before you reinforce the walls or build new defenses, you need to assess the vulnerabilities, weak points, and potential entryways that adversaries might exploit.

In the world of digital security, this initial step is equally critical, and it's often referred to as "Assessing the Current Security Posture." This process involves taking a close look at your organization's existing security measures, practices, and policies to identify strengths and weaknesses.

Picture an organization's digital landscape, with its various systems, networks, and applications. To assess the current security posture, cybersecurity professionals embark on a comprehensive examination. They delve into the existing security policies and protocols, scrutinize network configurations, and evaluate the effectiveness of access controls. This meticulous review is akin to conducting a thorough inspection of a fortress's defenses before devising a strategy to reinforce them.

One of the first aspects examined during this assessment is the organization's security policies and procedures. Think of these policies as the rulebook for cybersecurity within the organization. Are there well-defined policies in place, and are they consistently followed? Policies dictate everything from password requirements to incident response procedures. Ensuring that these policies align with best practices is a fundamental step in assessing the current security posture.

Imagine a scenario where an organization has a password policy that requires complex, regularly updated passwords. This is a positive aspect of their security posture. However, if employees are not consistently following this policy, it becomes a vulnerability. Assessing and addressing such discrepancies is crucial.

Network architecture is another critical aspect that undergoes scrutiny during this assessment. In the digital realm, networks are the highways through which data flows. Evaluating the design and segmentation of these networks is akin to inspecting the layout and accessibility of various sections within a castle.

Consider an organization's network design. Does it follow the principles of network segmentation, dividing the network into distinct zones to limit lateral movement by potential threats? Proper segmentation is a key factor in reducing the risk of breaches. Assessing the network design helps identify any areas where this segmentation might be lacking or improperly configured.

Access controls and user privileges are at the heart of any security posture assessment. Think of access controls as the gates and checkpoints within your digital fortress. They dictate who can enter, what resources they can access, and what actions they can perform. Assessing access controls involves scrutinizing user accounts, permissions, and authentication mechanisms.

Imagine an organization where employees have access to sensitive financial data without undergoing multi-factor authentication. This presents a significant vulnerability. A thorough assessment identifies these access control weaknesses and prompts the organization to strengthen them.

Vulnerability assessments play a pivotal role in evaluating the current security posture. Just as a castle's defenders would search for cracks in the walls or hidden entry points, cybersecurity professionals use vulnerability scanning tools to identify weaknesses in the digital infrastructure.

Think of a vulnerability assessment as a security team searching for unlocked doors or unpatched cracks in the digital fortress. Vulnerability scanning tools scan the organization's systems and applications, looking for known vulnerabilities that attackers could exploit. Identifying these vulnerabilities is the first step in addressing them.

Now, consider the concept of "Patch Management" in the context of a security assessment. Just as a castle's maintenance crew would regularly inspect and repair its physical defenses, organizations must regularly update and patch their software and systems. An assessment examines whether patch management processes are in place and effective. If not, it identifies potential entryways for attackers.

Imagine a scenario where an organization fails to apply critical security patches in a timely manner. This oversight can leave the organization exposed to known vulnerabilities that attackers are actively exploiting. Assessing the patch management process is vital for shoring up this potential weak point.

Security awareness and training are essential elements of a security posture assessment. Just as the inhabitants of a castle must be trained to recognize and respond to threats, employees within an organization must be educated about cybersecurity best practices.

Consider an organization that conducts regular phishing awareness training for its employees. This training helps employees recognize and avoid phishing attacks, reducing the likelihood of successful attacks. Assessing the effectiveness of security awareness programs helps organizations identify areas for improvement.

The assessment process also delves into incident response planning. Just as a castle's defenders would have a plan in place to respond to an enemy siege, organizations must have robust incident response procedures. Assessing these procedures involves examining how the organization prepares for and reacts to security incidents.

Imagine a cybersecurity incident where a breach occurs. An effective incident response plan would ensure that the organization responds promptly, containing the incident and minimizing damage. Assessing this aspect of the security posture helps organizations refine their incident response capabilities.

Data protection is a critical component of any security assessment. Data is often the treasure that adversaries seek to steal or compromise. Assessing data protection involves evaluating data encryption, access controls, and backup procedures.

Think of data protection as safeguarding the valuable artifacts within a castle's vault. Ensuring that sensitive data is encrypted, accessible only to authorized users, and regularly backed up is crucial for a robust security posture. Assessing these measures helps organizations protect their digital assets effectively.

In summary, assessing the current security posture is a foundational step in strengthening an organization's cybersecurity defenses. Just as a castle's defenders would thoroughly inspect their fortifications, organizations scrutinize their security policies, network architecture, access controls, vulnerability management, patch management, security awareness, incident response, and data protection measures. Identifying vulnerabilities and weaknesses during this assessment allows organizations to fortify their defenses, ensuring that their digital fortress remains secure in the face of evolving threats.

Embarking on the journey to implement Zero Trust Security within your organization is akin to setting out on a grand adventure, and like any significant undertaking, it's essential to have a clear roadmap to guide you through the twists and turns of the path ahead. Picture it as charting a course through uncharted waters, with the destination being a state of heightened cybersecurity and resilience.

Creating a Zero Trust roadmap is not just about deciding where you want to go; it's also about understanding where you are now and plotting the most effective route to your desired cybersecurity destination. Imagine this roadmap as a detailed itinerary, outlining the steps, milestones, and checkpoints along the way.

The first stop on this journey is "Assessment and Discovery." Just as an explorer would take stock of their supplies and equipment before setting out, organizations need to assess their current state of cybersecurity. This involves a deep dive into existing security policies, network configurations, access controls, and potential vulnerabilities.

Think of this assessment as creating a map of your organization's digital landscape. What are the strengths and weaknesses of your current security posture? Are there areas where the principles of Zero Trust can be applied immediately, or are there significant gaps that need immediate attention?

Next comes the critical step of "Defining Objectives and Priorities." Just as an adventurer must decide what landmarks to visit along the way, organizations need to set clear objectives for their Zero Trust journey. What are the specific security goals you aim to achieve with Zero Trust? Is it strengthening access controls, implementing micro-segmentation, or enhancing user authentication?

Imagine an organization setting a priority to improve access controls for its most critical data. This objective becomes a focal point for the roadmap, guiding subsequent steps to achieve this specific goal. Prioritizing objectives ensures that resources and efforts are concentrated where they will have the most significant impact.

With objectives in place, the roadmap takes us to "Planning and Design." Here, the organization outlines the strategies and tactics required to achieve the defined objectives. Just as an architect meticulously plans the construction of a building, cybersecurity professionals plan the implementation of Zero Trust principles.

Consider the planning phase as drafting the blueprint for your Zero Trust fortress. What technologies, tools, and processes will be necessary? How will access controls be tightened? How will user authentication be strengthened? Designing a comprehensive plan ensures that every aspect of the Zero Trust journey is well thought out.

Now, let's move to the "Pilot and Proof of Concept" phase. This step is akin to a test run before the grand expedition. Organizations select a smaller, controlled environment, often called a pilot group, to implement and test Zero Trust principles.

Imagine a ship captain navigating a smaller vessel into uncharted waters to ensure safe passage for the entire fleet. Similarly, a pilot group provides an opportunity to validate the planned strategies and iron out any issues on a smaller scale before rolling them out organization-wide.

Once the pilot phase is successful, the organization proceeds to "Deployment and Implementation." This is the phase where Zero Trust principles are put into practice across the entire organization. Access controls are tightened, micro-segmentation is implemented, and continuous monitoring becomes the norm.

Picture this phase as the construction of the main fortifications of your digital fortress. It's a deliberate and methodical process, ensuring that Zero Trust becomes ingrained in the organization's cybersecurity culture.

Now, consider the "Monitoring and Optimization" phase as the ongoing maintenance of your digital fortress. Just as a castle's defenses require constant upkeep, Zero Trust requires continuous monitoring, analysis, and fine-tuning.

Imagine security professionals reviewing logs, analyzing user behavior, and making adjustments as needed. This ongoing process ensures that the organization remains vigilant and responsive to emerging threats and evolving needs.

Education and Training play a crucial role in any successful Zero Trust implementation. Just as a crew must be well-prepared for the challenges of a long journey, employees need to be educated about Zero Trust principles and best practices.

Consider training as the compass that guides your team through the journey. Training ensures that everyone understands their role in maintaining a strong security posture and helps them recognize potential threats and vulnerabilities.

Regular Audits and Assessments are essential to ensure that your Zero Trust defenses remain robust and effective. These assessments are like periodic inspections of your digital fortress, ensuring that all gates and walls are secure.

Imagine an independent team of security experts reviewing your security measures to identify weaknesses and suggest improvements. These assessments help you stay proactive in addressing potential vulnerabilities.

Finally, the "Adaptation and Evolution" phase acknowledges that the cybersecurity landscape is ever-changing. Just as explorers adapt to changing weather and terrain, organizations must adapt to new threats and technologies.

Think of this phase as continually updating your map to account for new discoveries and challenges. It's an ongoing process of refinement and adaptation to ensure that your Zero Trust roadmap remains relevant and effective.

In summary, creating a Zero Trust roadmap is not just about setting out on a journey; it's about carefully planning and executing each step along the way. The roadmap encompasses assessment, objective setting, planning, testing, deployment, monitoring, education, audits, and adaptation. Just as a well-planned expedition can navigate treacherous terrain and reach its destination, a well-crafted Zero Trust roadmap guides organizations to a state of heightened cybersecurity and resilience in an ever-changing digital landscape.

**Chapter 3: Identity and Access Management in Zero Trust**

In the realm of cybersecurity, authentication is the process of verifying the identity of a user, device, or application attempting to access digital resources. It's the equivalent of proving your identity before gaining access to a highly secure facility. In the context of advanced user authentication methods, we're delving into the innovative techniques and technologies that are transforming the way we verify identities in our increasingly digital world.

Imagine traditional authentication methods as keys to a locked door. You have a key, and if it matches the lock, the door opens. While this approach has served us well, the modern digital landscape demands more robust and sophisticated methods. This is where advanced user authentication steps in, offering a multifaceted approach to identity verification.

One of the most prominent advancements in user authentication is Multi-Factor Authentication (MFA). MFA is like having multiple locks on a door, each requiring a different key. In this method, users are asked to provide two or more types of authentication factors before gaining access. These factors typically fall into three categories: something you know, something you have, and something you are.

Imagine a scenario where you log into your online banking account. In addition to your password (something you know), the system asks for a one-time code sent to your mobile device (something you have). This two-factor authentication significantly enhances security because even if an attacker knows your password, they can't access your account without your mobile device.

Biometric authentication is another advanced method that's becoming increasingly prevalent. Biometrics use unique physical or behavioral traits to verify identity. Think of it as a fingerprint scan or facial recognition. These traits are something you are, and they're incredibly difficult to forge or mimic.

Consider unlocking your smartphone with your fingerprint. The device scans your fingerprint, matches it to the stored biometric data, and grants access. Biometric authentication provides a high level of security because it's challenging for anyone to replicate your unique fingerprint or facial features.

Now, imagine the concept of Behavioral Biometrics. This method involves analyzing user behavior, such as typing patterns, mouse movements, and touchscreen gestures, to verify identity. Behavioral biometrics is like recognizing someone by the way they walk or talk. Each person has a distinct behavioral signature, making it a powerful authentication method.

Imagine logging into your computer, and as you type your password, the system analyzes your typing speed, rhythm, and keystroke patterns to ensure it's really you. If your behavior matches the established profile, access is granted. Behavioral biometrics adds an extra layer of security by continuously monitoring and adapting to changes in user behavior.

Adaptive Authentication takes user verification to the next level. This method is like having an intelligent gatekeeper who assesses the risk of each access attempt. It uses a variety of factors, such as user location, device information, and recent activity, to determine the level of authentication required.

Picture this scenario: You typically log in from your office computer during business hours. One day, you attempt to access your account from a foreign location at an unusual time. Adaptive authentication detects this anomaly and triggers a more rigorous verification process, such as MFA or biometric authentication, to ensure the legitimacy of the access attempt.

Passwordless Authentication is a revolutionary approach that aims to eliminate the traditional reliance on passwords. It's like having a door that opens when it recognizes your face but doesn't require a physical key. Instead of entering a password, users authenticate using methods like biometrics, smart cards, or mobile apps.

Imagine accessing your work computer without typing a password. Instead, you use your fingerprint or a mobile app that generates a one-time code. Passwordless authentication not only enhances security but also simplifies the user experience, reducing the risk of password-related vulnerabilities.

One-Time Passwords (OTP) provide an additional layer of security by generating a unique code for each authentication attempt. OTP is like having a constantly changing lock combination. Users receive a temporary code through SMS, email, or a mobile app, and they must enter it within a short timeframe to gain access.

Consider logging into your email account and receiving a one-time code on your mobile device. This code, valid for a limited time, ensures that even if an attacker intercepts it, they won't be able to use it later. OTPs are highly effective in thwarting unauthorized access attempts.

Imagine combining these advanced user authentication methods to create a robust security fortress. Users might start by providing a fingerprint (biometric authentication), followed by a one-time code (OTP) delivered to their mobile device (something they have). If their behavior (behavioral biometrics) matches their established profile, access is granted. This multifaceted approach significantly enhances security while ensuring a seamless user experience.

In summary, advanced user authentication methods are transforming the way we verify identities in the digital realm. MFA, biometrics, behavioral biometrics, adaptive authentication, passwordless authentication, and one-time passwords offer a multifaceted approach that goes beyond traditional passwords to provide enhanced security and user convenience. As the digital landscape continues to evolve, these methods will play a crucial role in safeguarding digital resources and protecting against emerging threats.

In the intricate world of cybersecurity, where safeguarding digital assets is paramount, the concept of Device Authentication and Authorization takes center stage. Imagine it as the process of granting access to digital resources not to just human users but to the very devices that seek entry, much like permitting trusted sentinels into a fortress. Now, consider the typical scenario in our digital age. You own a smartphone, a tablet, a laptop, and perhaps even smart home devices like thermostats and cameras. These devices communicate and interact with various online services and applications, from email and social media to online banking and cloud storage. They are your digital emissaries, carrying out your commands and storing your data. However, this interconnected web of devices also presents a security challenge. How can you ensure that each device accessing your digital world is genuinely yours and that it behaves as expected? This is where Device Authentication and Authorization come into play.

Authentication, in this context, is the process of verifying the identity of a device before granting it access. Think of it as confirming the identity of a visitor before allowing them inside your home. Device authentication ensures that only trusted devices gain entry to your digital realm.

The most basic form of device authentication involves passwords or cryptographic keys specific to the device. Imagine a device having a unique secret code that it must present to gain access to your network or digital services. This code serves as the digital equivalent of a device's ID card.

However, modern device authentication goes beyond mere passwords. Consider the use of digital certificates. Just as a medieval king might bestow a royal seal upon a trusted envoy, digital certificates are issued to devices as a mark of trust. These certificates contain cryptographic keys that prove a device's authenticity.

Imagine a scenario where your smartphone presents its digital certificate when connecting to your company's network. The network's authentication server verifies the certificate's validity, ensuring that the device is legitimate and trusted. If the certificate checks out, access is granted.

Biometric authentication adds an extra layer of security to device authentication. Just as a castle might have a guard who recognizes the faces of trusted visitors, biometric authentication uses unique physical or behavioral traits to verify a device's identity.

Consider facial recognition as an example. Your smartphone's front camera scans your face to determine if it matches the stored biometric data. If there's a match, the device gains access. Biometric authentication ensures that only the authorized user can unlock the device.

Now, think about behavioral biometrics in the context of device authentication. This method analyzes the device's behavior patterns to confirm its identity. It's like recognizing a trusted friend by their distinct gait or way of speaking.

Imagine a scenario where a device's behavioral biometrics are continuously monitored. If the device starts behaving unusually, indicating a potential security threat, access can be restricted until its identity is verified. Behavioral biometrics add an adaptive layer of security to device authentication.

Authorization, on the other hand, determines what actions a device is allowed to perform once authenticated. It's akin to specifying the privileges and responsibilities of a guest within your castle. Authorization ensures that even trusted devices only access the resources and data they are allowed to.

Consider the example of an Internet of Things (IoT) device, like a smart thermostat. You want it to have access to your home's temperature control but not to your personal emails. Authorization mechanisms ensure that the thermostat can only interact with the relevant services and data.

Role-based access control (RBAC) is a common method of authorization. Think of it as assigning different roles to devices within your digital kingdom. Each role comes with specific permissions. For instance, a work laptop might have administrative access to the company's servers, while a smart TV has access to streaming services only.

Imagine the importance of RBAC in a corporate setting. It ensures that devices used by employees are granted appropriate levels of access based on their job roles, preventing unauthorized access to sensitive data and systems.

Dynamic authorization policies take authorization to the next level. Imagine these policies as adaptive rules that can change based on the context and conditions. For example, a device's access permissions might change when it connects from a different location or exhibits unusual behavior.

Consider a scenario where a company laptop is normally granted access to sensitive financial data. However, if it connects from an unfamiliar location or behaves suspiciously, dynamic authorization policies can temporarily restrict its access until the situation is clarified.

Access control lists (ACLs) are another tool in the authorization toolbox. Think of ACLs as detailed lists of permissions for each device. These lists specify what resources a device can access, what actions it can perform, and under what conditions.

Imagine a scenario where an IoT device can access certain data during specific hours of the day. ACLs ensure that the device's access is limited to the predefined conditions, preventing unauthorized access outside those parameters.

The concept of Zero Trust Security, which we've explored earlier, aligns closely with device authentication and authorization. It assumes that no device, regardless of its origin or location, should be trusted by default. Instead, each device, even those within your trusted network, must continually prove its identity and adhere to strict authorization rules.

Think of Zero Trust as the ultimate security sentinel in your digital castle. It constantly verifies the identity of devices, monitors their behavior, and enforces authorization policies. Even if a device gains entry, it remains under the watchful eye of Zero Trust, ensuring that it behaves as expected and poses no threat.

In summary, device authentication and authorization form the foundation of a secure digital environment. They ensure that only trusted devices gain access, and even then, they limit what those devices can do. From passwords and digital certificates to biometric and behavioral authentication, these methods provide multiple layers of defense, while role-based access control and dynamic authorization policies ensure that devices operate within predefined boundaries. In an era of increasing digital connectivity, effective device authentication and authorization are paramount in safeguarding your digital kingdom.

## Chapter 4: Network Segmentation and Least Privilege Access

In the world of cybersecurity, network segmentation stands as a formidable defense mechanism, akin to building distinct walls within a fortress to compartmentalize and protect valuable assets. Imagine your network as a bustling city, and network segmentation as creating districts, each with its unique access controls and defenses, to safeguard critical resources.

At its core, network segmentation is the practice of dividing a large network into smaller, isolated segments or subnetworks. These segments, often referred to as VLANs (Virtual Local Area Networks), create a controlled environment where specific devices or user groups can communicate while limiting access to other segments. Picture it as having different districts in a city, each with its gates and guards, allowing only authorized individuals to pass through.

The first strategy in effective network segmentation is defining the segmentation scope. Think of this as determining the boundaries of each district within your network city. Which devices, services, or user groups need isolation, and what resources should be protected? Defining the scope ensures that you have a clear understanding of what you're protecting and what needs to be separated.

Consider a scenario where a company wants to segment its network to protect sensitive customer data. The segmentation scope would include identifying the servers, databases, and user groups that handle this data. Once the scope is defined, you can move on to implementing the segmentation.

Segmentation implementation involves creating the digital walls and gates that control access between segments. Imagine deploying firewalls, access control lists, and VLANs to establish clear boundaries. Firewalls act as guards at the gates, allowing or denying traffic based on predefined rules.

In the customer data protection scenario, you would set up firewalls to control access to the servers and databases holding that data. Only authorized personnel would be granted access, and any unauthorized attempts would be blocked at the firewall.

The next strategy revolves around access controls and policies. Consider these as the rules and regulations governing each district in your network city. Access controls define who can enter and what they can do once inside. Access policies determine the conditions under which access is granted.

Imagine a district where only employees with special clearance can enter, and they must adhere to specific rules while inside. Access controls can enforce user authentication, ensuring that only authorized users gain entry, while access policies might dictate that certain actions are allowed only during specific hours.

Network segmentation also benefits from continuous monitoring and auditing, forming another vital strategy. Think of this as having vigilant guards who patrol the district boundaries, ensuring that everything remains secure. Continuous monitoring involves tracking network traffic, identifying anomalies, and responding to potential threats in real-time.

Consider a situation where unusual activity is detected in a segmented district. Continuous monitoring would trigger alerts, enabling security teams to investigate and respond promptly. It's like having guards who sound the alarm at the first sign of trouble.

Segmentation strategies also encompass periodic assessments and adjustments. Picture these as routine inspections of your district walls and gates. Periodic assessments involve evaluating the effectiveness of your segmentation controls, ensuring that they remain robust and aligned with evolving security needs.

Imagine a scenario where your network expands, or new security threats emerge. Periodic assessments would prompt you to reevaluate your segmentation strategy, making necessary adjustments to address new challenges. It's like strengthening district defenses in response to changing threats.

Consider the concept of micro-segmentation as a strategy within network segmentation. This is like dividing a district into smaller neighborhoods, each with its unique security measures. Micro-segmentation enables even finer control over access and security within a network.

Imagine a district with highly sensitive areas, like a financial district within a city. Micro-segmentation would further divide this district, ensuring that only authorized individuals can access specific zones, such as the bank or stock exchange.

Additionally, think about the role of automation in network segmentation strategies. Automation is like having a team of efficient guards who can respond to threats in real-time. Automated systems can detect unusual behavior, isolate compromised devices, and update access controls dynamically.

Consider a scenario where a device within a segmented district exhibits suspicious activity. Automation would detect the anomaly and immediately isolate the device to prevent further harm, all without human intervention. It's like having security guards who can act swiftly and decisively.

Now, let's explore the concept of a Zero Trust approach within network segmentation strategies. This is akin to treating every district within your network city as a potential threat, regardless of its origin or location. Zero Trust principles ensure that trust is never assumed, and access is continually verified.

Imagine a scenario where a device from a trusted district attempts to access a sensitive resource. In a Zero Trust model, this access attempt would undergo rigorous authentication and verification, regardless of the device's origin. Zero Trust adds an extra layer of security to your segmented network.

The final strategy in effective network segmentation is communication and collaboration. This is like having a network of interconnected districts that share information about potential threats and vulnerabilities. Collaboration ensures that security teams across segments work together to address emerging challenges.

Consider a scenario where one district detects a new type of cyber threat. Effective communication and collaboration would enable this district to share its findings with other segments, allowing them to prepare and adapt their defenses. It's like having a network of vigilant neighborhoods that watch out for each other.

In summary, effective network segmentation strategies are crucial in today's complex cybersecurity landscape. These strategies involve defining the segmentation scope, implementing access controls and policies, continuous monitoring, periodic assessments, micro-segmentation, automation, Zero Trust principles, and fostering communication and collaboration. Much like dividing a city into well-protected districts, network segmentation safeguards digital assets and ensures that only authorized users and devices gain access. It's a multifaceted approach that adapts to evolving security challenges, providing layers of defense in an interconnected digital world.

In the intricate world of cybersecurity, Role-Based Access Control (RBAC) emerges as a powerful strategy, akin to assigning roles and responsibilities within a well-organized team, to govern who can access what resources in a digital environment. Think of it as creating a well-structured organization chart for your network, ensuring that every user and device has a defined role and corresponding access privileges.

Imagine a scenario where you're managing a bustling office. Each employee has a specific role, from the receptionist to the CEO, and with those roles come varying levels of access to different areas and resources. RBAC extends this organizational concept into the digital realm, where users and devices are assigned roles based on their responsibilities.

At its core, RBAC revolves around defining roles within your organization and associating each role with specific permissions and access rights. Think of it as giving employees job titles and responsibilities, along with clear instructions on what they can and cannot do. This organizational structure forms the basis of RBAC.

Consider a scenario in a healthcare setting. You have doctors, nurses, and administrative staff. Each role comes with its own set of responsibilities. Doctors need access to patient records and diagnostic tools, while nurses require access to patient charts and medication records. Administrative staff handle scheduling and billing. RBAC would assign distinct roles to each group, ensuring they have access to the necessary resources and nothing more.

Permissions, in the context of RBAC, are like keys that unlock specific doors within your organization. Each role is associated with a set of permissions that dictate what actions a user or device can perform. Think of permissions as the rules that govern access to different areas and assets.

Imagine a scenario in a financial institution. You have roles like tellers, financial analysts, and bank managers. Each role has its own set of permissions. Tellers can process transactions and handle customer accounts but are restricted from accessing sensitive financial data. Financial analysts have access to financial reports and data analysis tools. Bank managers have broader access, including the ability to approve large transactions and access sensitive financial information. RBAC ensures that these permissions align with the roles and responsibilities of each group.

Access control lists (ACLs) are the mechanisms through which RBAC enforces permissions. Think of ACLs as gatekeepers who check the credentials of users and devices against the predefined rules. ACLs grant or deny access based on whether a user or device matches the criteria set for their role.

Imagine a scenario where an employee attempts to access a confidential document. The ACL checks the user's role and permissions. If the user's role allows access to the document, it's granted. Otherwise, access is denied. ACLs ensure that permissions are consistently enforced across the organization.

The dynamic nature of RBAC allows for scalability and adaptability. Consider this as the ability to add new roles and adjust permissions as your organization evolves. RBAC is not a static hierarchy; it's a flexible system that accommodates growth and changing responsibilities.

Imagine your organization expands, and you introduce new job roles. RBAC allows you to create new roles and define their permissions, ensuring that each role aligns with the evolving needs of your organization. It's like updating your organizational chart to accommodate new departments and teams.

Role assignment and revocation are essential aspects of RBAC. Think of this as the process of hiring and terminating employees within your organization. When a user or device joins your network, they are assigned a role that matches their responsibilities. When they leave or change roles, their access is adjusted accordingly.

Imagine a scenario where an employee is promoted to a managerial position. RBAC ensures that the employee's access privileges are updated to reflect their new role. Conversely, when an employee leaves the company, their access is revoked immediately, reducing the risk of unauthorized access.

Consider the principle of least privilege (PoLP) within RBAC. This is like ensuring that employees have access only to the resources and data necessary for their job responsibilities. PoLP minimizes the potential for unauthorized access and data breaches.

Imagine an employee in a marketing role. Their access is limited to marketing tools and data, preventing them from accessing sensitive financial or HR information. PoLP ensures that each user or device has the minimum access required to perform their duties, reducing the attack surface.

Now, let's explore the integration of RBAC within the context of a Zero Trust model. Zero Trust is like the sentinel who never takes anything for granted and continually verifies the identity and permissions of every user and device, regardless of their location or origin.

Imagine a scenario where a user attempts to access a sensitive database from an external network. In a Zero Trust model with RBAC, the user's role and permissions are rigorously verified, even if they are connecting from a trusted location. Zero Trust ensures that trust is never assumed and that access is continually validated.

The role-based approach aligns seamlessly with Zero Trust principles. It's like having a well-structured security team that assigns roles, enforces permissions, and scrutinizes every access request. RBAC ensures that users and devices adhere to strict access controls, adding an additional layer of security to the Zero Trust model.

In summary, Role-Based Access Control (RBAC) is a cornerstone of effective access management in today's cybersecurity landscape. It's like creating a well-organized organization chart for your digital environment, assigning roles, defining permissions, and enforcing access controls. RBAC ensures that users and devices have appropriate access based on their responsibilities, aligning seamlessly with the Zero Trust model to continually verify and validate access requests. In a world of evolving security threats, RBAC provides a structured and adaptable approach to access control, safeguarding digital assets and reducing the risk of unauthorized access.

**Chapter 5: Implementing Zero Trust Controls**

Imagine your digital network as a grand castle, with multiple layers of walls and defenses protecting the invaluable treasures within. Now, envision the Zero Trust Firewall as the first line of defense, the gatekeeper that scrutinizes every visitor and ensures their legitimacy before granting access. It's like the castle's guardian who never assumes anyone's trustworthiness and always verifies their identity.

Zero Trust Firewall, in the realm of cybersecurity, embodies the core principles of the Zero Trust model. This model rejects the conventional notion of trusting entities based on their location within the network. Instead, it advocates the idea that trust should be earned and continuously verified, irrespective of a device's origin.

Consider a scenario where an employee wants to access a critical database from a remote location. In the traditional security paradigm, if the employee's device is within the corporate network, it's often assumed to be trusted. However, in a Zero Trust model with a Zero Trust Firewall, this assumption is challenged. The firewall rigorously checks the employee's identity, device health, and access privileges, ensuring that access is only granted if all criteria are met.

To grasp the significance of the Zero Trust Firewall, it's essential to delve into the concept of Micro-Segmentation. Micro-Segmentation is like creating multiple inner sanctums within your castle, each with its own set of guards and fortified walls. These inner sanctums isolate critical assets and limit access to a select few, even within your trusted network.

Imagine a scenario where your castle has a treasury, a library, and a laboratory, each housing priceless treasures.

Micro-Segmentation would create distinct zones around these areas, ensuring that only authorized personnel can access them. The Zero Trust Firewall acts as the guardian of these inner sanctums, verifying the identity and permissions of those seeking entry.

Micro-Segmentation, often implemented using network segmentation tools and techniques, divides your network into smaller, isolated segments or zones. These segments can be as granular as specific applications or resources. Think of it as subdividing your castle into separate chambers, each with its unique purpose and level of protection.

Consider a corporate network where sensitive customer data resides. Micro-Segmentation would create a dedicated zone for this data, surrounded by virtual walls and guarded by the Zero Trust Firewall. Only users and devices with explicit permissions can access this zone, regardless of their location within the network.

Now, let's delve into the role of the Zero Trust Firewall within Micro-Segmentation. Think of the Zero Trust Firewall as the vigilant gatekeeper at each chamber's entrance, ensuring that only those with the right credentials gain access. It's like having multiple layers of security checks for each inner sanctum in your castle.

Imagine an employee attempting to access the chamber housing sensitive customer data. The Zero Trust Firewall, as part of the Micro-Segmentation strategy, checks the employee's identity, device health, and access permissions. If any of these criteria are not met, access is denied. This multi-layered approach ensures that only authorized users and devices can enter.

Moreover, the Zero Trust Firewall continuously monitors and audits traffic within each segment. Picture it as the guardian who keeps a watchful eye on all activities within the castle's inner chambers. Any suspicious behavior or unauthorized access attempts are immediately detected and reported.

Consider a scenario where an employee, who normally has access to a specific segment, attempts to perform unusual actions or access unauthorized resources within that segment. The Zero Trust Firewall, through its monitoring capabilities, flags these actions as potential security threats, triggering immediate alerts and responses.

The dynamic nature of the Zero Trust Firewall and Micro-Segmentation allows for adaptability in the face of evolving threats. Think of it as being able to reinforce specific inner sanctums within your castle when new dangers arise. These security measures can be adjusted in real-time to address emerging challenges.

Imagine a scenario where a new type of cyber threat emerges, targeting a specific segment of your network. The Zero Trust Firewall and Micro-Segmentation enable you to promptly strengthen security measures for that segment. This adaptive approach ensures that your castle's inner chambers remain impervious to evolving threats.

Zero Trust Firewall also aligns closely with the principle of least privilege (PoLP) within Micro-Segmentation. PoLP is like granting limited access even within your inner sanctums. It ensures that users and devices have the minimum necessary privileges to perform their tasks, reducing the risk of unauthorized actions.

Consider an employee accessing a segment with sensitive financial data. PoLP ensures that the employee can only perform actions directly related to their responsibilities, such as viewing financial reports. Actions like modifying or deleting data are restricted. This fine-grained control minimizes the potential for errors or malicious activities.

Additionally, Zero Trust Firewall and Micro-Segmentation complement the principles of Zero Trust, which advocate for continuous verification and validation. Think of it as having sentinels who never let their guard down and always scrutinize every entity, even if it's from a trusted location within your castle.

Imagine a scenario where a device from a trusted network zone attempts to access a segment with sensitive intellectual property. In a Zero Trust model with Zero Trust Firewall and Micro-Segmentation, the device's identity and access permissions are rigorously verified, ensuring that trust is never assumed, and access is continually validated.

In summary, the synergy between the Zero Trust Firewall and Micro-Segmentation forms a robust defense strategy in today's cybersecurity landscape. It's like having multiple layers of guards and fortified walls within your castle, where trust is earned and continuously verified. This approach ensures that even within your trusted network, access is strictly controlled and monitored, reducing the risk of unauthorized access and safeguarding your most valuable digital assets.

Picture your organization's digital landscape as a sprawling city with countless entry points, and within this metropolis lies a network of interconnected devices - your endpoints. Now, envision the Zero Trust model as the vigilant guardian that watches over each endpoint, tirelessly verifying their identities and safeguarding against potential threats. It's a bit like having a dedicated security team for every device, ensuring that trust is never assumed and security is paramount.

In the realm of cybersecurity, endpoints encompass a wide range of devices, from traditional workstations and laptops to smartphones, tablets, and even Internet of Things (IoT) devices. Each of these devices, like citizens in your digital city, plays a unique role, but they all need protection.

Zero Trust fundamentally challenges the notion of trust based on a device's location within your network. In the past, if a device was within the corporate network's perimeter, it was often considered trusted. However, in a Zero Trust environment, trust is earned, not presumed, regardless of a device's location.

Imagine a scenario where an employee's laptop, connected to the corporate network, attempts to access sensitive financial data. In a traditional security setup, the device's location might lead to the assumption of trust. However, in a Zero Trust model, this trust is questioned. The system validates the device's identity, security posture, and access permissions before granting entry.

To fully appreciate the importance of endpoint protection in a Zero Trust environment, let's dive into the concept of continuous authentication. Think of it as a digital ID check that occurs not just when a user logs in but at various points during their digital journey.

Consider an employee working remotely who needs access to company resources. In a Zero Trust environment, the system continuously verifies the employee's identity as they move from one application to another, ensuring that access remains secure even after the initial login. It's akin to having a vigilant bouncer at each digital door, confirming identities each time someone enters.

Furthermore, endpoint protection extends beyond simple username and password authentication. Multi-Factor Authentication (MFA) enters the stage as a key player. MFA is like adding an extra layer of security to each entry point, requiring users to provide multiple forms of verification.

Imagine an employee accessing a critical application from their smartphone. MFA would prompt them to not only enter their password but also provide a one-time code generated on their smartwatch. This multi-layered approach significantly bolsters security, making it challenging for unauthorized access.

Now, let's explore the concept of Device Identity Verification within endpoint protection. It's akin to assigning a unique badge to each device in your digital city, enabling the system to recognize and validate them.

Consider a scenario where an IoT device, such as a sensor on a factory floor, needs to communicate with your network. Device Identity Verification ensures that the device's credentials and security posture are verified before it's granted access. It's like having a security guard check the identification of every device that enters your digital city.

Another critical aspect of endpoint protection is Device Health Assessment. Think of it as a regular check-up for your devices, ensuring that they meet specific security standards before they connect to your network.

Imagine an employee's laptop trying to access corporate resources. Before granting access, the system checks the device's health, verifying that it has the latest security updates and antivirus definitions. If the device doesn't meet the required health standards, access is denied until the necessary updates are applied. It's like ensuring that every device in your digital city is in good health before allowing them inside.

Within a Zero Trust environment, behavior analysis plays a pivotal role in endpoint protection. Think of it as having a behavioral psychologist for your devices, constantly monitoring their actions for unusual or suspicious behavior.

Consider a scenario where a user's laptop, which has a history of accessing financial data, suddenly starts attempting to download large volumes of sensitive information. Behavior analysis would flag this behavior as unusual, triggering alerts and potentially blocking further actions until the situation is investigated. It's like having a watchful eye on your devices, ready to intervene if their behavior raises concerns.

Moreover, endpoint protection encompasses real-time threat detection and response capabilities. Think of it as having a digital SWAT team on standby, ready to neutralize threats the moment they are detected.

Imagine a scenario where a malware infection is detected on an employee's smartphone. Endpoint protection systems can respond immediately, isolating the infected device from the network and initiating remediation processes. It's like having an emergency response team that springs into action the moment a threat is identified.

The Zero Trust model emphasizes the principle of least privilege (PoLP) within endpoint protection. It's akin to ensuring that each device only has access to what is necessary for its specific role and responsibilities.

Consider an employee's laptop. PoLP ensures that it has access only to the applications and data required for the employee's job function. Unnecessary access to sensitive resources is restricted, reducing the potential attack surface. It's like providing each citizen in your digital city with precisely the permissions they need, nothing more, and nothing less.

Furthermore, device hygiene is a crucial element of endpoint protection. Think of it as encouraging healthy habits among the inhabitants of your digital city. Users and device owners are encouraged to maintain their devices' security by keeping software up to date, using strong passwords, and adhering to security policies.

Imagine an employee receiving regular reminders to update their device's operating system and software. Device hygiene practices help ensure that every device in your digital city remains secure, reducing vulnerabilities that attackers might exploit.

In summary, endpoint protection is the guardian of your digital city within the Zero Trust model. It's like having a dedicated security team for each device, continuously verifying identities, enforcing security measures, and responding to threats in real-time. In a world of evolving cyber threats, endpoint protection ensures that trust is never assumed, and security remains paramount, safeguarding your digital assets and protecting your organization's sensitive data.

**Chapter 6: Monitoring and Incident Response in Zero Trust Environments**

Imagine your organization's cybersecurity as a digital fortress, with valuable assets housed within its walls. In this fortified environment, real-time threat monitoring serves as the vigilant sentry, tasked with identifying and thwarting potential dangers before they breach the gates. It's akin to having a watchful guardian who scans the horizon, always on the lookout for any signs of trouble.

In the realm of cybersecurity, real-time threat monitoring is not a passive endeavor but an active and continuous process. Picture it as an ongoing conversation between your digital fortress and the outside world, where your fortress constantly gathers intelligence and analyzes data to assess the security of its perimeter.

Consider a scenario where your organization's network faces a constant barrage of incoming traffic. Some of this traffic is legitimate, like authorized user access, while some may be malicious, like attempted cyberattacks. Real-time threat monitoring distinguishes between the two, identifying potentially harmful activity amidst the sea of data.

To appreciate the significance of real-time threat monitoring, let's delve into the concept of threat intelligence. Think of it as the vast library of knowledge that your digital fortress consults regularly, gathering information about known threats and emerging risks.

Imagine a situation where a new type of malware is unleashed into the digital world. Threat intelligence systems would promptly detect and analyze this threat, providing your organization with insights into its behavior, indicators of compromise, and recommended countermeasures. It's like having access to a global network of informants who tip you off about potential dangers.

In the context of real-time threat monitoring, consider the importance of Security Information and Event Management (SIEM) systems. SIEM systems act as the interpreters of the digital world, collecting and analyzing vast amounts of security-related data generated by your organization's systems, applications, and devices.

Imagine a scenario where multiple alarms are triggered within your digital fortress. These alarms could be related to failed login attempts, suspicious network traffic, or unusual system behavior. SIEM systems consolidate and correlate this information, helping your security team pinpoint the source of the threat and take timely action. It's like having a team of investigators who sift through clues to uncover the culprit. Real-time threat monitoring also involves the use of intrusion detection systems (IDS) and intrusion prevention systems (IPS). Think of these as the gatekeepers who scrutinize every entity attempting to enter your digital fortress. Consider an outsider attempting to breach your network's defenses. IDS systems would detect this intrusion attempt in real-time, raising an alert. IPS systems can take immediate action to block the intruder's access, preventing any potential harm. It's like having a security detail that intervenes the moment an unauthorized individual tries to breach the gates.

Moreover, behavioral analytics plays a pivotal role in real-time threat monitoring. Think of this as having a keen observer who profiles the behavior of users, devices, and entities within your digital fortress.

Imagine an employee, whose usual behavior involves accessing certain applications and data during specific hours, suddenly attempting to access sensitive financial records at an unusual time. Behavioral analytics would flag this behavior as suspicious, prompting further investigation. It's like having a digital psychologist who identifies anomalies in behavior patterns.

In the dynamic landscape of real-time threat monitoring, consider the role of Security Orchestration, Automation, and Response (SOAR) systems. Think of these as the enablers of rapid response, orchestrating security measures and automating responses to identified threats.

Imagine a situation where a security breach is detected. SOAR systems can initiate predefined response actions, such as isolating affected systems, blocking malicious IP addresses, or alerting the incident response team. It's like having an emergency response plan that is executed swiftly and efficiently.

Furthermore, threat intelligence sharing is a collaborative aspect of real-time threat monitoring. Think of it as being part of a neighborhood watch program, where neighboring organizations share information about security incidents and threats to collectively enhance their defenses.

Consider a scenario where a neighboring organization experiences a cyberattack. By sharing threat intelligence, your organization can proactively take measures to defend against a similar attack, fortifying your digital fortress. It's like having a network of allies who provide early warnings about potential threats.

The Zero Trust model aligns seamlessly with real-time threat monitoring. It's like having a philosophy that advocates continuous scrutiny, regardless of the source or location of an entity. In a Zero Trust environment, trust is never assumed, and access is continually verified.

Imagine a situation where a user within your network attempts to access a critical database. In a Zero Trust model with real-time threat monitoring, the user's identity, behavior, and access request are scrutinized, even if they are connecting from a trusted location. Zero Trust ensures that access remains contingent on continuous validation.

In summary, real-time threat monitoring is the ever-watchful guardian of your digital fortress in the world of cybersecurity. It's like having a vigilant sentry who tirelessly scans the horizon for potential threats, continuously assesses the security of your perimeter, and responds swiftly to any signs of trouble. In a world where cyber threats constantly evolve, real-time threat monitoring ensures that your organization's defenses remain robust, safeguarding your valuable digital assets and sensitive data. Imagine your organization's cybersecurity as a bustling city, with various departments and services working in harmony. Now, envision an incident as a sudden disturbance, like a fire breaking out in one of the city's buildings. Incident response within a Zero Trust framework is akin to a well-coordinated emergency response team, ready to swiftly and efficiently address any unexpected events, ensuring minimal disruption and damage. In the realm of cybersecurity, incidents can take various forms, from data breaches and malware infections to insider threats and system vulnerabilities. Regardless of the nature of the incident, a Zero Trust framework dictates that trust should never be assumed, even within the confines of your organization's digital city.

Consider a scenario where an employee's credentials are compromised, and an unauthorized user gains access to sensitive company data. In a traditional security paradigm, the trust placed in the employee's identity might lead to delayed detection and response. However, in a Zero Trust framework, this trust is questioned, and an incident response plan is activated.

To grasp the significance of incident response within a Zero Trust framework, let's delve into the concept of continuous monitoring. It's like having surveillance cameras and alarms throughout your digital city, constantly vigilant for any signs of trouble.

Imagine a situation where unusual network activity is detected, such as an employee's device attempting to access unauthorized resources. Continuous monitoring systems raise alerts, prompting further investigation. It's like having sensors that can detect early indicators of a fire before it spreads.

Furthermore, incident response within a Zero Trust framework relies on Security Information and Event Management (SIEM) systems. Think of these systems as the nerve center of your digital city, collecting and analyzing vast amounts of security-related data.

Consider a scenario where multiple alarms are triggered within your organization's network, indicating potential security incidents. SIEM systems consolidate and correlate this information, providing a centralized view that helps your incident response team assess the situation and take appropriate action. It's like having a command center that coordinates emergency responses across the city.

Real-time threat monitoring, another component of the Zero Trust framework, plays a pivotal role in incident response. Think of it as having a network of informants who tip you off about potential dangers.

Imagine a situation where a new type of malware is identified in the wild. Real-time threat monitoring systems promptly detect and analyze this threat, providing your organization with valuable intelligence to strengthen its defenses. It's like receiving early warnings from trusted sources within your digital city.

Incident response also involves the use of intrusion detection and prevention systems (IDS/IPS). Think of these systems as the gatekeepers who scrutinize every entity attempting to enter your digital city.

Consider an outsider attempting to breach your organization's network. IDS systems detect this intrusion attempt in real-time, raising an alert. IPS systems can take immediate action to block the intruder's access, preventing any potential harm. It's like having a dedicated security detail that intervenes the moment an unauthorized individual tries to enter.

Moreover, behavioral analytics is a key element of incident response within a Zero Trust framework. Think of it as having a digital psychologist who profiles the behavior of users, devices, and entities within your digital city.

Imagine an employee, whose usual behavior involves accessing certain applications and data during specific hours, suddenly attempting to access sensitive financial records at an unusual time. Behavioral analytics would flag this behavior as suspicious, prompting further investigation. It's like having a keen observer who identifies anomalies in behavior patterns.

Furthermore, Security Orchestration, Automation, and Response (SOAR) systems come into play during incident response. Think of these systems as the coordinators of your emergency response team, orchestrating actions and automating responses to identified threats.

Imagine a situation where a security breach is detected. SOAR systems can initiate predefined response actions, such as isolating affected systems, blocking malicious IP addresses, or alerting the incident response team. It's like having an emergency response plan that is executed swiftly and efficiently.

In the context of incident response within a Zero Trust framework, consider the importance of collaboration and threat intelligence sharing. Think of it as being part of a neighborhood watch program, where neighboring organizations share information about security incidents and threats to collectively enhance their defenses.

Consider a scenario where a neighboring organization experiences a cyberattack. By sharing threat intelligence, your organization can proactively take measures to defend against a similar attack, fortifying your digital city. It's like having a network of allies who provide early warnings about potential threats.

The Zero Trust model aligns seamlessly with incident response. It's like having a philosophy that advocates continuous scrutiny, regardless of the source or location of an incident. In a Zero Trust environment, trust is never assumed, and incident response is guided by a proactive and cautious approach.

Imagine a situation where an employee within your network inadvertently clicks on a phishing email link. In a Zero Trust model with robust incident response capabilities, the incident is detected and contained swiftly, minimizing the potential damage. Zero Trust ensures that incident response is part of your organization's DNA, ready to address any security incidents, regardless of their origin.

In summary, incident response within a Zero Trust framework is the well-coordinated emergency response team for your digital city. It's like having a dedicated team of professionals who are always prepared to address unexpected events, ensuring minimal disruption and damage. In a world where cyber threats are ever-evolving, incident response within a Zero Trust framework ensures that your organization remains resilient and capable of swiftly addressing security incidents, safeguarding your digital assets, and maintaining trust in the digital landscape.

## Chapter 7: Cloud Adoption and Zero Trust

Imagine the vast digital landscape of cloud computing, where your organization's data and applications reside in a virtual realm, accessible from anywhere in the world. In this expansive cloud city, security challenges can be as diverse and complex as the skyline itself, but fear not, for Zero Trust solutions stand ready to provide a fortified defense, ensuring the safety of your digital assets.

The journey into the cloud brings forth a multitude of security considerations. Picture it as venturing into a bustling city where different neighborhoods represent various cloud providers, each with its unique characteristics and potential risks. These cloud neighborhoods are your chosen cloud service providers, such as Amazon Web Services (AWS), Microsoft Azure, or Google Cloud Platform.

In this urban analogy, each cloud provider offers its version of security measures, similar to distinct city police departments patrolling their respective neighborhoods. While these security measures are robust, they are designed to protect the overall environment, not necessarily the specific assets your organization houses within.

This is where the concept of Shared Responsibility comes into play. Think of it as a collaborative effort between you, the cloud tenant, and the cloud service provider. You're responsible for securing your data and applications within the cloud, while the provider ensures the security of the underlying cloud infrastructure.

In this shared responsibility model, it's essential to delineate responsibilities clearly, much like having a neighborhood watch program where each resident knows their role in securing their property. This distinction helps avoid potential security gaps and ensures comprehensive protection.

The move to the cloud often entails a significant shift in the security paradigm. Imagine transitioning from a fortified physical office building with well-defined perimeters to a virtual workspace accessible from anywhere. This shift brings about a change in the security landscape, where traditional security models may not suffice.

In a traditional office environment, the security model is often perimeter-centric, akin to a gated community with strict access controls. However, the cloud's borderless nature challenges this traditional approach. In the cloud city, there are no fixed gates; instead, access can occur from any location and device. This shift necessitates a more dynamic and adaptable security model.

Zero Trust solutions step in as the architects of this new security paradigm. Imagine them as the city planners who redesign the urban layout to accommodate the changing landscape. Zero Trust operates on the fundamental principle that trust is never assumed, regardless of a user's location or device.

In a Zero Trust cloud environment, each user and device must continually authenticate and validate their identity before accessing resources, much like having to show identification every time you enter a new building. Access is determined based on factors such as user identity, device health, and context, ensuring that trust is earned with each interaction.

Furthermore, the concept of Micro-Segmentation becomes crucial in a Zero Trust cloud strategy. Think of it as dividing the cloud city into smaller, isolated districts, each with its security controls. These districts are like secure enclaves where specific applications and data reside, accessible only to authorized individuals.

Imagine an employee attempting to access sensitive financial data within the cloud city. Micro-Segmentation ensures that the employee can access only the specific district containing the financial data, limiting their reach to other parts of the city. This granular approach significantly reduces the potential attack surface.

Multi-Factor Authentication (MFA) also plays a pivotal role in a Zero Trust cloud environment. Think of it as having multiple layers of security clearance before entering a secure facility within the cloud city.

Consider an employee accessing critical applications within the cloud. MFA prompts the employee not only to enter their password but also to provide an additional verification, such as a one-time code generated on their mobile device. This multi-layered approach adds a robust security barrier, making it challenging for unauthorized access.

Moreover, the Zero Trust model advocates the principle of Least Privilege Access, similar to granting specific permissions only to individuals who require them. Imagine being given access to only the floors you need in a multi-story building, rather than having access to the entire structure.

In a Zero Trust cloud environment, permissions are granted based on a user's role and responsibilities, ensuring that they can access only the resources necessary for their tasks. This approach minimizes the risk of unauthorized access and potential data breaches.

Zero Trust solutions also emphasize the importance of continuous monitoring, much like having security cameras in every corner of the cloud city. These monitoring systems continually assess user behavior, device health, and network traffic for any signs of suspicious activity.

Imagine an employee, whose usual pattern involves accessing specific cloud resources during regular working hours, suddenly attempting to access sensitive data late at night. Continuous monitoring systems would flag this behavior as unusual, triggering alerts and potential security responses.

Furthermore, Zero Trust solutions enable organizations to implement stringent security policies, much like establishing rules and regulations within a city. These policies govern access, data handling, and security controls, ensuring that all residents (users) adhere to a common set of security guidelines.

Imagine an organization specifying that all cloud data must be encrypted and that access to sensitive information requires multi-factor authentication. These policies serve as the digital laws of the cloud city, enforced consistently to maintain security standards.

Zero Trust also extends its reach to remote and mobile device security, much like ensuring that all vehicles within a city meet safety and emissions standards. In a cloud environment, remote and mobile devices are like vehicles traveling in and out of the city, potentially carrying sensitive cargo (data).

Zero Trust solutions ensure that these devices meet security standards before granting access to cloud resources. They may require devices to have up-to-date security software, encryption, and remote wipe capabilities to protect data in case of loss or theft.

Imagine your organization's journey into the cloud as a grand adventure, with your data and applications embarking on a new digital frontier. As you set sail into this vast virtual realm, it's essential to consider the integration of Zero Trust principles with your chosen cloud service provider, as this integration will be your trusted guide through uncharted territories.

In this digital journey, your cloud service provider becomes your trusted companion, akin to a skilled navigator on a seafaring voyage. Each cloud provider, whether it's Amazon

Web Services (AWS), Microsoft Azure, Google Cloud Platform, or others, offers its unique set of tools, services, and security measures. However, it's important to remember that their primary responsibility is to secure the underlying cloud infrastructure, much like ensuring the seaworthiness of the ship.

In this partnership, it's crucial to establish a clear division of responsibilities, much like delineating roles among a ship's crew. Your organization assumes the responsibility of securing the data and applications hosted within the cloud, while the cloud service provider takes care of the infrastructure's security.

Consider the cloud service provider's security measures as the sturdy hull of the ship, safeguarding it from external threats. While this hull is formidable, your organization's data and applications are like precious cargo within the ship, requiring additional protection.

This concept aligns with the Shared Responsibility Model, much like having a cooperative effort among crew members to ensure the safe passage of the ship. You and your cloud service provider must work together to navigate the digital seas safely.

In this collaborative journey, your organization's responsibilities include configuring and securing the cloud environment, much like setting the sails and rigging on a ship. This entails configuring access controls, encrypting data, and implementing security policies, all of which are essential aspects of Zero Trust.

Imagine configuring access controls within your cloud environment as setting strict admission requirements for passengers boarding your ship. Zero Trust principles advocate that trust should never be assumed, and access should always be contingent on continuous verification.

Multi-Factor Authentication (MFA) plays a pivotal role in this verification process, much like requiring passengers to provide multiple forms of identification before embarking on a journey. MFA adds an extra layer of security by ensuring that users authenticate themselves through something they know (like a password) and something they have (like a mobile device).

Moreover, the principle of Least Privilege Access applies to your cloud environment, similar to providing passengers access only to specific areas of the ship based on their roles and responsibilities. This principle ensures that users and applications have access only to the resources necessary for their tasks, minimizing the potential attack surface.

Micro-Segmentation, a key concept in Zero Trust, is like dividing the ship into separate compartments, each with its security controls. Just as compartments restrict access to specific areas of the ship, Micro-Segmentation limits access within your cloud environment, isolating applications and data to reduce the impact of potential breaches.

Think of Micro-Segmentation as having secure vaults within the ship where valuable cargo is stored. Even if one compartment is breached, the others remain secure, preventing unauthorized access to critical resources.

Continual monitoring, another cornerstone of Zero Trust, is like having a vigilant lookout on the ship's crow's nest, constantly scanning the horizon for potential threats. In your cloud environment, continuous monitoring systems assess user behavior, network traffic, and device health for any signs of suspicious activity.

These systems serve as the digital eyes and ears, alerting your organization to potential security incidents. Imagine a lookout spotting a distant storm cloud, giving you ample time to adjust course and avoid potential danger.

Security Information and Event Management (SIEM) systems are like the ship's communication network, relaying information from various parts of the vessel to a centralized command center. SIEM systems collect and analyze security-related data, providing a holistic view of your cloud environment's security.

Consider SIEM systems as the means by which you receive reports about the ship's condition, enabling you to make informed decisions and take immediate action if necessary. In the cloud, SIEM systems offer insights into security incidents and potential threats, facilitating a proactive response. Real-time threat monitoring, much like having a weather radar on the ship, scans the digital skies for any approaching storms. These monitoring systems detect and analyze emerging threats, ensuring that your cloud environment remains resilient and prepared to face evolving challenges.

Imagine the radar detecting a sudden change in atmospheric pressure, alerting you to an incoming squall. Real-time threat monitoring provides early warnings about potential cyber threats, allowing your organization to respond swiftly and effectively.

Behavioral analytics, akin to studying the behavior of the ship's crew and passengers, profiles the actions and interactions of users, devices, and entities within your cloud environment. This analysis helps identify anomalies and potential security risks.

Think of behavioral analytics as having a digital psychologist who can detect unusual behavior patterns. For example, if an employee typically accesses specific resources during regular working hours but suddenly attempts to access sensitive data late at night, behavioral analytics would flag this as suspicious, prompting further investigation.

Security Orchestration, Automation, and Response (SOAR) systems within your cloud environment are like having an efficient crew that can respond rapidly to changing conditions. These systems coordinate security measures and automate responses to identified threats, ensuring swift and efficient incident handling.

Consider SOAR systems as the crew members who follow established emergency response protocols, taking immediate action to mitigate potential risks. In the cloud, these systems can initiate predefined response actions, such as isolating affected resources or alerting the incident response team.

Moreover, threat intelligence sharing becomes an integral part of your cloud security strategy. Imagine your cloud environment as a vast sea, and threat intelligence sharing as a network of lighthouses that signal impending dangers.

In this network, you and other organizations share information about security incidents and emerging threats, providing early warnings to one another. This collaborative effort enhances your collective defenses, much like ships communicating to navigate safely through treacherous waters.

In summary, integrating Zero Trust principles with your cloud service provider is like embarking on a digital voyage with a reliable navigator by your side. Together, you and your cloud service provider can navigate the complexities of the cloud, secure your data and applications, and respond effectively to emerging challenges. Zero Trust serves as your guiding star, ensuring that trust is never assumed, and security remains a top priority throughout your cloud journey.

## Chapter 8: Integrating Zero Trust with Existing Security Frameworks

Imagine a world where security is an ever-evolving puzzle, with threats constantly morphing and adapting, much like a chessboard where adversaries maneuver to gain an advantage. In this complex landscape, traditional security measures serve as the foundational pieces of defense, providing essential protection to your organization's assets.

Traditional security, much like the initial moves of a chess game, encompasses well-established practices such as firewalls, intrusion detection systems, and antivirus software. These measures are the stalwart guardians, defending against known threats and maintaining a baseline level of security.

Think of them as the initial line of defense, much like the front row of chess pieces protecting the rest of the board. They establish a perimeter, monitor incoming and outgoing traffic, and identify known malicious patterns. However, as the chess game progresses, adversaries employ advanced tactics, necessitating a more adaptable strategy.

This is where Zero Trust steps onto the chessboard, like a chess grandmaster with a deep understanding of the game's intricacies. Zero Trust, as a security concept, challenges the traditional notion of trust, advocating that trust should never be assumed, even within your organization's walls.

Imagine traditional security measures as the castle walls of your organization, providing a sense of security within a defined perimeter. However, as threats become more sophisticated, it's crucial to recognize that adversaries might already be inside the castle, much like an opponent's pieces infiltrating your territory.

Zero Trust principles take this reality into account. They encourage organizations to scrutinize every user, device, and interaction, much like examining each move on the chessboard for potential threats. In a Zero Trust model, trust is not granted based on location, and access is not assumed simply because a user is within the castle walls.

Multi-Factor Authentication (MFA) plays a pivotal role in this approach, much like requiring players to validate each move with multiple strategies. MFA ensures that users must provide more than just a username and password to gain access. This multi-layered verification process adds a robust layer of security, making it challenging for adversaries to breach the defenses.

Moreover, the principle of Least Privilege Access is like the strategic placement of pieces on the chessboard, ensuring that each piece has a specific role and cannot move beyond its designated capabilities. In a Zero Trust model, users are granted access only to the resources necessary for their roles and responsibilities, reducing the attack surface.

Imagine a chessboard where each piece is carefully positioned to protect the king. Similarly, in a Zero Trust model, access controls are meticulously configured to safeguard critical assets, much like positioning the most critical chess pieces to ensure the king's safety.

Micro-Segmentation, another essential element of Zero Trust, is like dividing the chessboard into smaller, isolated sections, each with its security measures. Just as chess pieces are confined to specific areas of the board, Micro-Segmentation limits access within the network, isolating applications and data to contain potential breaches.

Picture a game of chess where only certain pieces can interact with one another while others remain isolated. Similarly, Micro-Segmentation ensures that only authorized entities can access specific parts of the network, limiting lateral movement for potential threats.

Continuous monitoring in a Zero Trust model is like a vigilant chess player constantly analyzing the board for enemy moves. These monitoring systems assess user behavior, device health, and network traffic, flagging any deviations from expected patterns.

Consider a chess player who notices an opponent's piece advancing unexpectedly. Continuous monitoring systems in a Zero Trust model would similarly detect unusual behavior, prompting further investigation and potential response.

Furthermore, the concept of Behavioral Analytics is like studying an opponent's gameplay over time, learning their strategies and tendencies. In a Zero Trust model, behavioral analytics profile user actions and interactions, identifying anomalies and potential risks based on historical data.

Think of it as recognizing patterns in your opponent's moves and adjusting your strategy accordingly. Behavioral analytics help organizations detect unusual behavior patterns, alerting them to potential security threats.

Security Information and Event Management (SIEM) systems within Zero Trust are like having a seasoned chess coach providing insights and guidance during a match. These systems collect and analyze security-related data, offering a comprehensive view of the organization's security posture.

Imagine a chess coach offering advice on strategy and tactics based on the unfolding game. SIEM systems, similarly, provide valuable information about security incidents and potential threats, enabling organizations to make informed decisions and take immediate action if necessary.

Zero Trust also emphasizes the importance of security policies, much like establishing rules and strategies for a successful chess game. These policies govern access, data handling, and security controls, ensuring that all players (users) adhere to a common set of guidelines.

Consider it as having a rulebook for the chess match, ensuring that both players abide by a standardized set of rules. In the digital realm, security policies enforce security standards, guiding users and applications towards secure behavior.

Zero Trust extends its reach to remote and mobile device security, similar to ensuring that chess pieces meet certain criteria for participation. In a Zero Trust model, remote and mobile devices must meet security standards before gaining access to resources, much like chess pieces must adhere to specific rules to be part of the game.

Think of it as verifying that each chess piece is made of the right material and conforms to the game's regulations. Similarly, Zero Trust ensures that remote and mobile devices are equipped with security measures such as up-to-date software and encryption.

In summary, Zero Trust acts as a strategic chess player in the realm of security, complementing traditional security measures to adapt to the evolving threat landscape. While traditional security establishes the initial defenses, Zero Trust continuously assesses and adapts, ensuring that trust is earned with each move, and security remains resilient in the face of ever-changing challenges.

Imagine your organization's security landscape as a well-constructed house, with various layers of defenses built over the years to safeguard your valuable assets. These layers, much like the foundation, walls, and roof of a house, have served their purpose, providing protection against known threats and vulnerabilities. However, as the digital world evolves, so do the tactics of adversaries, making it imperative for your organization to consider transitioning from legacy security to a more adaptive and resilient approach, such as Zero Trust.

Picture your legacy security measures as the original components of your house, designed with care and expertise at the time of their installation. Firewalls, intrusion detection systems, and antivirus software are the building blocks of this security architecture, forming the outer shell of protection.

Think of them as the sturdy walls that have protected your organization from intruders for years. While these measures have served you well, they rely on the concept of trust within your network. Once an entity is inside the perimeter, it is often trusted implicitly, much like trusted occupants inside a house.

However, the digital landscape has evolved, introducing new challenges and threats, much like the changing climate and weather patterns affecting your physical house. Adversaries have become more sophisticated, targeting vulnerabilities within your organization's network and exploiting the inherent trust that legacy security measures often assume.

This is where the concept of Zero Trust enters the picture, acting as an adaptive blueprint to retrofit your existing security framework. Zero Trust recognizes that trust should never be assumed, even for entities within your network, much like installing modern security features in your house to enhance protection.

Consider Multi-Factor Authentication (MFA) as one of these modern security features, much like a smart lock system for your home. MFA requires users to authenticate themselves through multiple verification methods, ensuring that access is granted only to those who can prove their identity beyond a doubt.

Think of it as requiring both a physical key and a unique passcode to unlock your front door. Similarly, MFA adds an extra layer of security by requiring users to provide something they know (like a password) and something they have (like a smartphone).

Furthermore, the principle of Least Privilege Access is like installing specialized locks on different rooms within your house. In a Zero Trust model, users and entities are granted access only to the resources necessary for their roles and responsibilities, reducing the potential attack surface.

Imagine having keys that open only specific doors in your house, limiting access to authorized areas. Similarly, Least Privilege Access ensures that users can interact with only the resources essential to their tasks, minimizing the risk of unauthorized access to critical assets.

Micro-Segmentation, another crucial aspect of Zero Trust, is akin to dividing your house into separate, secure zones. Just as you might compartmentalize your house to prevent the spread of fire or contain potential threats, Micro-Segmentation isolates applications and data within your network, limiting lateral movement for potential threats.

Think of it as having firewalls between different sections of your house, preventing the spread of flames from one room to another. Similarly, Micro-Segmentation ensures that even if one part of your network is breached, the rest remains secure, minimizing the impact of potential security incidents.

Continuous monitoring, a cornerstone of Zero Trust, is like having a vigilant security system in your house that constantly watches for unusual activity. These monitoring systems assess user behavior, network traffic, and device health, flagging any deviations from expected patterns.

Imagine having motion sensors and surveillance cameras in your home that alert you to any suspicious movements. Continuous monitoring in a Zero Trust model provides real-time insights into potential security threats, allowing you to respond promptly.

Behavioral analytics within a Zero Trust framework are like having a smart home system that learns your daily routines and can detect anomalies. These analytics profile user actions and interactions, identifying unusual behavior patterns that might indicate security risks.

Think of it as your smart home system noticing a change in your regular schedule and alerting you to potential issues. Similarly, behavioral analytics in a Zero Trust model help organizations detect deviations from normal behavior, enabling them to investigate and address potential threats.

Security Information and Event Management (SIEM) systems within Zero Trust are like having a central command center in your house that monitors all security-related activities. SIEM systems collect and analyze data from various sources, offering a holistic view of your organization's security posture.

Consider SIEM systems as the central hub where all security information converges, allowing you to see the bigger picture. In the event of a security incident, SIEM systems provide valuable insights, enabling your organization to respond effectively.

In summary, transitioning from legacy security to Zero Trust is like modernizing your house to adapt to changing security needs. While legacy security measures have provided a strong foundation, Zero Trust enhances your security posture, ensuring that trust is earned with each interaction and that your organization remains resilient in the face of evolving threats.

## Chapter 9: Real-world Case Studies of Successful Implementations

Imagine a bustling financial institution, where the security of sensitive financial data is paramount, and customer trust is the bedrock of its success. This case study delves into the journey of this institution as it embraced the principles of Zero Trust to fortify its security posture and ensure the confidentiality, integrity, and availability of its financial services.

Picture the financial institution's security landscape as a vault safeguarding immense wealth, with traditional security measures serving as the initial layers of defense. Firewalls, intrusion detection systems, and access controls are like the heavy, reinforced doors guarding access to the vault.

Think of them as the vigilant sentinels at the entrance, ensuring that only authorized personnel can gain access to the financial data within. However, as cyber threats evolve, the institution recognized the need to adopt a more proactive and adaptable approach to security.

This is where the concept of Zero Trust entered the equation, like a new layer of security measures designed to enhance the existing defenses. Zero Trust challenges the traditional notion of trust, advocating that trust should never be assumed, even within the institution's network.

Imagine a scenario where access to the vault requires multiple layers of verification, even for employees. Multi-Factor Authentication (MFA) became an integral part of the institution's security strategy, much like requiring employees to present both a keycard and a unique PIN to enter secure areas.

Think of it as adding an extra layer of security, ensuring that access is granted only to individuals who can provide multiple forms of authentication. MFA made it significantly more challenging for unauthorized users to gain entry, enhancing security.

Furthermore, the principle of Least Privilege Access was like refining the institution's internal processes, much like delegating specific tasks to employees based on their roles and responsibilities. In a Zero Trust model, users and systems are granted access only to the resources necessary for their functions.

Imagine assigning employees specific access levels and permissions, limiting their abilities to interact with certain data or systems. Least Privilege Access minimized the risk of unauthorized access and reduced the attack surface, strengthening the institution's defenses.

Micro-Segmentation, another pivotal aspect of Zero Trust, is akin to dividing the institution's network into secure zones, much like isolating different sections of a fortified castle. Micro-Segmentation ensured that even if one part of the network was compromised, the rest remained secure, preventing lateral movement for potential threats.

Consider it as creating distinct compartments within the institution's network, each with its access controls and security measures. Micro-Segmentation allowed for granular control over network traffic and limited the spread of potential security incidents.

Continuous monitoring within a Zero Trust framework is like having vigilant security personnel stationed throughout the institution, constantly watching for unusual activity. These monitoring systems assessed user behavior, network traffic, and device health, flagging any deviations from expected patterns.

Imagine security personnel scrutinizing every person entering the institution for suspicious behavior or items. Continuous monitoring provided real-time insights into potential security threats, allowing the institution to respond promptly.

Behavioral analytics within the Zero Trust model are like having an advanced profiling system that learns the typical behavior of employees and customers. These analytics identified anomalies and potential risks based on historical data, much like recognizing unusual patterns in customer behavior.

Consider it as a system that detects deviations from the norm, such as irregular transaction patterns or unusual data access requests. Behavioral analytics became a valuable tool in identifying potential security incidents early.

Security Information and Event Management (SIEM) systems within Zero Trust served as the institution's central command center, much like the nerve center of a military operation. SIEM systems collected and analyzed security-related data from across the institution, providing a comprehensive view of the security landscape.

Imagine a control room where data from various sources converged, allowing security personnel to monitor and respond to security events effectively. SIEM systems offered valuable insights into security incidents and potential threats, enabling the institution to make informed decisions.

Zero Trust policies within the institution were like the institution's rulebook, guiding employees and systems toward secure behavior. These policies governed access, data handling, and security controls, ensuring that all users adhered to a common set of guidelines.

Think of it as setting the ground rules for employees and systems to follow, establishing a unified approach to security. Zero Trust policies ensured that security standards were upheld throughout the institution.

Remote and mobile device security in the Zero Trust model resembled stringent entry requirements for visitors, much like ensuring that guests meet specific criteria before entering a secure facility. Remote and mobile devices had to meet security standards before gaining access to the institution's network, much like requiring visitors to undergo security checks.

Imagine a visitor's center where individuals must pass through security checkpoints before entering a secure area. Similarly, remote and mobile devices were subjected to security checks, ensuring they met the institution's requirements for secure access.

In summary, the financial institution's journey toward embracing Zero Trust was like fortifying the vault that held its most valuable assets. By adopting the principles of Zero Trust, the institution enhanced its security posture, ensuring that trust was never assumed, and security remained at the forefront of its operations. This case study highlights the importance of adaptability and proactive security measures in safeguarding critical financial services.

Let's journey into the intricate world of healthcare, where patient privacy and data security are paramount. In this case study, we'll explore how a healthcare facility implemented the principles of Zero Trust to enhance its security posture, safeguard sensitive patient information, and ensure the uninterrupted delivery of critical healthcare services.

Imagine the healthcare facility as a sanctuary of healing, with traditional security measures serving as the initial barriers to protect patient data. Firewalls, antivirus software, and access controls are like the sturdy walls guarding the sanctity of patient records and sensitive medical information.

Think of them as the vigilant guardians at the facility's entrance, ensuring that only authorized personnel can access the invaluable data within. However, as the healthcare landscape evolves, so do the tactics of cyber adversaries, necessitating a more proactive and adaptive security approach.

This is where the concept of Zero Trust comes into play, acting as an additional layer of security measures designed to augment the existing defenses. Zero Trust challenges the traditional notion of trust within the network, advocating that trust should never be assumed, even within the healthcare facility's walls.

Imagine a scenario where access to patient records requires multiple layers of verification, even for healthcare professionals. Multi-Factor Authentication (MFA) became a crucial part of the healthcare facility's security strategy, much like requiring healthcare staff to provide both a secure ID card and a unique PIN to access patient records.

Think of it as adding an extra layer of security, ensuring that access is granted only to individuals who can provide multiple forms of authentication. MFA made it significantly more challenging for unauthorized users to access patient data, enhancing security.

Furthermore, the principle of Least Privilege Access was like refining the healthcare facility's internal processes, much like assigning specific roles and responsibilities to healthcare professionals based on their qualifications and duties. In a Zero Trust model, users and systems are granted access only to the resources essential for their functions.

Imagine assigning healthcare professionals specific access levels and permissions, limiting their abilities to view or modify patient records. Least Privilege Access minimized the risk of unauthorized access and reduced the attack surface, strengthening the healthcare facility's defenses.

Micro-Segmentation, another critical component of Zero Trust, is akin to creating distinct, secure wards within the healthcare facility. Micro-Segmentation ensured that even if one section of the network was breached, the rest remained secure, preventing lateral movement for potential threats.

Consider it as establishing secure zones within the healthcare facility, each with its access controls and security measures. Micro-Segmentation allowed for granular control over network traffic and limited the spread of potential security incidents.

Continuous monitoring within a Zero Trust framework is like having diligent security personnel stationed throughout the healthcare facility, constantly vigilant for unusual activity. These monitoring systems assessed user behavior, network traffic, and device health, flagging any deviations from expected patterns.

Imagine security personnel scrutinizing every individual entering the healthcare facility for unusual behavior or signs of unauthorized access. Continuous monitoring provided real-time insights into potential security threats, allowing the healthcare facility to respond promptly.

Behavioral analytics within the Zero Trust model are like having an advanced profiling system that learns the typical behavior of healthcare professionals. These analytics identified anomalies and potential risks based on historical data, much like recognizing unusual patterns in healthcare staff behavior.

Consider it as a system that detects deviations from the norm, such as irregular data access or unexpected patient record requests. Behavioral analytics became a valuable tool in identifying potential security incidents early.

Security Information and Event Management (SIEM) systems within Zero Trust served as the healthcare facility's central command center, much like the nerve center coordinating critical medical operations. SIEM systems collected and analyzed security-related data from across the healthcare facility, providing a comprehensive view of the security landscape.

Imagine a control room where data from various sources converged, allowing security personnel to monitor and respond to security events effectively. SIEM systems offered valuable insights into security incidents and potential threats, enabling the healthcare facility to make informed decisions.

Zero Trust policies within the healthcare facility were like the institution's rulebook, guiding healthcare professionals and systems toward secure behavior. These policies governed access, data handling, and security controls, ensuring that all users adhered to a common set of guidelines.

Think of it as setting the ground rules for healthcare professionals and systems to follow, establishing a unified approach to security. Zero Trust policies ensured that security standards were upheld throughout the healthcare facility.

Remote and mobile device security in the Zero Trust model resembled stringent access requirements for visitors, much like ensuring that guests meet specific criteria before entering a highly secure area. Remote and mobile devices had to meet security standards before gaining access to the healthcare facility's network, much like requiring visitors to pass through multiple security checkpoints.

Imagine a visitor's center where individuals must undergo rigorous checks before entering a secure area. Similarly, remote and mobile devices were subjected to stringent security assessments, ensuring they met the healthcare facility's requirements for secure access.

In summary, the healthcare facility's journey toward implementing Zero Trust was like fortifying the sanctum of patient data and medical services. By embracing the principles of Zero Trust, the facility enhanced its security posture, ensuring that trust was never assumed, and patient data remained confidential and secure. This case study underscores the critical role of proactive and adaptable security measures in safeguarding the integrity of healthcare services and patient well-being.

## Chapter 10: Continuous Improvement: Evolving Your Zero Trust Strategy

Imagine a scenario where you've laid the foundation for a secure and dynamic security environment through Zero Trust principles, but the journey doesn't stop there. Now, it's time to delve into the crucial process of evaluating and adapting your Zero Trust policies to maintain a robust and resilient security posture.

Picture your Zero Trust policies as the rules governing access and behavior within your security ecosystem. These policies are like the guardrails along a highway, ensuring that your security remains on the right path. However, as the threat landscape evolves and your organization grows, these policies must adapt accordingly.

Think of your organization as a bustling city with various entry points, including employees, partners, contractors, and remote workers. Zero Trust policies, much like traffic rules, are designed to maintain order and security within this city. They dictate who can access what, under what conditions, and for how long.

Imagine a situation where a new technology or application is introduced into your organization. This is akin to adding a new type of vehicle to your city's streets. As new technologies emerge, your policies must adapt to accommodate them. Otherwise, you risk security gaps that could be exploited by malicious actors.

Consider a scenario where a critical security vulnerability is discovered in one of your applications. This is like discovering a hazardous road condition in your city. Zero Trust policies should be agile enough to respond quickly to these vulnerabilities, ensuring that the affected application is isolated or patched promptly.

Think of your security policies as constantly evolving road signs. Just as road signs are updated to reflect changing traffic conditions, Zero Trust policies should be adjusted to reflect the evolving threat landscape. For example, if a new type of cyber threat emerges, your policies must incorporate measures to counteract it.

Imagine that your organization is expanding into new markets or collaborating with different partners. This expansion is akin to building new roads and bridges in your city. As your organization's footprint grows, your policies should extend to cover these new areas and partnerships, ensuring that security remains comprehensive.

Consider a situation where your organization undergoes a merger or acquisition. This is like merging two cities into one. In such cases, your Zero Trust policies should seamlessly integrate the security measures of both entities, creating a unified security framework that spans the entire organization.

Think of your security policies as adaptable traffic signals. Just as traffic signals adjust the flow of vehicles to prevent congestion and accidents, your Zero Trust policies should adjust access and permissions to prevent security bottlenecks and breaches. For example, during peak usage times, policies may temporarily restrict access to certain resources to ensure optimal performance and security.

Imagine a scenario where a user's role within your organization changes. This is like a change in a driver's license category. When employees take on new responsibilities or roles, your policies should reflect these changes by adjusting their access and privileges accordingly.

Consider a situation where a third-party vendor needs access to your organization's systems. This is akin to granting access to a guest driver on your city's roads. While you want to accommodate their needs, your policies must ensure that their access is limited and closely monitored to prevent any security risks.

Think of your security policies as the navigation system for your organization's security journey. Just as a GPS guides you to your destination, your policies should guide users and systems through the security landscape, ensuring that they follow the correct path to access resources securely.

Imagine a scenario where an employee's device is compromised. This is like discovering a vehicle with a faulty brake system on your city's streets. In such cases, your policies should have mechanisms in place to quickly isolate the compromised device and prevent it from causing further harm.

Consider a situation where a security incident occurs within your organization. This is akin to a traffic accident in your city. Your policies should include incident response procedures that outline how to address and mitigate the impact of security incidents, minimizing disruption and damage.

Think of your security policies as the traffic management center for your organization's security operations. Just as a traffic management center monitors and responds to traffic incidents, your policies should enable your security team to monitor and respond to security incidents in real-time.

Imagine a scenario where regulatory requirements change, requiring your organization to comply with new standards. This is like a change in traffic laws that require drivers to follow new rules. Your policies must adapt to these changes to ensure that your organization remains compliant and avoids potential penalties.

Consider a situation where your organization undergoes a significant restructuring. This is akin to redesigning the road network in your city. During such transitions, your policies should be reviewed and adjusted to align with the new organizational structure and security needs.

Think of your security policies as the rulebook that governs your organization's security game. Just as athletes adapt their strategies to the changing dynamics of a game, your policies should adapt to the evolving security landscape, ensuring that your organization remains agile and resilient in the face of threats.

In summary, evaluating and adapting your Zero Trust policies is an ongoing and essential aspect of maintaining a strong security posture. Much like the ever-changing traffic patterns in a bustling city, your organization's security landscape will evolve, and your policies must evolve with it. By embracing adaptability and proactive adjustments, your organization can navigate the complex security journey with confidence and resilience.

Imagine your organization as a sentinel standing guard over its digital domain, facing a never-ending onslaught of cyber threats. In this ever-evolving landscape, the value of threat intelligence shines brightly as a beacon guiding you toward continuous improvement in your cybersecurity posture.

Think of threat intelligence as a network of informants, each providing valuable insights into the activities and intentions of potential adversaries. These informants are like the eyes and ears of your organization, collecting information from various sources, such as dark web forums, malware analysis, and incident reports.

Consider a scenario where a new type of malware is detected in the wild. This is akin to receiving a tip-off about a previously unknown criminal activity in your neighborhood. Threat intelligence provides you with the details of this malware, including its behavior, indicators of compromise, and potential impact.

Imagine your organization as a detective, tasked with solving the mystery of a cyber threat. Threat intelligence serves as the case file, providing you with the clues and evidence needed to identify, investigate, and respond to the threat effectively.

Think of threat intelligence as a comprehensive map of the cyber threat landscape, complete with markers indicating the locations of potential threats and vulnerabilities. This map helps you navigate the complex terrain of cyberspace and make informed decisions about where to allocate your resources for maximum impact.

Consider a situation where a security breach occurs within your organization. This is like a breach in the perimeter defenses of your fortress. Threat intelligence helps you understand how the breach occurred, what data may have been compromised, and whether it is part of a larger, coordinated attack.

Imagine your organization as a guardian responsible for protecting sensitive information. Threat intelligence is your trusted advisor, providing you with real-time information about emerging threats and vulnerabilities that could jeopardize your organization's security.

Think of threat intelligence as a library of knowledge, continuously updated with the latest insights into cyber threats. This library is like a reference guide that empowers your security team with the information they need to stay ahead of evolving threats.

Consider a scenario where your organization is planning a major software update. This is like preparing for a significant renovation of your digital infrastructure. Threat intelligence can help you assess the potential security risks associated with the update and develop strategies to mitigate them.

Imagine your organization as a chess player, constantly strategizing to outmaneuver its opponents. Threat intelligence provides you with the moves and countermoves of cyber adversaries, enabling you to anticipate their actions and plan your defense accordingly.

Think of threat intelligence as a crystal ball, offering glimpses into the future of cyber threats. While it can't predict every move of adversaries, it can provide you with valuable insights into emerging tactics, techniques, and procedures (TTPs) that may be used against your organization.

Consider a situation where a zero-day vulnerability is discovered in a widely used software application. This is like finding a hidden trapdoor in your castle's defenses. Threat intelligence can alert you to the existence of this vulnerability and provide guidance on how to protect your organization until a patch is available.

Imagine your organization as a vigilant guardian of its digital assets, committed to staying one step ahead of cyber adversaries. Threat intelligence is your trusted ally in this ongoing battle, providing you with the knowledge and awareness needed to make informed decisions and take proactive measures to safeguard your organization.

Think of threat intelligence as a radar system, constantly scanning the digital skies for signs of impending threats. When a potential threat is detected, it provides you with early warning, allowing you to respond swiftly and decisively to protect your organization.

Consider a scenario where your organization is targeted by a sophisticated phishing campaign. This is like being lured into a carefully laid trap. Threat intelligence can help you recognize the signs of phishing attempts, such as malicious email addresses or deceptive URLs, and educate your employees on how to spot and report such threats.

Imagine your organization as a community, where every member plays a role in its security. Threat intelligence is the neighborhood watch, keeping a vigilant eye on the digital streets and alerting you to any suspicious activity or potential threats.

Think of threat intelligence as a force multiplier, amplifying the effectiveness of your cybersecurity efforts. With the right threat intelligence, you can prioritize your security investments, focus on the most critical threats, and allocate your resources where they will have the greatest impact.

Consider a situation where your organization faces a data breach. This is like a breach in the walls of your fortress. Threat intelligence can help you identify the source of the breach, assess the extent of the damage, and formulate a response plan to contain and mitigate the incident.

Imagine your organization as a learning institution, committed to continuous improvement in its cybersecurity practices. Threat intelligence is the curriculum, providing you with valuable lessons on the evolving tactics and techniques of cyber adversaries.

Think of threat intelligence as a compass, guiding you toward the right direction in the ever-changing landscape of cyber threats. With the right threat intelligence, you can make informed decisions, adapt your security strategies, and stay ahead of the curve in the ongoing battle against cyber adversaries.

In summary, leveraging threat intelligence is not just about defending against cyber threats; it's about continuously improving your organization's ability to detect, respond to, and mitigate those threats. By embracing threat intelligence as a critical component of your cybersecurity strategy, you can navigate the complex world of cyber threats with confidence and resilience.

## BOOK 3
## ADVANCED ZERO TRUST ARCHITECTURES
## CYBER RESILIENCE AND EXPERT STRATEGIES

## ROB BOTWRIGHT

# Chapter 1: Foundations of Advanced Zero Trust Security

Picture a time when cybersecurity relied heavily on the concept of a trusted perimeter—a virtual fortress around an organization's network. In this bygone era, once someone or something breached the outer defenses, they often enjoyed a degree of implicit trust within the network, akin to a guest who had gained entry to a well-guarded castle.

Imagine this trust-centric model as a medieval castle with its sturdy walls and moat. Just as the castle protected its inhabitants from external threats, the perimeter-based approach aimed to shield an organization's digital assets from malicious actors lurking in the outside world.

Think of the traditional security model as a set of heavily fortified gates leading into the castle. These gates were guarded by various security mechanisms, such as firewalls and intrusion detection systems, designed to keep unauthorized intruders at bay.

Consider the notion of the trusted insider—someone within the castle walls, be it a nobleman, a servant, or a guest. In the traditional model, once an individual was inside the perimeter, they were often granted broad access privileges, similar to the way a trusted castle resident could freely roam the castle grounds.

Imagine a scenario where an intruder cunningly infiltrates the castle, perhaps by impersonating a trusted guest or using stealthy tactics. In the traditional security model, once inside, the intruder might have had ample opportunities to move freely and exploit vulnerabilities, much like a cyber attacker maneuvering through a network once past the outer defenses.

Think of the traditional security mindset as being akin to fortifying the castle walls even further, adding more layers of protection to the already formidable barriers. While this approach aimed to deter attackers, it often relied on the assumption that the perimeter would remain impervious.

Consider the limitations of this approach in the face of modern cyber threats. As technology evolved and the digital landscape expanded, the castle walls began to show cracks. The rise of remote work, cloud computing, and mobile devices blurred the boundaries of the traditional perimeter, creating new entry points for cyber attackers.

Imagine a scenario where an organization's sensitive data resided not just within the castle walls but also in various outposts and remote locations. In this distributed landscape, the traditional perimeter model struggled to provide the same level of protection, much like trying to defend multiple castles scattered across a vast kingdom.

Think of the evolving threat landscape as a collection of crafty adversaries who recognized the weaknesses in the traditional model. These adversaries exploited the gaps in the castle's defenses, targeting vulnerabilities both inside and outside the perimeter, much like cybercriminals targeting vulnerabilities within and beyond an organization's network.

Consider the need for a paradigm shift in cybersecurity—a new approach that would adapt to the changing digital landscape. Enter the concept of Zero Trust, a cybersecurity philosophy that challenges the notion of implicit trust and advocates for continuous verification and validation of every user and device, regardless of their location.

Imagine Zero Trust as a new way of thinking—a departure from the castle-and-moat mindset. Instead of assuming trust once someone or something gained entry, Zero Trust introduced the principle of "never trust, always verify," much like a vigilant guard who checks the credentials of everyone seeking access to the castle.

Think of Zero Trust as a network without a trusted perimeter—a network where security is not based on the location of users or devices but on their identity and behavior. In this model, each user and device is treated as if they were accessing the network for the first time, subject to rigorous authentication and authorization, similar to how a security checkpoint screens every visitor to the castle.

Consider the core principles of Zero Trust—verify explicitly, least privilege access, and assume breach. These principles are the foundation of the Zero Trust philosophy, emphasizing the need to authenticate and authorize users and devices rigorously, restrict access to the bare minimum required, and always be prepared for the possibility of a security breach.

Imagine the transformation underway in cybersecurity as organizations adopted the Zero Trust model. Instead of relying solely on the strength of perimeter defenses, they began implementing comprehensive identity and access management solutions, enforcing strict access controls, and continuously monitoring user and device behavior.

Think of the Zero Trust model as a dynamic security posture, one that adapts to the evolving threat landscape. In this model, security is not a static castle wall but a constantly shifting and evolving defense system, capable of responding to emerging threats and vulnerabilities in real-time.

Consider the importance of visibility and analytics in the Zero Trust approach. With the ability to monitor and analyze user and device behavior across the network, organizations gained a deeper understanding of their security posture, much like having watchful guards who patrol the castle grounds and report any suspicious activity.

Imagine a world where organizations no longer relied solely on a trusted perimeter but embraced a holistic and proactive approach to cybersecurity. This shift in mindset marked the evolution of Zero Trust principles from a theoretical concept to a practical and necessary security strategy.

Think of Zero Trust as a journey, one that organizations embarked on to enhance their cybersecurity resilience. It was not a destination but an ongoing process of strengthening security measures, adapting to new threats, and continually refining access controls, similar to a castle that constantly reinforces its defenses.

Consider the role of technology in enabling Zero Trust. From multi-factor authentication and identity management solutions to advanced analytics and threat intelligence, technology played a pivotal role in helping organizations implement and maintain the Zero Trust model.

Imagine a future where Zero Trust principles continue to evolve, adapting to emerging technologies and cyber threats. In this ever-changing landscape, the castle walls may have crumbled, but the spirit of vigilance and resilience lives on, guiding organizations toward a more secure and adaptable future. Think of the evolution of Zero Trust as a testament to the adaptability of cybersecurity practices. In a world where the digital landscape is in constant flux, the principles of Zero Trust serve as a beacon of trustworthiness and security, guiding organizations through the complexities of the modern cybersecurity landscape.

In the realm of advanced Zero Trust security, there are key concepts that form the bedrock of a robust and adaptive cybersecurity strategy. These concepts go beyond the basics, delving into the intricacies of securing a modern digital landscape. Let's explore these concepts and their significance in the world of advanced Zero Trust security.

Think of the first key concept as "Continuous Authentication." In the advanced Zero Trust model, authentication is not a one-time event but an ongoing process. It's like having a digital bouncer at the door, constantly verifying the identity of users and devices as they move throughout the network. Continuous authentication ensures that access remains restricted to authorized individuals or entities and responds swiftly to any suspicious activity. Consider "Dynamic Access Controls" as the second key concept. In advanced Zero Trust security, access control goes beyond traditional role-based permissions. It's like having an intelligent access manager who evaluates not only who you are but also what you're trying to access and why. Dynamic access controls adapt in real-time, granting or revoking privileges based on the context of the request and the user's behavior. Now, let's delve into the third key concept: "Adaptive Policies." In the advanced Zero Trust model, policies are not static rules but dynamic guidelines that adjust to changing conditions. It's like having a chameleon-like security policy that blends in with its surroundings. Adaptive policies consider factors such as user behavior, device health, and network conditions, allowing organizations to respond effectively to evolving threats.

Think of "Behavioral Analytics" as the fourth key concept. Advanced Zero Trust security employs machine learning and artificial intelligence to analyze user and device behavior. It's like having a digital detective who can spot anomalies and potential threats in the vast sea of network activity. Behavioral analytics provide organizations with early warning signs of security incidents and help identify insider threats. Consider "Threat Intelligence Integration" as the fifth key concept. In the advanced Zero Trust model, threat intelligence is not an isolated function but an integral part of the security ecosystem. It's like having a network of informants who feed real-time data about emerging threats and vulnerabilities. Threat intelligence integration empowers organizations to proactively defend against new attack vectors and stay ahead of cyber adversaries.

Now, let's explore the sixth key concept: "Micro-Segmentation." Advanced Zero Trust security takes network segmentation to the next level. It's like having a set of digital barriers that divide your network into micro-environments, each with its unique security policies. Micro-segmentation limits lateral movement for attackers, containing potential breaches and minimizing the impact of security incidents.

Think of "Zero Trust for Critical Infrastructure" as the seventh key concept. In advanced Zero Trust security, critical infrastructure is a focal point. It's like safeguarding the vital systems that power a city's infrastructure. Zero Trust principles are applied rigorously to protect critical assets, ensuring that they remain resilient in the face of cyber threats and potential disruptions.

Consider "Endpoint Detection and Response (EDR)" as the eighth key concept. Advanced Zero Trust security extends its reach to endpoints, such as laptops, desktops, and mobile devices. It's like having a network of sentinels that constantly monitor and respond to suspicious activity at the endpoint level. EDR solutions provide real-time threat detection, containment, and response capabilities, bolstering an organization's overall security posture.

Now, let's delve into the ninth key concept: "Zero Trust in Cloud-Native Environments." As organizations embrace cloud technologies, advanced Zero Trust security extends its principles to the cloud. It's like extending the castle's defenses into the cloud kingdom. Zero Trust for cloud-native environments ensures that data and applications are protected regardless of their location, whether on-premises or in the cloud.

Think of "Integration with Existing Security Frameworks" as the tenth key concept. Advanced Zero Trust security complements existing security investments rather than replacing them. It's like adding a new layer of security that seamlessly integrates with your current defenses. Integration with existing frameworks allows organizations to leverage their previous investments while enhancing their security posture.

Consider "Cyber Resilience" as the eleventh key concept. In advanced Zero Trust security, the focus goes beyond just prevention to include rapid response and recovery. It's like having a robust disaster recovery plan for your digital assets. Cyber resilience ensures that organizations can bounce back from security incidents swiftly, minimizing downtime and data loss.

Now, let's explore the twelfth key concept: "Zero Trust for IoT." As the Internet of Things (IoT) expands, advanced Zero Trust security extends its principles to IoT devices. It's like adding layers of security to a smart city's infrastructure. Zero Trust for IoT ensures that connected devices are rigorously authenticated, monitored, and secured, preventing them from becoming entry points for cyber threats.

Think of "Future-Proofing" as the final key concept. In advanced Zero Trust security, the approach is designed to evolve with the ever-changing threat landscape. It's like building a digital fortress that can adapt to new challenges and technologies. Future-proofing ensures that organizations remain resilient and agile in the face of emerging cyber threats and technological advancements.

These key concepts collectively form the foundation of advanced Zero Trust security. They empower organizations to adapt, respond, and thrive in the dynamic and challenging world of modern cybersecurity. By embracing these concepts, organizations can strengthen their defenses, protect critical assets, and stay ahead of cyber adversaries in an ever-evolving digital landscape.

**Chapter 2: Deep Dive into Zero Trust Architectures**

In the realm of advanced Zero Trust security, architectural components play a pivotal role in shaping the security posture of an organization. These components provide the framework and infrastructure needed to implement and maintain a robust Zero Trust model. Let's explore these advanced architectural components and their significance in the context of Zero Trust security.

Imagine "Multi-Layered Authentication" as the first architectural component. In advanced Zero Trust, authentication is not a single gatekeeper but a series of checkpoints, much like having multiple layers of security clearance. Multi-layered authentication ensures that users and devices go through a rigorous identity verification process, reducing the risk of unauthorized access.

Consider "Identity and Access Management (IAM)" as the second architectural component. IAM is the cornerstone of advanced Zero Trust security, akin to having a digital ID card for each user and device. IAM solutions centralize identity management, making it easier to enforce strict access controls and authentication policies across the organization.

Think of "Device Trustworthiness Assessment" as the third architectural component. In advanced Zero Trust, it's essential to evaluate the trustworthiness of devices, similar to checking the health of soldiers before they enter a secure facility. Device trustworthiness assessments determine whether a device meets security standards and can be granted access to the network.

Imagine "Network Segmentation" as the fourth architectural component. Advanced Zero Trust extends network segmentation to a granular level, dividing the network into smaller segments, each with its unique access policies. It's like creating distinct zones within a castle, with different levels of security clearance required to enter each zone. Network segmentation limits lateral movement for attackers and contains security incidents.

Consider "Secure Access Service Edge (SASE)" as the fifth architectural component. In advanced Zero Trust, SASE combines network security and wide-area networking (WAN) capabilities into a unified cloud-based service. It's like having a digital security checkpoint at the edge of the network, where all traffic is inspected and secured before entering or leaving the organization's network.

Think of "Security Orchestration and Automation" as the sixth architectural component. Advanced Zero Trust leverages automation to respond swiftly to security incidents, much like having a team of digital responders who can react in real-time. Security orchestration and automation streamline incident response, reducing the time it takes to mitigate threats and vulnerabilities.

Imagine "User and Entity Behavior Analytics (UEBA)" as the seventh architectural component. In advanced Zero Trust, UEBA solutions analyze user and device behavior patterns, similar to studying the habits of residents in a secure community. UEBA identifies anomalies and potential threats, allowing organizations to proactively address security issues.

Consider "Continuous Monitoring and Threat Detection" as the eighth architectural component. In advanced Zero Trust, continuous monitoring is a cornerstone, much like having surveillance cameras throughout a castle that never sleep. Continuous monitoring and threat detection ensure that security teams are alerted to suspicious activities in real-time, enabling rapid response.

Think of "Secure Cloud Gateway" as the ninth architectural component. In advanced Zero Trust, a secure cloud gateway acts as a secure entry point to cloud resources and services. It's like having a fortified gateway that verifies users and devices before granting access to cloud resources, ensuring that cloud-based assets are protected.

Imagine "Endpoint Detection and Response (EDR)" as the tenth architectural component. In advanced Zero Trust, EDR solutions extend their coverage to endpoints, continuously monitoring and responding to threats. It's like having a network of digital sentinels guarding every device, ready to take action against security incidents.

Consider "Zero Trust Network Access (ZTNA)" as the eleventh architectural component. In advanced Zero Trust, ZTNA solutions provide secure remote access, ensuring that users and devices can connect to the network securely, even from remote locations. It's like having a digital drawbridge that can be raised and lowered as needed to allow safe passage.

Think of "Security Information and Event Management (SIEM)" as the twelfth architectural component. In advanced Zero Trust, SIEM solutions collect and analyze security data from various sources, similar to having a team of vigilant analysts who sift through information to identify security threats. SIEM enhances threat visibility and helps organizations make informed security decisions.

Imagine "Threat Intelligence Integration" as the thirteenth architectural component. In advanced Zero Trust, threat intelligence feeds real-time data about emerging threats and vulnerabilities, much like having a network of informants who provide timely information. Threat intelligence integration empowers organizations to stay ahead of cyber adversaries and proactively defend against new threats.

Consider "Zero Trust for Internet of Things (IoT)" as the fourteenth architectural component. In advanced Zero Trust, IoT devices are rigorously authenticated, monitored, and secured. It's like adding layers of security to a smart city's infrastructure, ensuring that connected devices do not become entry points for cyber threats.

Think of "Integration with Cloud-Native Security Controls" as the fifteenth architectural component. In advanced Zero Trust, the model seamlessly integrates with cloud-native security controls, extending its principles to cloud environments. It's like extending the castle's defenses into the cloud kingdom, ensuring that data and applications are protected regardless of their location.

These advanced architectural components collectively form the infrastructure of advanced Zero Trust security. They empower organizations to build a dynamic, adaptive, and resilient security posture that can withstand the challenges of the modern threat landscape. By embracing these components, organizations can enhance their security defenses, protect critical assets, and respond effectively to emerging cyber threats.

Designing resilient Zero Trust architectures is like constructing a digital fortress, ensuring that your organization's data and assets are safeguarded in an ever-evolving threat landscape. It's a strategic approach that encompasses multiple layers of security and adaptability to counter emerging cyber threats. Resilience is not about being impervious to attacks but rather about the ability to withstand, recover from, and adapt to disruptions while maintaining essential functions.

To start, one of the foundational principles of a resilient Zero Trust architecture is "Assume Breach." This means acknowledging that no network or system is entirely immune to potential breaches. In a world where cyberattacks are constant, assuming a breach allows organizations to be prepared for the worst-case scenario and respond effectively when it occurs.

The first step in designing resilience is to establish a comprehensive "Risk Assessment." This involves identifying potential threats, vulnerabilities, and consequences of security incidents. By understanding the risks, organizations can prioritize their security efforts and allocate resources to areas that need the most protection.

A resilient Zero Trust architecture also places a strong emphasis on "Continuous Monitoring." This means having a constant and vigilant eye on network traffic, user behavior, and system health. Advanced monitoring tools, such as Security Information and Event Management (SIEM) systems, help organizations detect anomalies and potential threats in real-time, allowing for swift response.

Furthermore, a resilient architecture incorporates "Redundancy and Failover Mechanisms." Redundancy means having backup systems and components that can take over in case of a failure. Failover mechanisms ensure that critical services remain available even when certain components are compromised. Redundancy and failover contribute to the overall availability and reliability of the network.

Another crucial aspect of resilience is "Incident Response Planning." Organizations should have well-defined incident response plans in place, outlining the steps to take when a security incident occurs. These plans should include roles and responsibilities, communication protocols, and procedures for containing and mitigating the incident.

Incorporating "Backup and Recovery Strategies" is essential for resilience. Regularly backing up data and systems ensures that in the event of a cyberattack or data breach, organizations can restore their operations quickly. Backup and recovery strategies help minimize downtime and data loss.

A resilient Zero Trust architecture also integrates "User Training and Awareness." Human error is a common factor in security incidents. Therefore, educating users about security best practices and raising awareness about potential threats can significantly reduce the risk of breaches. Users become the first line of defense in recognizing and reporting suspicious activity.

Moreover, "Patch Management" is a critical element of resilience. Keeping software and systems up to date with the latest security patches helps close vulnerabilities that attackers could exploit. Automated patch management tools streamline this process, ensuring that patches are applied promptly.

To enhance resilience, organizations should also consider implementing "Security Orchestration and Automation." Automation can help respond to security incidents rapidly by executing predefined actions based on identified threats. It streamlines incident response and reduces the manual effort required during an attack.

Furthermore, a resilient Zero Trust architecture includes "Threat Intelligence Integration." Staying informed about emerging threats and vulnerabilities is vital. Threat intelligence feeds real-time data that can help organizations proactively defend against new attack vectors and tailor their security measures accordingly.

In addition to these technical aspects, a resilient architecture considers "Business Continuity and Disaster Recovery." It involves planning for situations where the organization's operations are severely disrupted, such as natural disasters or large-scale cyberattacks. Business continuity and disaster recovery plans ensure that essential functions can continue even in the face of adversity.

In the context of resilience, "Cloud-Native Security Controls" play a significant role. As organizations increasingly adopt cloud technologies, integrating Zero Trust principles into cloud environments becomes crucial. Cloud-native security controls extend the same level of security to cloud-based assets as on-premises ones.

Moreover, "Zero Trust for IoT" is a growing concern. With the proliferation of IoT devices, organizations need to apply the same rigorous security principles to these devices as they do to traditional endpoints. IoT devices can become entry points for cyber threats if not properly secured.

Lastly, "Cyber Resilience Strategies" involve continuously evolving and adapting security measures to stay ahead of the ever-changing threat landscape. It's an ongoing process that requires organizations to regularly reassess their security posture, update policies and procedures, and invest in emerging technologies to counter new threats.

In summary, designing resilient Zero Trust architectures is an intricate but necessary endeavor in today's cybersecurity landscape. It involves assuming breach, comprehensive risk assessments, continuous monitoring, redundancy, incident response planning, backup and recovery, user training, patch management, automation, threat intelligence, business continuity, cloud-native security, IoT security, and ongoing cyber resilience strategies. These elements collectively create a fortified digital fortress that can withstand, adapt to, and recover from security incidents, ensuring the protection of critical data and assets.

## Chapter 3: Zero Trust and Threat Intelligence Integration

In the ever-evolving landscape of cybersecurity, staying ahead of emerging threats is paramount. Leveraging threat intelligence has become a crucial component of advanced threat detection strategies. Picture threat intelligence as a network of informants who provide real-time data on potential threats and vulnerabilities. It's like having a digital early warning system that helps organizations anticipate and defend against cyberattacks.

To begin with, let's delve into the concept of "Threat Intelligence." Threat intelligence encompasses a wide range of information related to cybersecurity threats. It includes data about the tactics, techniques, and procedures (TTPs) of cyber adversaries, indicators of compromise (IOCs), vulnerabilities, and emerging attack trends. This wealth of information enables organizations to understand the evolving threat landscape.

Threat intelligence comes in various forms, such as "Open Source Intelligence (OSINT)," "Human Intelligence (HUMINT)," and "Technical Intelligence (TECHINT)." OSINT involves collecting information from publicly available sources, much like gathering news reports from various outlets. HUMINT involves human sources providing insights into the activities of threat actors, similar to intelligence agencies gathering information from informants. TECHINT involves technical data, such as analyzing malware code or network traffic patterns.

Effective threat intelligence relies on the aggregation and analysis of data from multiple sources, both internal and external. This process, known as "Threat Data Collection and Aggregation," involves gathering information from various security tools, logs, and external feeds. It's like piecing together a puzzle where each data point contributes to the overall threat picture.

Once data is collected, it undergoes "Threat Data Analysis." This involves dissecting the information to identify patterns, anomalies, and potential threats. Advanced analytics and machine learning play a crucial role in this phase, helping security teams spot subtle indicators that may go unnoticed by traditional methods.

"Indicator of Compromise (IOC) Management" is a key aspect of threat intelligence. IOCs are pieces of data that signify a potential security incident. They can include IP addresses, domain names, file hashes, and more. IOCs are used to detect and respond to security threats. Threat intelligence platforms help organizations manage and use IOCs effectively, allowing for rapid threat detection.

Threat intelligence feeds "Security Information and Event Management (SIEM)" systems, which serve as the nerve center of advanced threat detection. SIEM solutions correlate and analyze data from various sources, including threat intelligence feeds, to identify suspicious activities and potential threats in real-time. It's like having a team of vigilant analysts who sift through data to uncover hidden dangers.

Moreover, threat intelligence enables the creation of "Threat Models." These models depict potential attack scenarios and help organizations understand how threat actors might target their assets. By simulating these scenarios, organizations can proactively implement defenses and monitor for signs of impending attacks.

"Real-time Threat Detection" is where threat intelligence truly shines. With up-to-the-minute information about emerging threats, organizations can identify and respond to incidents faster than ever. This is akin to having an early warning system that alerts you to potential dangers as they unfold.

Furthermore, threat intelligence contributes to "Behavioral Analytics." By analyzing user and device behavior patterns alongside threat intelligence data, organizations can identify deviations from normal behavior that may indicate a security incident. It's like having a digital detective who notices when something doesn't quite add up.

Threat intelligence also aids in "Incident Correlation and Prioritization." When security incidents occur, threat intelligence helps security teams understand the context and severity of the incident. It assists in determining which incidents require immediate attention and which can be addressed later.

In addition to real-time threat detection, threat intelligence plays a pivotal role in "Incident Response." When a security incident is confirmed, organizations can rely on threat intelligence to guide their response efforts. It provides insights into the tactics and techniques used by threat actors, allowing for a more effective and targeted response.

Moreover, threat intelligence is an essential component of "Proactive Threat Hunting." Security teams actively seek out potential threats within their networks by leveraging threat intelligence data. It's like having digital detectives who investigate the network for signs of hidden dangers.

Threat intelligence also extends its benefits to "Cyber Threat Sharing and Collaboration." Organizations can share threat intelligence with trusted partners and industry peers to collectively defend against common threats. This collaborative approach strengthens the overall cybersecurity posture.

Furthermore, "Threat Intelligence Enrichment" enhances the value of existing security data. By enriching security logs and events with threat intelligence data, organizations gain additional context and can make more informed decisions about potential threats.

Lastly, threat intelligence is instrumental in "Adaptive Security Strategies." As threat landscapes evolve, organizations must adapt their security measures. Threat intelligence provides the insights needed to adjust security controls, update policies, and prioritize investments in cybersecurity.

In summary, leveraging threat intelligence for advanced threat detection is like having a crystal ball that reveals potential dangers in the ever-evolving cybersecurity landscape. It involves collecting, analyzing, and applying data from various sources to identify threats, detect incidents in real-time, and respond effectively. Threat intelligence is a critical component of modern cybersecurity strategies, helping organizations stay one step ahead of cyber adversaries and protect their digital assets.

In the dynamic and constantly evolving world of cybersecurity, real-time threat response within a Zero Trust environment is akin to a finely tuned orchestra, where every instrument plays a crucial role in maintaining the harmony of your digital ecosystem. Imagine a scenario where your cybersecurity measures are so finely attuned that they can instantly detect and respond to threats as they materialize, preventing potential breaches and safeguarding your organization's assets.

The concept of real-time threat response in a Zero Trust environment starts with the fundamental principle that no one and nothing should be trusted implicitly, regardless of their location within the network. It's a paradigm shift from the traditional perimeter-based security model, where once inside, entities were often considered safe. In a Zero Trust environment, trust is not assumed; it's continuously verified and never taken for granted.

At the heart of real-time threat response is the concept of "Continuous Authentication." In a Zero Trust model, users and devices must prove their identity and trustworthiness continuously, not just at the initial login. This is akin to having a bouncer at a nightclub who checks your identification every time you enter a different section of the venue, ensuring that only authorized individuals gain access.

Moreover, "Micro-Segmentation" is a key architectural component that enables real-time threat response. Networks are divided into smaller, isolated segments, each with its own access controls. These segments act like secure compartments that contain threats, preventing lateral movement within the network. When a threat is detected in one segment, it can be contained without affecting the rest of the network, like isolating a contagious patient in a hospital room.

Real-time threat response leverages "Behavioral Analytics" to detect anomalies in user and device behavior. It's like having a security guard who knows the usual behavior of every employee in your organization and can immediately spot when someone's actions deviate from the norm. This helps identify potential threats as they happen.

In a Zero Trust environment, "Continuous Monitoring" of network traffic, user behavior, and device activity is a constant process. Advanced monitoring tools analyze data in real-time, looking for suspicious patterns and signs of potential threats. Think of it as having a team of vigilant detectives who keep a close eye on your organization's digital activities, ready to pounce on any sign of trouble.

"User and Entity Behavior Analytics (UEBA)" is another critical aspect of real-time threat response. UEBA solutions profile user and entity behavior, creating a baseline of normal activity. When deviations from this baseline occur, it raises a red flag, much like a security camera system that triggers an alarm when it detects unusual movement.

When a potential threat is detected, "Automated Response" mechanisms kick into action. These mechanisms can include isolating the affected device or user, blocking suspicious network traffic, and initiating incident response workflows. It's like having an emergency response team that springs into action the moment a security breach is detected.

Furthermore, real-time threat response is closely tied to "Incident Orchestration and Automation." This involves predefined workflows and playbooks that guide security teams through the steps required to mitigate and resolve security incidents. Automation streamlines these processes, reducing response times and ensuring consistent actions are taken.

"Threat Intelligence Integration" is a vital component of real-time threat response. Threat intelligence feeds provide real-time data about emerging threats and vulnerabilities. When integrated into security systems, this intelligence helps organizations proactively defend against new attack vectors and tailor their responses to specific threats.

Moreover, "Security Information and Event Management (SIEM)" systems are at the core of real-time threat response. They aggregate data from various sources, including threat intelligence feeds, continuous monitoring tools, and behavioral analytics solutions. SIEM systems correlate this data to identify potential threats in real-time, acting as the central nervous system of your cybersecurity infrastructure.

In addition to automated response, "Human Intervention" is crucial in real-time threat response. Security analysts play a vital role in investigating and mitigating complex threats that automated systems may not fully understand. Their expertise is akin to having experienced detectives who can dig deep into the intricacies of a security incident.

"Incident Triage" is a critical step in real-time threat response. Security teams must quickly assess the severity of an incident and prioritize their actions accordingly. It's like having paramedics on the scene of an accident who determine which injuries require immediate attention and which can wait.

Moreover, real-time threat response involves "Incident Containment." When a threat is detected, security teams work to isolate and contain it to prevent further damage. This containment strategy is akin to firefighters creating a perimeter around a wildfire to prevent it from spreading.

Lastly, "Post-Incident Analysis" is a crucial part of real-time threat response. After an incident is resolved, organizations conduct thorough post-mortems to understand what happened, how it happened, and how to prevent similar incidents in the future. It's like conducting a detailed investigation after a crime to gather evidence and learn from the experience.

In summary, real-time threat response within a Zero Trust environment is a dynamic and proactive approach to cybersecurity. It involves continuous authentication, micro-segmentation, behavioral analytics, continuous monitoring, UEBA, automated response, incident orchestration, threat intelligence integration, SIEM systems, human intervention, incident triage, incident containment, and post-incident analysis. By embracing these elements, organizations can swiftly detect, respond to, and mitigate security threats as they occur, enhancing their cybersecurity resilience and protecting their digital assets.

## Chapter 4: Advanced Identity and Access Management Techniques

Role-Based Access Control (RBAC) is like assigning specific keys to employees in an office building - it ensures that individuals only have access to the areas and resources necessary for their job responsibilities. At an advanced level, RBAC takes this concept to new heights, allowing organizations to finely tune access permissions with precision.

Imagine an organization with a complex network of employees, each with different roles, responsibilities, and levels of access. Advanced RBAC simplifies this intricate web of permissions, making it manageable and secure. It's like having a master key that can open multiple doors, but only granting it to those who truly need it.

At its core, RBAC assigns access rights based on roles rather than individual users. This simplifies access management by grouping users with similar job functions into predefined roles. It's like categorizing employees into departments, such as marketing, finance, or IT, each with its own set of access permissions.

Roles in advanced RBAC are more than just labels; they come with a well-defined set of privileges. Think of privileges as the keys that allow access to specific resources or actions within an organization's systems. For instance, a role might have privileges to read, write, or delete files in a particular directory, or to access certain applications and databases.

One of the key benefits of advanced RBAC is "Granularity." This means that access permissions can be finely tuned to match the specific needs of each role. It's like having a control panel with sliders that allow you to adjust access levels with precision. For example, a junior developer might have read-only access to certain code repositories, while a senior developer has full read-write access.

Moreover, "Dynamic Role Assignment" is a feature that allows roles to be assigned and revoked automatically based on certain criteria. Imagine a scenario where an employee's role changes from junior developer to senior developer. With dynamic role assignment, their access permissions are adjusted automatically to align with their new responsibilities.

Furthermore, "Role Hierarchies" are a fundamental concept in advanced RBAC. In large organizations, roles can be organized in a hierarchical fashion, with higher-level roles inheriting permissions from lower-level roles. It's like a family tree, where each role inherits traits and privileges from its parent role. For example, a manager role might inherit all the permissions of the employee roles within their team.

"Separation of Duties (SoD)" is another critical aspect of advanced RBAC. It's like having checks and balances in place to prevent conflicts of interest. SoD ensures that no single role has too much power or control over critical systems or processes. For instance, a role responsible for initiating payments should not also be able to approve them.

Moreover, "Least Privilege Principle" is at the core of RBAC. It means that users should only have the minimum level of access required to perform their job functions. It's like providing employees with exactly the tools they need for their tasks and nothing more. This minimizes the potential impact of security breaches.

"Role-Based Access Control Policies" are the rules that govern access permissions within an organization. These policies define which roles have access to specific resources and under what conditions. Think of them as the guidelines that dictate who can enter which rooms in an office building and when.

To implement advanced RBAC, organizations often rely on "Access Control Lists (ACLs)" and "Role-Based Access Control Lists (RBACLs)." ACLs specify access permissions for individual resources, while RBACLs define access permissions for roles. It's like having a library catalog that lists which books can be borrowed by each role, ensuring that only the right people have access to specific titles.

Moreover, "Attribute-Based Access Control (ABAC)" is an extension of RBAC that considers additional factors, such as user attributes, resource attributes, and environmental conditions, when granting access. It's like a combination lock that requires the correct sequence of attributes to open a door. For example, an employee's access to sensitive data might depend on their department, location, and the time of day.

In an advanced RBAC system, "Auditing and Monitoring" play a crucial role. It's like having security cameras in every corner of your building, recording who accessed what and when. Auditing and monitoring tools track user activities, ensuring that any unauthorized or suspicious access attempts are flagged for review.

"Role-Based Access Control Implementation" requires careful planning and management. It involves defining roles and their associated privileges, assigning users to roles, configuring access policies, and continuously monitoring and updating permissions as roles change or new ones are introduced. It's like orchestrating a symphony, where every instrument has its part to play.

Lastly, "Role-Based Access Control in a Zero Trust Environment" takes RBAC to the next level by aligning it with the overarching Zero Trust security model. In a Zero Trust environment, trust is never assumed, and RBAC helps ensure that access is continually verified and granted only when necessary. It's like having a security guard at every door, checking credentials every time someone enters.

In summary, advanced Role-Based Access Control is a sophisticated system that simplifies access management by grouping users into roles with specific privileges. It offers granularity, dynamic role assignment, role hierarchies, separation of duties, and enforces the least privilege principle. By carefully implementing and managing RBAC, organizations can strike the right balance between security and usability, ensuring that the right people have access to the right resources at the right time.

Advanced authentication methods are like adding multiple layers of security to your digital world, making it nearly impenetrable for unauthorized access. These methods go beyond traditional usernames and passwords, providing a robust defense against cyber threats.

Picture this: You're not just relying on a single key to your house; you have a fingerprint scanner, a retinal scanner, and a voice recognition system in place. Each of these methods verifies your identity in a unique way, ensuring that only you can gain access.

One of the most powerful advanced authentication methods is "Biometric Authentication." It's like having your body serve as the key to your digital kingdom. With biometrics, your unique physical characteristics, such as fingerprints, facial features, or even the pattern of your iris, are used to confirm your identity. It's nearly impossible for someone to replicate these traits, making it an extremely secure way to authenticate.

"Multi-Factor Authentication (MFA)" is another critical advanced authentication method. Think of it as having multiple locks on your front door, each requiring a different key. MFA combines two or more authentication factors:

something you know (like a password), something you have (like a mobile device or a smart card), and something you are (like a fingerprint or a face scan). This multi-layered approach makes it significantly more challenging for unauthorized users to gain access.

Moreover, "Smart Cards" are like digital IDs that you carry with you. These small, portable devices store cryptographic keys and require a PIN or biometric verification to use. It's like having a secure vault for your digital identity in your pocket. Smart cards are commonly used in government and corporate settings to enhance security.

"Hardware Tokens" are another form of advanced authentication. These physical devices generate time-based or one-time passwords that change periodically. It's like having a new combination for your lock every minute. Users enter the current token code along with their password for access, providing an extra layer of security.

Imagine you have a smartphone that not only recognizes your face but also generates a unique access code every minute. That's the power of "Mobile Authentication Apps." These apps use factors like biometrics or time-based codes to verify your identity. Even if someone steals your password, they won't be able to access your account without your mobile device.

"Push Notifications" are a user-friendly form of advanced authentication. When you log in from a new device, a notification is sent to your registered mobile app asking for confirmation. It's like receiving a text message that asks, "Are you trying to access your account?" You simply tap "Yes" or "No" to allow or deny access.

"Behavioral Biometrics" is a fascinating advanced authentication method. It analyzes how you interact with your device, such as your typing speed, the angle at which you hold your phone, or the way you swipe your touchscreen. It creates a unique behavioral profile for each user, making it challenging for impostors to mimic.

Additionally, "Location-Based Authentication" adds another layer of security. This method verifies your identity based on your physical location. It's like saying, "I should be in New York right now; if someone tries to access my account from another country, that's suspicious." Location-based authentication can be especially useful for mobile banking and remote work scenarios.

"Certificate-Based Authentication" relies on digital certificates to verify identity. These certificates are issued by a trusted authority and provide strong proof of identity. It's like having an official document that confirms who you are. Certificate-based authentication is commonly used in secure communication protocols like SSL/TLS.

"Passwordless Authentication" is a game-changer in the world of advanced authentication. It eliminates the need for passwords altogether, replacing them with more secure methods like biometrics or hardware tokens. It's like getting rid of keys and using your fingerprint or face to unlock your front door. Passwordless authentication not only enhances security but also simplifies the user experience.

Moreover, "Adaptive Authentication" is a smart way to adapt security measures based on the situation. It's like having a security guard who assesses the level of risk and adjusts the security protocols accordingly. For example, if you're logging in from a familiar device and location, adaptive authentication might require only a single factor, making it convenient. However, if the system detects a suspicious login attempt, it can escalate to a multi-factor authentication process.

"Single Sign-On (SSO)" is a convenience-oriented form of advanced authentication. It allows users to access multiple services with a single set of credentials. It's like having a universal key that unlocks all your doors. While SSO streamlines access, it's essential to secure the initial login with strong authentication methods.

"Risk-Based Authentication" takes a proactive approach to security. It evaluates the risk associated with each login attempt, considering factors like device, location, and user behavior. If a login seems risky, it can prompt additional authentication steps. It's like having an alarm system that triggers when something seems amiss.

In the realm of advanced authentication, "Continuous Authentication" is a continuous watchful eye. It monitors user behavior even after login and can prompt for re-authentication if it detects suspicious activity. It's like having a guardian angel that stays by your side, ensuring your digital safety.

Furthermore, "Password Managers" are not just about convenience; they enhance security too. These tools generate and store complex passwords for various accounts, reducing the risk of weak or reused passwords. It's like having a personal secretary who creates and manages your keys.

The adoption of advanced authentication methods is essential in today's digital landscape, where cyber threats are constantly evolving. By implementing these robust security measures, organizations can significantly reduce the risk of unauthorized access and data breaches. It's like fortifying the walls of a fortress, ensuring that only those with the right credentials can enter. Advanced authentication methods are the future of secure digital interactions, offering both protection and user-friendly experiences.

## Chapter 5: Cutting-edge Network Segmentation Strategies

Implementing Zero Trust Micro-Segmentation is like creating a digital maze within your network, where every pathway is carefully guarded and only authorized individuals can navigate.

Picture this: You have a large office building, and you want to ensure that only employees from certain departments can access specific areas. Micro-segmentation lets you create digital barriers that are as impenetrable as physical walls.

So, what is micro-segmentation exactly? It's a network security technique that divides your network into small, isolated segments or zones. Each segment has its own set of security rules and policies, which determine who can communicate with whom and under what conditions.

Imagine your network as a city, and each micro-segment is like a neighborhood. In this analogy, only residents of a neighborhood can move freely within it, and they need special permissions to enter other neighborhoods. This is the essence of micro-segmentation: strict control over lateral movement within your network.

Now, let's delve into how to implement this powerful security strategy. The first step is to identify your network's assets and the data you want to protect. Think of this as making a list of your most valuable possessions in each room of your digital house.

Next, you'll define the micro-segments. This involves grouping assets with similar security requirements into segments. For example, you might have a segment for your finance department, another for human resources, and one for research and development.

Once you've defined your segments, it's time to set access policies. These policies determine who can access what within each micro-segment. It's like giving keys to certain doors in your digital house but keeping others locked.

Access policies can be based on a variety of factors, such as user roles, device types, and even the time of day. For example, you can allow HR employees to access their segment during office hours but restrict access at night.

Now, let's talk about enforcement. Micro-segmentation relies on network controls to enforce access policies. Firewalls, both physical and virtual, play a crucial role here. Think of them as the guards stationed at the entrances to each neighborhood in our city analogy.

These firewalls inspect network traffic and ensure that only authorized traffic flows between segments. Any unauthorized attempts to cross the boundaries are blocked, just like a guard denying entry to an uninvited guest.

In addition to firewalls, you can use intrusion detection and prevention systems (IDS/IPS) to monitor traffic within each micro-segment. These systems act as vigilant sentinels, alerting you to any suspicious activity or potential breaches.

Furthermore, encryption is your ally in micro-segmentation. It ensures that even if an intruder manages to breach a segment, the data they access is unreadable without the encryption keys. It's like having secret codes for your most valuable documents.

Remember, micro-segmentation isn't a one-time setup; it's an ongoing process. Regularly review and update your access policies to adapt to changing security needs and threats. It's like periodically changing the locks on your doors to maintain security.

Testing is a crucial part of the implementation process. Before fully deploying micro-segmentation, it's wise to conduct tests and simulations to ensure that your policies are effective and don't disrupt legitimate operations. It's like running a fire drill to make sure everyone knows what to do in an emergency.

Another key consideration is visibility. You need to be able to see what's happening within each micro-segment. This requires robust monitoring and logging tools that provide insights into network traffic and security events.

Think of it as having security cameras in every room of your digital house. These tools not only help you detect and respond to threats but also enable you to audit and fine-tune your access policies.

Education and training are essential components of micro-segmentation. Make sure your employees understand the new security measures and how to navigate within the segmented network. It's like teaching them the layout of the city and the rules for accessing different neighborhoods.

Finally, keep in mind that micro-segmentation is not a silver bullet. While it greatly enhances security, it should be part of a broader security strategy that includes other layers of defense, such as strong authentication, threat detection, and incident response.

In summary, implementing Zero Trust Micro-Segmentation is like constructing a fortified city within your network, where access is tightly controlled, and security is paramount. It involves defining segments, setting access policies, enforcing security controls, and continuously monitoring and adapting to evolving threats. With micro-segmentation, you can create a network that's resilient and resistant to lateral movement by cyber threats, safeguarding your digital assets effectively.

Network segmentation in cloud-native environments is a strategic approach to enhancing security and improving the overall resilience of your digital infrastructure. Imagine your cloud environment as a bustling city, with various services and applications representing different neighborhoods within that city.

Just as in a city, you want to ensure that each neighborhood operates independently while allowing controlled interaction between them. This is where network segmentation comes into play. It's about creating distinct virtual boundaries that restrict unauthorized traffic while enabling essential communication.

Now, let's delve into the details of network segmentation in cloud-native environments. First, you need to understand that the cloud offers unique advantages but also introduces new challenges. Unlike traditional on-premises networks, cloud-native environments are highly dynamic and elastic, with resources that can be provisioned or decommissioned in seconds.

This dynamism demands an equally agile approach to network segmentation. In the cloud, you can't rely on fixed physical boundaries; instead, you must leverage software-defined networking (SDN) to create and manage segments. Think of it as having the ability to reshape your city's neighborhoods with a few clicks.

One fundamental principle of network segmentation is the concept of trust zones. These zones define the level of trust and security required for different parts of your cloud environment. For example, your database servers may reside in a high-trust zone, while public-facing web servers are in a lower-trust zone.

To establish trust zones effectively, you need to classify your assets based on their importance and sensitivity. This is akin to categorizing buildings in a city as residential, commercial, or government properties. Each category requires a different level of security.

Access control is at the heart of network segmentation. Just as a city has checkpoints and gates to control who enters certain areas, your cloud environment must have robust access controls. This includes identity and access management (IAM) policies that define who can access specific resources and under what conditions.

In a cloud-native environment, IAM policies are like the keys that grant or deny entry to different parts of the city. By carefully configuring these policies, you can ensure that only authorized individuals, applications, or services are allowed access.

Now, let's discuss the importance of micro-segmentation within cloud-native environments. Micro-segmentation takes network segmentation to a granular level by creating small, isolated segments for individual workloads or resources. It's like dividing a neighborhood into houses, each with its own security measures.

Micro-segmentation is particularly valuable in cloud-native environments because it prevents lateral movement within your infrastructure. Just as a well-fortified house deters intruders from entering neighboring properties, micro-segmentation restricts lateral movement by cyber threats.

To implement micro-segmentation effectively, you can leverage cloud-native security groups or firewall rules. These controls allow you to specify which resources can communicate with each other and which ports and protocols are permitted. It's like having a detailed map that shows the permissible routes between houses in your neighborhood.

Visibility is a critical aspect of network segmentation. Just as a city's authorities need to monitor traffic and security across various neighborhoods, you must have tools in place to monitor network traffic and security events in your cloud-native environment. This includes logging, monitoring, and auditing mechanisms.

Think of these tools as surveillance cameras that capture activity throughout the city. They provide insights into who is accessing what, helping you detect anomalies or potential security breaches.

In addition to security tools, cloud-native environments often offer advanced threat detection and prevention services. These services use machine learning and behavioral analysis to identify suspicious activities. It's like having a team of vigilant inspectors who spot unusual behavior in the city.

Regular assessments and audits are essential to ensuring the effectiveness of your network segmentation strategy. Just as city officials periodically review safety measures and infrastructure, you should regularly assess your cloud-native network's security posture. This helps you identify vulnerabilities and adapt your segmentation policies accordingly.

Remember that network segmentation is not a one-time setup but an ongoing process. As your cloud environment evolves and expands, so should your segmentation strategy. It's like continually refining the city's layout and infrastructure to meet the changing needs of its residents.

In summary, network segmentation in cloud-native environments is a dynamic and essential practice for enhancing security and resilience. It involves creating trust zones, defining access controls, implementing micro-segmentation, ensuring visibility, and regularly assessing and adapting your strategy. By effectively segmenting your cloud environment, you can create a digital city that's both secure and responsive to the evolving landscape of cyber threats.

## Chapter 6: Endpoint Security in Advanced Zero Trust Environments

Advanced endpoint security solutions represent the frontline defense against an increasingly sophisticated landscape of cyber threats, ensuring that your digital devices remain safe and your data remains protected.

In today's interconnected world, our devices are like gateways to the digital realm, and they are under constant siege from a wide range of threats. These threats can come in the form of malware, ransomware, zero-day exploits, and sophisticated phishing attempts.

Imagine your endpoint devices as the guardians of your digital kingdom, standing resolute against these threats. The term "endpoint" refers to any device that connects to your network, such as computers, smartphones, tablets, and even IoT devices.

To effectively secure these endpoints, advanced endpoint security solutions employ a multifaceted approach that goes beyond traditional antivirus programs. These solutions are designed to provide comprehensive protection, often utilizing a combination of technologies and strategies.

One of the core components of advanced endpoint security is real-time threat detection and prevention. It's like having a vigilant sentry who not only guards your castle gates but also constantly scans the horizon for potential threats. These solutions employ sophisticated algorithms and machine learning to identify unusual or suspicious behavior on your devices, allowing for the rapid detection and blocking of threats before they can cause harm.

Another vital element is endpoint detection and response (EDR) capabilities. EDR is like having a team of investigators who can analyze security incidents in detail. It provides visibility into the activities of both known and unknown threats, allowing security teams to investigate and respond effectively.

Additionally, advanced endpoint security solutions often include behavioral analysis. This is akin to studying the behavior of potential intruders and identifying patterns that could indicate malicious intent. It helps in catching threats that might not have a recognizable signature but exhibit suspicious behavior.

To fortify your digital defenses, these solutions also offer application control. Think of it as setting strict rules about who can enter your castle. Application control allows you to specify which software is allowed to run on your endpoints, preventing unauthorized or malicious programs from executing.

Furthermore, advanced endpoint security emphasizes the importance of patch management. It's like ensuring that the drawbridge to your castle is always in good repair. Regularly updating and patching your software and operating systems is crucial to closing vulnerabilities that attackers might exploit.

Endpoint security solutions also emphasize the necessity of strong access controls and identity management. They ensure that only authorized users can access your devices and data, utilizing multi-factor authentication and role-based access policies.

To effectively manage these security measures, centralized management consoles are often employed. These consoles act as the control center for your digital defenses, allowing you to monitor and manage security policies across all your endpoints from a single interface.

Now, let's discuss the importance of threat intelligence in advanced endpoint security. It's like having a network of informants who provide you with the latest information on potential threats. Threat intelligence feeds help security solutions stay up-to-date with emerging threats, allowing them to adapt their defenses accordingly.

In addition to protecting against known threats, advanced endpoint security solutions are designed to defend against zero-day vulnerabilities. These are like secret tunnels that attackers exploit before they are discovered. Advanced solutions use techniques such as sandboxing and heuristics to identify and block threats that have no known signature.

Moreover, endpoint security solutions often incorporate data loss prevention (DLP) capabilities. Think of DLP as an invisible shield around your sensitive information. It helps prevent unauthorized users from accessing, copying, or transmitting sensitive data, reducing the risk of data breaches.

To stay ahead of attackers, advanced endpoint security solutions prioritize continuous improvement. It's like constantly reinforcing the walls of your fortress. Security vendors release regular updates and enhancements to ensure that their solutions can adapt to the ever-evolving threat landscape.

Now, let's talk about the importance of education and training. Just as knights undergo rigorous training to defend the kingdom, users must be educated about security best practices. Many endpoint security solutions include user awareness training to help individuals recognize and respond to security threats effectively.

Endpoint security is not just about defense; it's also about response and recovery. Advanced solutions often include incident response capabilities that help organizations quickly contain and mitigate security incidents. This is like having a well-practiced emergency response plan in place.

In summary, advanced endpoint security solutions are the knights of the digital realm, standing guard over your devices and data. They employ real-time threat detection, EDR, behavioral analysis, application control, patch management, access controls, and threat intelligence to provide comprehensive protection. These solutions evolve to counter known and unknown threats, with a focus on continuous improvement and user education. By adopting advanced endpoint security, you can fortify your digital defenses and protect your kingdom from the ever-present dangers of the cyber world.

In a world where Bring Your Own Device (BYOD) policies have become increasingly common, implementing Zero Trust principles becomes all the more crucial. Imagine your network as a carefully guarded castle, and each device that connects to it as a potential entry point. With BYOD, these devices include not only company-owned assets but also personal smartphones, tablets, and laptops belonging to your employees.

Now, the challenge is to ensure that each of these devices, regardless of ownership, adheres to the same stringent security standards. This is where Zero Trust approaches for BYOD environments come into play.

First and foremost, Zero Trust emphasizes the principle of "Verify Explicitly." In a BYOD setting, this means that every device must prove its trustworthiness before gaining access to your network. It's like having a gatekeeper at the castle entrance who checks the credentials of every visitor, regardless of whether they are a loyal subject or a stranger.

To implement this, organizations often employ Multi-Factor Authentication (MFA) as a baseline security measure. MFA adds an extra layer of protection by requiring users to provide multiple forms of verification before granting access. This could include something they know (like a password), something they have (like a mobile device), and something they are (like a fingerprint or facial recognition).

In the context of BYOD, ensuring the identity of the user becomes paramount. It's like making sure that everyone who enters the castle is who they claim to be. Advanced identity and access management techniques are used to achieve this. This includes robust user authentication methods, such as biometrics or smart cards, combined with strict access control policies that limit what users can do and access based on their roles.

Network segmentation, a fundamental component of Zero Trust, also plays a crucial role in BYOD environments. It's like dividing the castle into different sections, each with its own level of security. With BYOD, organizations implement micro-segmentation, which involves creating small, isolated network segments for specific device types or user groups. This ensures that even if one segment is compromised, the rest of the network remains protected.

For BYOD devices, mobile security becomes a focal point. Just as knights wear armor to protect themselves, these devices need robust endpoint security solutions. This includes features like application whitelisting and blacklisting, which dictate which apps are allowed to run on the device. It's like controlling what kind of weapons are allowed within the castle walls.

Moreover, cloud-native security controls are essential in a BYOD environment. As more organizations migrate their resources to the cloud, it's like extending the castle's defenses beyond its physical walls. BYOD devices need to access these cloud resources securely, and this is where cloud-native security measures come into play.

Now, let's consider the integration of BYOD with Zero Trust. BYOD policies often involve employees using personal devices for work-related tasks, such as accessing company email or documents. Zero Trust principles require that these devices be treated with the same level of suspicion and scrutiny as any other endpoint. It's like ensuring that every traveler who wishes to enter the castle is subject to the same security checks, regardless of their purpose.

To achieve this, organizations need to enforce strict security policies on BYOD devices. This includes ensuring that they have the latest security updates and patches installed. It's like making sure that every traveler's armor is in good condition before allowing them entry.

Mobile Device Management (MDM) solutions become indispensable in BYOD environments. MDM is like having a team of guards who oversee and manage the security of all the devices that connect to your network. These solutions allow organizations to enforce security policies, remotely wipe devices if they are lost or stolen, and ensure that only authorized devices can access corporate resources.

In the context of BYOD, mobile app security becomes paramount. Just as guards keep an eye on the activities within the castle, organizations need to monitor and control the apps running on employee devices. This includes identifying and addressing vulnerabilities in mobile apps and ensuring that they adhere to security best practices.

BYOD environments also require a strong focus on user education and awareness. Just as knights are trained to defend the castle, employees must be educated about the risks associated with using their personal devices for work. Security training and awareness programs help users recognize phishing attempts, malware threats, and other security risks.

In summary, Zero Trust approaches for BYOD environments are like fortifying the castle's defenses to protect against both external and internal threats. These approaches emphasize strict verification, identity and access management, network segmentation, endpoint security, cloud-native security, and the integration of BYOD policies with Zero Trust principles. By implementing these strategies, organizations can ensure that their network remains secure, even as the number of devices connecting to it continues to grow.

# Chapter 7: Advanced Monitoring and Threat Detection

In the world of cybersecurity, staying one step ahead of threats is a never-ending challenge. This is where real-time threat analytics in advanced Zero Trust security comes into play, like having a vigilant sentry who scans the horizon for potential dangers and alerts the castle's defenders at the first sign of trouble.

Real-time threat analytics is a critical component of Zero Trust security because it enables organizations to continuously monitor their network for suspicious activities. It's like having a network of spies and informants who provide real-time intelligence on potential threats.

In this advanced Zero Trust paradigm, every user, device, and application is treated as untrusted until proven otherwise. It's akin to suspecting everyone who approaches the castle until they can prove they have a legitimate reason to be there. Real-time threat analytics is the tool that helps organizations enforce this zero-trust posture effectively.

Imagine a scenario where an employee's device, which has access to sensitive company data, starts exhibiting unusual behavior. It's like noticing a member of the castle staff acting strangely within the walls. Real-time threat analytics tools can detect these anomalies, such as unusual data access patterns or login attempts from unusual locations, and raise immediate red flags.

One of the key advantages of real-time threat analytics is its ability to detect and respond to threats as they happen. It's like having guards who not only detect an intruder at the castle gates but also take immediate action to apprehend them. In the cybersecurity context, this means the ability to isolate compromised devices, block malicious activities, and mitigate potential damage swiftly.

Advanced Zero Trust environments often leverage behavioral analytics as part of their real-time threat analytics arsenal. This involves analyzing user and device behavior over time to establish a baseline of what is normal. Any deviation from this baseline is treated as a potential threat. It's like recognizing when someone within the castle starts acting out of character and investigating the reason behind it.

Machine learning and artificial intelligence are integral to real-time threat analytics. These technologies are like having highly skilled detectives who can sift through vast amounts of data to identify patterns and anomalies that human analysts might miss. Machine learning models can continuously adapt and improve their threat detection capabilities, just as a seasoned investigator gains experience over time.

Furthermore, real-time threat analytics can integrate with threat intelligence feeds from various sources. It's like having access to a network of informants who provide information about the latest threats and attack techniques. By staying up-to-date with the threat landscape, organizations can better defend against emerging threats.

Cloud-native environments are increasingly common in today's IT landscape, and real-time threat analytics must extend to the cloud. It's like expanding the castle's defenses to include not only its physical walls but also the entire surrounding territory. Cloud security posture management tools help organizations monitor their cloud resources in real-time, ensuring that security policies are consistently applied across all environments.

In the context of real-time threat analytics, automation plays a crucial role. It's like having a team of security experts who can respond to threats 24/7 without rest. Automated incident response workflows can be triggered when suspicious activities are detected, allowing organizations to contain and mitigate threats swiftly. Integration with Security Information and Event Management (SIEM) systems is another facet of real-time threat analytics. It's like having a centralized command center where all security events and alerts are monitored and managed. SIEM systems provide a holistic view of an organization's security posture and enable rapid response to security incidents.

As organizations embrace real-time threat analytics in their advanced Zero Trust security strategies, they become better equipped to handle the evolving threat landscape. It's like fortifying the castle's defenses with advanced surveillance technology and a highly skilled security team. With real-time threat analytics, organizations can proactively identify and thwart cyber threats, ensuring the safety of their digital kingdom. In the ever-evolving landscape of cybersecurity, the concept of threat hunting has emerged as a proactive and strategic approach to identifying and mitigating threats within a Zero Trust security framework. Picture it as a relentless quest for hidden adversaries within the walls of your digital kingdom, where every corner and shadow is scrutinized for signs of danger.

Threat hunting in a Zero Trust landscape is akin to deploying skilled trackers and investigators throughout your realm, searching for any traces of malicious activity. Instead of waiting for alarms to sound or breaches to occur, threat hunters actively seek out threats, just as a vigilant guard patrols the castle walls to prevent intrusions.

Zero Trust security, with its foundational principle of "never trust, always verify," sets the stage for proactive threat hunting. It operates on the assumption that threats are omnipresent, both outside and inside the network, and it aims to uncover these threats before they can wreak havoc. It's like having a dedicated team of detectives who question every user, device, and application's intentions and actions, seeking inconsistencies or anomalies.

The role of a threat hunter is to continuously investigate the network, endpoints, and data flows, looking for any signs of abnormal behavior or potential threats. It's like having a team of watchful guardians who inspect every guest at the castle gate, verifying their identities and intentions. In the cybersecurity realm, this verification process involves scrutinizing user behavior, network traffic, and system logs for deviations from established norms.

Threat hunters often rely on advanced analytics and machine learning algorithms to sift through vast amounts of data. Think of these technologies as the keen senses of a tracker, enabling them to detect even the subtlest signs of danger. Machine learning models can analyze historical data to identify patterns and anomalies, allowing threat hunters to focus their efforts on areas that require attention.

Behavioral analytics is a critical tool in threat hunting. Just as a seasoned investigator can detect when someone's behavior is out of character, behavioral analytics can identify deviations from normal user or device behavior. It's like noticing when a castle resident suddenly starts acting suspiciously, prompting an investigation into their activities.

Threat hunting often involves the use of threat intelligence feeds from various sources. These feeds provide information about the latest threats, attack techniques, and indicators of compromise. It's like having a network of informants who share valuable intelligence about potential threats lurking in the kingdom.

One of the key benefits of threat hunting in a Zero Trust landscape is its ability to uncover threats that may have gone unnoticed by traditional security measures. It's like discovering hidden traps and secret passages within the castle that adversaries could exploit. Threat hunters can uncover insider threats, zero-day vulnerabilities, and sophisticated attack techniques that evade standard security defenses.

As organizations adopt Zero Trust principles, threat hunting becomes an integral part of their security strategy. It's like fortifying the castle's defenses with a dedicated team of scouts and spies who continuously assess the threat landscape. Threat hunters not only detect threats but also gather intelligence on adversary tactics, techniques, and procedures, which can inform the organization's overall security posture.

Collaboration between threat hunters and incident responders is essential in a Zero Trust security environment. When a threat is detected, it's like sounding the alarm within the castle. Threat hunters work closely with incident responders to assess the threat's severity, contain the incident, and initiate the appropriate response actions.

Threat hunting is not a one-time endeavor; it's an ongoing process. Just as a vigilant castle guard must remain ever watchful, threat hunters continuously refine their techniques and adapt to evolving threats. They leverage automation and orchestration tools to streamline their investigations and responses, ensuring that the kingdom's defenses stay ahead of the adversaries.

In summary, threat hunting in a Zero Trust landscape is a proactive and strategic approach to cybersecurity. It's like having a dedicated team of detectives who tirelessly search for hidden threats within your digital realm. By actively seeking out and mitigating threats, organizations can bolster their security posture and protect their digital kingdom from adversaries.

## Chapter 8: Zero Trust in Cloud-Native Environments

In the ever-evolving landscape of cybersecurity, the emergence of serverless and containerized environments has brought about new challenges and opportunities for organizations seeking to secure their digital assets. Imagine these environments as futuristic cityscapes, where applications and services are no longer confined to traditional servers but are distributed across a dynamic and interconnected network.

Securing serverless and containerized environments is like protecting a city with constantly changing streets and buildings. These environments are built on the principles of flexibility, scalability, and efficiency, allowing organizations to deploy and manage applications in a more agile manner. However, this agility comes with its own set of security considerations.

Serverless computing, characterized by the absence of traditional servers, offers organizations the ability to execute code in a highly scalable and event-driven manner. It's like having an army of autonomous messengers who respond to specific signals and deliver messages instantaneously. However, securing serverless functions requires a shift in mindset, as traditional security measures designed for server-based applications may not apply.

Containerization, on the other hand, enables organizations to package applications and their dependencies into isolated units called containers. Think of containers as portable and self-contained apartments within the city. They can be easily moved from one environment to another, providing consistency and efficiency. However, securing containers involves ensuring that each one is properly sealed, preventing unauthorized access.

One of the fundamental principles of securing serverless and containerized environments is the principle of least privilege. It's like assigning access permissions based on specific roles and responsibilities within the city. Only those who need access to certain resources or services should be granted permissions, reducing the attack surface.

Access control within these environments is critical. It's like having security checkpoints at the entrances to different districts within the city. Organizations must implement robust identity and access management (IAM) policies to authenticate and authorize users and applications. This ensures that only trusted entities can interact with the serverless functions or containers.

Encryption plays a vital role in securing data within serverless and containerized environments. Imagine it as securing valuable assets in locked vaults within the city. Data at rest and in transit should be encrypted to prevent unauthorized access or interception. Encryption keys should be managed securely, ensuring that only authorized parties can decrypt the data.

Monitoring and visibility are essential components of security in these dynamic environments. It's like having surveillance cameras and sensors throughout the city, constantly monitoring for unusual activity. Organizations should implement robust logging and monitoring solutions to detect and respond to security incidents in real-time.

Just as a city relies on law enforcement agencies to maintain order, organizations need incident response plans in place. These plans outline the steps to take when a security incident occurs. It's like having an emergency response team ready to react to various scenarios, from a minor disturbance to a full-blown crisis.

Securing serverless and containerized environments also involves regular vulnerability assessments and patch management. Think of it as conducting routine inspections and maintenance on the city's infrastructure to identify and fix weaknesses. Vulnerabilities should be patched promptly to prevent exploitation by malicious actors.

Organizations should adopt a proactive and continuous approach to security. This means regularly conducting security assessments, penetration testing, and code reviews to identify and address vulnerabilities. It's like ensuring that the city's defenses are always up-to-date and capable of withstanding new threats.

In addition to securing the serverless and containerized environments themselves, organizations must also consider the security of the orchestration and management tools used to deploy and manage these environments. Just as a city needs secure command and control centers, organizations must protect their management interfaces and APIs.

Security should be integrated into the development and deployment pipelines. It's like having quality control checkpoints throughout the city's manufacturing process to ensure that products meet safety standards. Security should not be an afterthought but rather a fundamental aspect of the development lifecycle.

Zero-trust principles, as discussed earlier, are also applicable in securing serverless and containerized environments. Trust is never assumed, and verification is required for every interaction. It's like ensuring that every visitor to the city presents valid identification and a purpose for their visit.

Securing serverless and containerized environments is an ongoing effort. Just as a city evolves and grows, these environments change over time. Security policies and measures should be continuously reviewed and adapted to address new threats and vulnerabilities.

In summary, securing serverless and containerized environments is like safeguarding a dynamic and interconnected city. It requires a proactive and comprehensive approach that includes access control, encryption, monitoring, incident response, and ongoing assessments. By adopting these security practices, organizations can harness the benefits of these modern computing paradigms while mitigating the associated risks.

In today's digital landscape, organizations are increasingly adopting multi-cloud strategies to harness the benefits of multiple cloud service providers. It's like having access to different neighborhoods within a city, each offering unique services and amenities. However, with this expansion comes the need for robust security measures, and the principles of Zero Trust become even more critical in multi-cloud environments.

Imagine managing multiple properties in different parts of the city; you want to ensure that each one is secure and protected. The same principle applies to multi-cloud deployments. Each cloud environment must be treated as a separate entity, and trust is never assumed by default. This is where Zero Trust strategies come into play.

The first key element of a Zero Trust approach in multi-cloud deployments is identity and access management (IAM). Think of it as the keys and locks for each property. Organizations need to establish a strong foundation of user and device authentication, ensuring that only authorized individuals or entities gain access to cloud resources. This extends to both human users and machine identities.

Just as you would verify the identity of someone entering your property, Zero Trust requires organizations to verify the identity of users and devices seeking access to cloud resources. Multi-factor authentication (MFA) is a crucial tool in this regard, adding an extra layer of security by requiring multiple forms of verification before granting access.

Once access is granted, the principle of least privilege access comes into play. It's like granting different levels of access to different areas of a property, depending on the role and responsibility of the individual. In multi-cloud environments, organizations must define and enforce access policies that limit permissions to the minimum necessary for each user or system. This reduces the attack surface and minimizes the potential impact of a security breach.

Encryption is another fundamental component of Zero Trust in multi-cloud deployments. Think of it as securing your belongings within each property. Data, both in transit and at rest, should be encrypted to protect it from unauthorized access. Cloud providers often offer encryption services, and organizations should leverage these capabilities to safeguard their data.

Just as you would have security cameras and alarms in place to monitor your properties, real-time monitoring and visibility are crucial in multi-cloud environments. Organizations need comprehensive logging and monitoring solutions to detect and respond to security incidents promptly. This includes monitoring user activities, network traffic, and application behavior across all cloud platforms.

Incident response plans are like having a well-trained security team ready to respond to any security breach in your properties. In multi-cloud environments, organizations must have clear and tested incident response plans in place. These plans outline the steps to take when a security incident occurs, ensuring that threats are contained and mitigated swiftly.

Security assessments and vulnerability management are essential for maintaining the security of multi-cloud deployments. Think of them as routine inspections and maintenance for each property in your portfolio. Regular security assessments, penetration testing, and vulnerability scanning help identify weaknesses that need to be addressed promptly.

Zero Trust extends beyond the cloud resources themselves to include the management interfaces and APIs used to control and orchestrate those resources. These interfaces should be secured with the same rigor as the resources they manage. It's like ensuring that the control centers for your properties are fortified against unauthorized access.

In multi-cloud environments, automation and orchestration play a significant role in ensuring consistent and secure deployments. Just as you would have standardized security protocols for each property, organizations should implement security policies as code. This allows security measures to be integrated into the deployment pipeline, ensuring that security is an integral part of the development lifecycle.

Zero Trust principles also apply when data flows between different cloud environments. Imagine it as securely transferring assets between different properties. Organizations should implement secure data transit mechanisms, such as encrypted tunnels or virtual private networks (VPNs), to protect data as it moves between cloud providers.

Cloud service providers offer a range of security tools and services that organizations can leverage to enhance their Zero Trust posture. These tools may include threat detection and response solutions, identity and access management services, and security information and event management (SIEM) platforms. Organizations should take advantage of these offerings to bolster their security capabilities.

Regular security audits and compliance assessments are like conducting periodic inspections to ensure that each property meets safety and regulatory standards. In multi-cloud environments, organizations should continuously evaluate their security posture against industry best practices and compliance requirements.

The journey to implementing Zero Trust in multi-cloud deployments is ongoing. Just as you would adapt your security measures as new risks emerge in different neighborhoods of the city, organizations must continuously assess and adapt their security strategies to address evolving threats in the cloud landscape.

In summary, Zero Trust strategies are a crucial foundation for securing multi-cloud deployments. By applying the principles of identity and access management, least privilege access, encryption, monitoring, incident response, and automation, organizations can protect their assets and data across multiple cloud environments. In the dynamic and interconnected world of multi-cloud, Zero Trust is the key to ensuring a secure and resilient infrastructure.

## Chapter 9: Zero Trust for Critical Infrastructure

In the realm of industrial control systems (ICS), where the physical world meets the digital, security is paramount. Imagine an intricate ballet of machines, sensors, and controllers working together to manage critical infrastructure like power plants, water treatment facilities, or manufacturing plants. The seamless operation of these systems is not only essential for efficiency but also for public safety and environmental protection.

Historically, industrial control systems operated in isolated environments, hidden from the broader internet and potential cyber threats. But as technology evolves and the need for remote monitoring and control grows, ICS environments have become more connected. This connectivity has introduced new challenges and risks, making the implementation of Zero Trust principles in ICS a pressing necessity.

Zero Trust, in the context of ICS, signifies a fundamental shift in the approach to security. It begins with the recognition that trust should not be assumed based on location or network boundaries. In the past, once you were inside the perimeter of an ICS network, you were often trusted implicitly. However, this trust can be exploited by malicious actors, leading to potentially catastrophic consequences.

Authentication is the cornerstone of Zero Trust in ICS. Think of it as the keys to access the control room of a critical infrastructure facility. Every user, device, or application attempting to access the ICS environment must undergo rigorous authentication and validation. Multi-factor authentication (MFA) is a powerful tool to ensure that only authorized individuals gain access, and it should be a mandatory component of any ICS security strategy.

Once authenticated, the principle of least privilege access is vital. It's akin to granting different levels of access to different parts of a control room, depending on an individual's role and responsibilities. In ICS, it means that users or systems should only have the permissions necessary to perform their specific functions. This minimizes the risk of unauthorized access or unintended actions within the ICS environment.

Encryption is another critical component of Zero Trust in ICS. Imagine securing the communications between controllers, sensors, and the central monitoring system as you would secure sensitive conversations within a control room. Data in transit and at rest within the ICS environment should be encrypted to prevent eavesdropping or data breaches.

Continuous monitoring is essential for early threat detection. Imagine having surveillance cameras and alarms in place within the control room to spot any unusual activity. In ICS, real-time monitoring and anomaly detection systems are crucial to identifying potential security threats or operational anomalies. This proactive approach allows for swift responses to any suspicious activities.

Incident response plans in ICS are like well-drilled emergency procedures in the event of a crisis. Organizations must develop and regularly test incident response plans tailored to ICS environments. These plans should outline the steps to take when a security incident occurs, ensuring that the impact is minimized and operations can be restored safely.

Security assessments and vulnerability management in ICS are akin to routine inspections and maintenance of critical machinery. Regular security assessments, penetration testing, and vulnerability scanning help identify weaknesses that could be exploited by adversaries. These vulnerabilities should be addressed promptly to ensure the resilience of the ICS environment.

Access control within the ICS environment extends to the management interfaces and application programming interfaces (APIs) used to control and monitor industrial processes. Just as the physical control room must be fortified, the digital interfaces must be secured against unauthorized access. This includes robust authentication and access controls for all management interfaces.

In ICS, Zero Trust principles apply not only to the digital systems but also to the physical components. Access to the physical infrastructure, including control panels and sensors, should be strictly controlled and monitored. Unauthorized physical access can have severe consequences, making physical security an integral part of the Zero Trust strategy.

Zero Trust can also be complemented by network segmentation in ICS. Imagine dividing the control room into separate sections, each with its own security measures. In ICS, network segmentation helps isolate critical systems from less critical ones, reducing the attack surface and limiting the potential impact of a breach.

In the context of ICS, Zero Trust principles extend to third-party connections and remote access. Just as you would scrutinize anyone seeking access to your control room, third-party vendors and remote users should undergo thorough vetting and adhere to strict security protocols before connecting to the ICS environment.

Regular audits and compliance assessments are like regulatory inspections for your control room. In ICS, organizations must ensure that their security practices align with industry standards and regulatory requirements. Compliance audits help identify areas that may need improvement and ensure that the ICS environment meets necessary security standards.

Implementing Zero Trust in ICS is not a one-time effort but an ongoing journey. Security measures must evolve to counter new and emerging threats. This involves staying informed about the latest security threats and technologies, as well as regularly updating security policies and practices.

In summary, implementing Zero Trust principles in industrial control systems is crucial to safeguard critical infrastructure and protect against evolving cyber threats. By focusing on authentication, least privilege access, encryption, monitoring, incident response, security assessments, physical security, network segmentation, and compliance, organizations can establish a robust Zero Trust framework that ensures the security and resilience of ICS environments. In an interconnected world, where the digital and physical realms converge, Zero Trust is the key to maintaining the reliability and safety of critical infrastructure.

Imagine a nation's critical infrastructure as the lifeblood of a country, comprising power grids, transportation systems, water supplies, and communication networks. These vital systems are the backbone of modern society, providing the essential services we rely on daily. The security of national critical infrastructure is not only a matter of economic stability but also a matter of national security.

Historically, the protection of critical infrastructure relied on physical barriers and isolated systems, safeguarding them from physical threats. However, as our world becomes increasingly digitized and interconnected, the threat landscape has expanded to include cyberattacks. These attacks, often carried out by sophisticated threat actors, pose a significant risk to national critical infrastructure.

The concept of Zero Trust is a paradigm shift in how we approach security for critical infrastructure. Traditionally, there was a level of trust once a user or device was inside the network perimeter. However, this trust can be exploited by cybercriminals seeking to infiltrate and disrupt essential services. In a Zero Trust model, trust is never assumed, and every user, device, or application is rigorously verified and authenticated.

Authentication is the cornerstone of Zero Trust in critical infrastructure. Just as you would verify the identity of individuals entering a secure facility, in the digital realm, you must verify the identity of anyone attempting to access critical infrastructure systems. Multi-factor authentication (MFA) plays a pivotal role in ensuring that only authorized individuals gain access to critical systems.

Once authenticated, the principle of least privilege access comes into play. Imagine granting access to different parts of a critical infrastructure facility based on an individual's role and responsibilities, similar to providing different levels of access within a secure facility. In the digital world, this means that users or systems should only have the permissions necessary to perform their specific functions. This minimizes the risk of unauthorized access or unintended actions within critical systems.

Encryption is another vital component of Zero Trust in critical infrastructure. Just as you would secure sensitive communications within a secure facility, data in transit and at rest within critical systems must be encrypted. This safeguards against eavesdropping and data breaches, ensuring the confidentiality and integrity of critical data.

Continuous monitoring and anomaly detection are essential for early threat detection within critical infrastructure. Think of it as having a vigilant security team in place to spot any unusual activity. Real-time monitoring and advanced analytics systems are crucial for identifying potential security threats or operational anomalies. This proactive approach allows for swift responses to any suspicious activities, minimizing potential damage.

Incident response plans are akin to well-practiced emergency procedures within critical infrastructure. Organizations must develop and regularly test incident response plans tailored to the unique challenges of protecting critical systems. These plans should outline the steps to take when a security incident occurs, ensuring that the impact is minimized, and services can be restored safely and swiftly.

Security assessments and vulnerability management in critical infrastructure are similar to routine inspections and maintenance of vital machinery. Regular security assessments, penetration testing, and vulnerability scanning help identify weaknesses that could be exploited by malicious actors. Addressing these vulnerabilities promptly is crucial to the resilience of critical systems.

Access control within critical infrastructure extends to the management interfaces and application programming interfaces (APIs) used to control and monitor essential processes. Just as the physical security of critical infrastructure is paramount, the digital interfaces must be secured against unauthorized access. This includes robust authentication and access controls for all management interfaces.

Physical security remains a critical component of Zero Trust for critical infrastructure. Access to the physical infrastructure, such as power plants or water treatment facilities, must be strictly controlled and monitored. Unauthorized physical access can have severe consequences, making physical security an integral part of the Zero Trust strategy.

Zero Trust principles also apply to third-party connections and remote access within critical infrastructure. Just as you would thoroughly vet anyone seeking access to a secure facility, third-party vendors and remote users must undergo stringent vetting and adhere to strict security protocols before connecting to critical systems.

Regular audits and compliance assessments are similar to regulatory inspections within critical infrastructure. Organizations must ensure that their security practices align with industry standards and regulatory requirements. Compliance audits help identify areas that may need improvement and ensure that critical systems meet necessary security standards.

Implementing Zero Trust in critical infrastructure is not a one-time effort but an ongoing journey. Security measures must continuously evolve to counter new and emerging threats. This involves staying informed about the latest security threats and technologies, as well as regularly updating security policies and practices.

In summary, the application of Zero Trust principles to protect national critical infrastructure is of paramount importance in our increasingly interconnected world. By focusing on authentication, least privilege access, encryption, monitoring, incident response, security assessments, physical security, network segmentation, and compliance, nations can establish a robust Zero Trust framework that ensures the security and resilience of critical infrastructure. In an era where cyber threats pose significant risks to national security, Zero Trust is the key to safeguarding the essential services that underpin modern society.

## Chapter 10: Cyber Resilience and Future-Proofing Your Zero Trust Strategy

In today's ever-evolving cybersecurity landscape, the ability to develop resilience against advanced threats is not just a goal but a necessity. Cyber threats have become increasingly sophisticated, and organizations of all sizes must adapt to the changing landscape to protect their digital assets effectively.

To understand how to develop resilience against advanced threats, it's essential to grasp the nature of these threats and the principles that underpin a resilient cybersecurity strategy. Advanced threats encompass a wide range of malicious activities, from nation-state-sponsored cyberattacks to financially motivated cybercrime. These threats are often characterized by their sophistication, stealth, and ability to bypass traditional security measures.

One of the fundamental principles in developing resilience against advanced threats is the adoption of a proactive cybersecurity posture. This means that organizations should not wait for an attack to occur before taking action. Instead, they should continuously assess their cybersecurity posture, identify vulnerabilities, and implement proactive measures to mitigate potential risks.

One of the key proactive measures is threat intelligence. Threat intelligence involves collecting and analyzing information about current and emerging threats in the cybersecurity landscape. It provides organizations with valuable insights into the tactics, techniques, and procedures used by threat actors. Armed with this knowledge, organizations can better prepare for and defend against potential attacks.

An essential aspect of developing resilience against advanced threats is the concept of "assume breach." In today's threat environment, organizations must assume that their networks and systems may already be compromised. This assumption drives the need for continuous monitoring and detection capabilities to identify unauthorized activities and intrusions promptly.

Advanced threat actors often use sophisticated techniques to gain initial access to a target's network. This may involve spear-phishing campaigns, exploiting unpatched vulnerabilities, or leveraging supply chain attacks. To develop resilience against such tactics, organizations must prioritize cybersecurity hygiene practices. This includes regular software patching, secure configuration management, and user awareness training.

Another critical element in resilience development is network segmentation. By segmenting their networks, organizations can limit the lateral movement of attackers within their systems. This containment strategy isolates compromised segments, preventing threats from spreading throughout the entire network.

Encryption plays a crucial role in developing resilience against advanced threats. Encrypting sensitive data both in transit and at rest adds an additional layer of protection. Even if a threat actor gains access to encrypted data, they would still need to decrypt it to extract meaningful information, which is a complex and time-consuming task.

Zero Trust security principles are also integral to resilience development. In a Zero Trust model, trust is never assumed, and strict access controls are enforced. This approach aligns well with the "assume breach" mindset and helps organizations protect their critical assets effectively.

Developing resilience against advanced threats requires robust incident response capabilities. Organizations should have well-defined incident response plans, including procedures for containing and mitigating threats, preserving evidence, and notifying relevant parties. Regularly testing and updating these plans is crucial to their effectiveness.

An often-overlooked aspect of resilience development is the importance of employee training and awareness. Human error remains a significant factor in successful cyberattacks. Employees should receive training on identifying phishing attempts, practicing good password hygiene, and understanding their role in the organization's overall cybersecurity posture.

To further enhance resilience, organizations can leverage advanced technologies such as artificial intelligence and machine learning. These technologies can help detect anomalies and potential threats in real time, allowing for rapid response and mitigation.

Collaboration and information sharing within the cybersecurity community are essential components of resilience development. Threat information sharing allows organizations to benefit from collective knowledge and insights, helping them better understand and defend against advanced threats.

Lastly, compliance with industry-specific regulations and standards can also contribute to resilience development. These frameworks often provide guidelines and best practices for enhancing cybersecurity, ensuring that organizations are well-prepared to face advanced threats.

In summary, developing resilience against advanced threats is an ongoing process that requires a proactive approach, a strong cybersecurity posture, continuous monitoring and detection capabilities, network segmentation, encryption, adherence to Zero Trust principles, robust incident response plans, employee training and awareness, advanced technologies, information sharing, and compliance with industry regulations and standards. By embracing these principles and practices, organizations can significantly enhance their ability to withstand and recover from advanced cyber threats in an ever-changing digital landscape.

As we delve into the realm of tomorrow's cybersecurity challenges, it becomes evident that the landscape is constantly evolving. The strategies and principles of today may not suffice in the face of emerging threats and technologies. Therefore, the need to adapt your Zero Trust strategy for tomorrow's challenges is of paramount importance.

One of the fundamental aspects of this adaptation is recognizing the ever-changing nature of cyber threats. Threat actors are becoming increasingly sophisticated, employing new techniques and technologies to breach even the most robust defenses. To adapt, organizations must adopt a proactive stance, staying ahead of potential threats rather than reacting to them.

A key element in adapting your Zero Trust strategy is embracing a holistic approach to security. This means going beyond traditional network-centric models and considering all entry points and potential vulnerabilities. With the proliferation of remote work, IoT devices, and cloud services, the attack surface has expanded exponentially. Consequently, your Zero Trust strategy should encompass not only the network but also endpoints, applications, and data.

The Zero Trust concept of "never trust, always verify" remains relevant, but verification methods must evolve to keep pace with tomorrow's challenges. This includes adopting advanced authentication methods such as biometrics, behavioral analytics, and continuous authentication. These methods provide a more robust and adaptive way to ensure that only authorized individuals and devices access critical resources.

Machine learning and artificial intelligence are poised to play a significant role in adapting Zero Trust for the future. These technologies enable organizations to analyze vast amounts of data in real-time, identifying anomalies and potential threats more effectively. By leveraging machine learning algorithms, organizations can enhance their ability to detect and respond to emerging threats promptly.

The perimeter, once defined by physical boundaries, has dissolved into the digital realm. As a result, the concept of "micro-segmentation" is gaining prominence in Zero Trust strategies. Micro-segmentation allows organizations to create granular security zones within their networks, limiting lateral movement and containing potential breaches. In tomorrow's landscape, where attackers may already be inside the network, micro-segmentation becomes a critical defense mechanism.

Cloud-native environments are becoming increasingly prevalent, offering scalability and flexibility. However, they also introduce new security challenges. Adapting your Zero Trust strategy for cloud-native deployments involves extending the same principles and controls to these environments. This includes ensuring robust identity and access management, encryption, and continuous monitoring in the cloud.

The Internet of Things (IoT) is another area where Zero Trust must adapt. IoT devices are often vulnerable and can serve as entry points for attackers. Integrating IoT security into your Zero Trust strategy involves strict access controls, device authentication, and continuous monitoring to detect unusual device behavior.

In tomorrow's cybersecurity landscape, threat intelligence becomes even more crucial. Organizations must stay informed about emerging threats and vulnerabilities specific to their industry and region. Threat intelligence feeds can provide real-time insights into evolving attack tactics, allowing organizations to adjust their security measures accordingly.

A key challenge for organizations is striking the right balance between security and user experience. As Zero Trust strategies become more complex, there's a risk of creating cumbersome authentication and verification processes that hinder productivity. Striking this balance involves implementing adaptive access controls that consider user behavior, context, and risk levels.

Collaboration and information sharing will continue to be vital components of adapting your Zero Trust strategy. Threat information sharing among organizations and across industries helps create a collective defense against evolving threats. Additionally, partnerships with cybersecurity vendors and service providers can provide access to cutting-edge technologies and expertise.

The regulatory landscape is also evolving, with new privacy laws and compliance requirements emerging. Adapting your Zero Trust strategy means staying abreast of these regulations and ensuring that your security measures align with legal obligations.

As we adapt Zero Trust for tomorrow's challenges, it's essential to recognize that there is no one-size-fits-all solution. Each organization's needs, risks, and resources are unique. Therefore, customization and continuous assessment are key. Regularly reassess your Zero Trust strategy to identify areas that require adjustment based on evolving threats and technologies.

In summary, adapting your Zero Trust strategy for tomorrow's challenges involves recognizing the ever-changing nature of cybersecurity threats and adopting a holistic approach to security that encompasses all potential entry points. It also involves leveraging advanced authentication methods, machine learning, micro-segmentation, and cloud-native security controls. Staying informed through threat intelligence, striking the right balance between security and user experience, fostering collaboration, and staying compliant with evolving regulations are all essential elements of this adaptation. By remaining proactive, agile, and open to customization, organizations can navigate the evolving cybersecurity landscape with confidence.

# *BOOK 4*
# *MASTERING ZERO TRUST SECURITY*
# *CYBER RESILIENCE IN A CHANGING*
# *LANDSCAPE*

## *ROB BOTWRIGHT*

## Chapter 1: The Evolution of Cyber Threats and the Need for Zero Trust

In our journey to understand the ever-evolving landscape of cyber threats, it's essential to start with a historical perspective. Looking back, we can trace the roots of cyber threats to the early days of computer technology, a time when the digital world was still in its infancy.

During these nascent stages, computer networks were isolated, and security wasn't a significant concern. The primary focus was on functionality and innovation. However, as computer systems became more interconnected, the vulnerabilities began to surface.

One of the earliest forms of cyber threats came in the form of viruses and worms. These malicious programs were designed to infiltrate computer systems, spread rapidly, and wreak havoc. The infamous Morris Worm of 1988, created by a computer science student, became one of the first well-known instances of a worm causing widespread disruption.

As the internet emerged in the 1990s, the landscape of cyber threats expanded dramatically. The World Wide Web brought new opportunities for communication and commerce, but it also opened the door to a new breed of cybercriminals. Hacking became more organized and financially motivated, leading to attacks on websites, data theft, and extortion.

The late 1990s and early 2000s saw a surge in distributed denial-of-service (DDoS) attacks. These attacks flooded websites and networks with traffic, rendering them inaccessible. Cybercriminals used DDoS attacks to disrupt services, extort businesses, or exact revenge.

The rise of e-commerce and online banking introduced a new threat vector: cyber fraud. Phishing, a technique in which attackers tricked individuals into revealing sensitive information like login credentials and credit card numbers, became prevalent. Email phishing campaigns posed significant risks to individuals and organizations alike.

The early 2000s also marked the emergence of ransomware attacks. Cybercriminals encrypted victims' data and demanded a ransom for its release. While ransomware dates back to the late 1980s, it gained notoriety with the advent of cryptocurrency, which made ransom payments more difficult to trace.

In the mid-2000s, state-sponsored cyberattacks came to the forefront. Nation-states leveraged cyber capabilities for espionage, intellectual property theft, and even attacks on critical infrastructure. Stuxnet, a worm discovered in 2010, was a watershed moment, as it was allegedly developed by a nation-state to target Iran's nuclear program.

Social engineering attacks, such as spear-phishing, advanced alongside technological advancements. These attacks preyed on human psychology, exploiting trust to gain access to sensitive information. Highly targeted and convincing, spear-phishing attacks posed significant challenges for organizations.

The proliferation of mobile devices brought forth mobile-specific threats, including mobile malware and data breaches. As smartphones became integral to our personal and professional lives, they became lucrative targets for cybercriminals.

Fast forward to the present day, and cyber threats have continued to evolve at an alarming rate. The digital transformation of businesses, the growth of the Internet of Things (IoT), and the increasing sophistication of threat actors have created a complex and ever-changing cybersecurity landscape.

Ransomware attacks have escalated, with cybercriminals demanding exorbitant sums and targeting critical infrastructure, healthcare systems, and municipalities. Nation-state actors engage in cyber-espionage, launching sophisticated campaigns to gather intelligence and disrupt rival nations.

The emergence of cryptocurrencies has enabled cybercriminals to launder money more effectively and extort victims with greater anonymity. Dark web marketplaces offer a thriving ecosystem for the sale of stolen data, hacking tools, and cybercrime services.

The advent of artificial intelligence and machine learning has introduced a new dimension to cyber threats. Threat actors can leverage these technologies to automate attacks, evade detection, and tailor their tactics to individual targets.

As we look ahead, it's clear that cyber threats will continue to evolve in tandem with technology. The digitalization of critical infrastructure, the expansion of 5G networks, and the increasing connectivity of IoT devices present both opportunities and challenges.

In this ever-changing landscape, organizations and individuals must remain vigilant and proactive in their approach to cybersecurity. Threat intelligence, advanced security measures, employee training, and collaboration among stakeholders will play essential roles in mitigating cyber risks.

As we navigate the historical perspective on cyber threats, we must recognize that our journey through the digital age is ongoing. The lessons of the past inform our understanding of the present and help us prepare for the challenges that lie ahead. In the chapters to come, we will delve deeper into the strategies and technologies that can help us combat these evolving threats and build a more secure digital future. In today's interconnected world, the modern threat landscape has become a vast and intricate web of challenges that individuals and organizations must navigate. As we examine this landscape, we find that it's characterized by a myriad of evolving threats, each presenting unique risks and complexities.

Cyberattacks have grown in sophistication and scale, posing significant challenges to cybersecurity professionals and individuals alike. One of the most prevalent and pernicious threats in recent years is ransomware, which has gained notoriety for its ability to cripple organizations and extort substantial sums of money. Ransomware attacks often involve encrypting critical data, making it inaccessible to the victim until a ransom is paid. These attacks can have far-reaching consequences, affecting everything from healthcare institutions to municipal services.

Another pressing concern is the rise of nation-state-sponsored cyberattacks. State actors are increasingly leveraging their cyber capabilities for espionage, intellectual property theft, and even disrupting critical infrastructure. The Stuxnet worm, which targeted Iran's nuclear program, was a watershed moment that highlighted the potential of state-sponsored cyberattacks. Such incidents underscore the need for robust defenses and international cooperation in cyberspace.

Phishing attacks remain a prevalent threat, but they have evolved to become more sophisticated and convincing. Spear-phishing, in particular, targets individuals or organizations with highly personalized and deceptive emails, often exploiting trust to gain access to sensitive information. This human-centric approach makes spear-phishing campaigns challenging to detect and defend against.

The digital transformation of businesses and the proliferation of Internet of Things (IoT) devices have expanded the attack surface for cybercriminals. IoT devices, ranging from smart thermostats to industrial sensors, are often poorly secured, making them attractive targets for attackers. These devices can be leveraged to launch attacks on larger networks or used as entry points into organizations.

The growth of cryptocurrency has introduced new challenges in the realm of cybersecurity. Cryptocurrencies provide a level of anonymity that can facilitate money laundering and ransom payments, making it difficult to trace and apprehend cybercriminals. Dark web marketplaces offer a thriving ecosystem for the sale of stolen data, hacking tools, and cybercrime services, further fueling cybercriminal activities.

Artificial intelligence (AI) and machine learning (ML) have become a double-edged sword in the modern threat landscape. While they hold promise for enhancing cybersecurity through automated threat detection and response, threat actors are also leveraging these technologies to automate attacks and evade detection. AI-powered attacks can adapt to evolving defenses and target vulnerabilities more effectively.

Supply chain attacks have emerged as a growing concern, exemplified by the SolarWinds breach. Cybercriminals exploit vulnerabilities within a trusted vendor's software or services to infiltrate their targets, often remaining undetected for extended periods. These attacks can have cascading effects, compromising numerous organizations connected to the compromised supply chain.

The modern threat landscape is not limited to the digital realm. Physical security threats, such as insider threats and social engineering, continue to pose risks to organizations.

Insider threats involve employees or individuals with insider knowledge exploiting their access to data or systems for malicious purposes. Social engineering attacks manipulate individuals into revealing sensitive information, often through psychological manipulation or deception.

With the advent of 5G networks and the digitalization of critical infrastructure, the potential attack surface continues to expand. Critical infrastructure, such as power grids and water treatment facilities, is increasingly connected to the internet, making it susceptible to cyberattacks that can have far-reaching societal impacts.

In response to these challenges, cybersecurity professionals must adopt a proactive and multi-faceted approach to defense. Threat intelligence, which involves monitoring and analyzing emerging threats, plays a crucial role in staying ahead of cyber adversaries. Organizations must invest in advanced security measures, including intrusion detection systems, firewalls, and endpoint protection, to fortify their defenses.

Employee training and awareness are essential components of cybersecurity. Ensuring that individuals within organizations are educated about the latest threats and best practices can help prevent successful attacks, particularly when it comes to phishing and social engineering attempts.

Collaboration among stakeholders, both within and across industries, is increasingly vital. Sharing threat intelligence, best practices, and incident response strategies can bolster collective cybersecurity efforts. International cooperation is also essential in addressing state-sponsored cyber threats and establishing norms in cyberspace.

As we navigate the complexities of the modern threat landscape, it's clear that cybersecurity is an ongoing and dynamic challenge. Threat actors will continue to adapt and innovate, necessitating a continuous commitment to evolving defense strategies and technologies. In the following chapters, we will explore these strategies in more detail, equipping readers with the knowledge and tools needed to navigate and mitigate the ever-changing cybersecurity landscape.

**Chapter 2: Advanced Principles of Zero Trust Security**

As we delve deeper into the realm of cybersecurity and Zero Trust, it's crucial to understand that the principles we've discussed thus far serve as a foundation upon which more advanced strategies are built. In this chapter, we'll explore the concept of "Advanced Zero Trust Principles" and how they enhance an organization's security posture in an ever-evolving threat landscape.

**Authentication Redefined**: Beyond the fundamental principle of "Verify Explicitly," advanced Zero Trust introduces multifaceted authentication methods that adapt to contextual factors. Biometric authentication, such as fingerprint or facial recognition, adds an extra layer of identity verification. Continuous authentication, where a user's identity is continuously verified during a session, helps thwart unauthorized access even after initial login.

**Dynamic Least Privilege Access**: While "Least Privilege Access" restricts user permissions to the minimum necessary, advanced Zero Trust takes it further by making these privileges dynamic. Instead of granting static permissions, advanced systems adjust access rights in real-time based on the user's behavior, location, and the context of their actions. This dynamic approach minimizes the risk of privilege escalation during an attack.

**Risk-Based Access Control**: Advanced Zero Trust integrates risk assessment into access control decisions. A risk-based approach evaluates various factors, including a user's behavior, device health, and network conditions, to assign risk scores. If a user's actions or context raise concerns, their access can be restricted or monitored more closely, ensuring proactive security measures.

**Continuous Monitoring and Behavioral Analysis**: The principle of "Continuous Monitoring" extends beyond network traffic. Advanced Zero Trust employs behavioral analytics to create user and device profiles. Machine learning algorithms analyze patterns and anomalies, instantly identifying deviations from normal behavior. This allows organizations to respond swiftly to emerging threats.

**Zero Trust for Workloads**: In addition to user and device-centric security, advanced Zero Trust principles apply to workloads, such as applications and services. Every interaction between workloads is treated as untrusted, necessitating rigorous authentication and encryption for data in transit and at rest. This approach secures the heart of an organization's digital infrastructure.

**Advanced Threat Detection and Response**: Modern threats require advanced detection mechanisms. Advanced Zero Trust environments leverage AI-driven threat detection systems that analyze vast datasets for unusual patterns and known attack signatures. Automated incident response capabilities can contain threats swiftly, limiting potential damage.

**Extended to IoT and Critical Infrastructure**: Advanced Zero Trust is adaptable to secure the rapidly expanding Internet of Things (IoT) landscape and critical infrastructure. By applying the same principles to these domains, organizations can safeguard smart devices, industrial control systems, and the essential services they support.

**Cyber Resilience Integration**: Recognizing that breaches are inevitable, advanced Zero Trust principles emphasize cyber resilience. Organizations implement strategies for rapid incident response, data recovery, and business continuity. This ensures that even in the face of a successful breach, the impact is minimized.

**Zero Trust for Cloud-Native Environments**: Cloud-native applications and microservices present unique security challenges. Advanced Zero Trust extends protection to cloud environments, utilizing native cloud security controls and leveraging API-driven security policies to secure data and applications in the cloud.

**Machine-to-Machine Trust**: In advanced Zero Trust architectures, machine-to-machine trust is paramount. Automated processes and AI-driven systems must establish trust with minimal human intervention. Advanced encryption and identity management techniques are employed to ensure the integrity of these interactions.

**Zero Trust for the Evolving Threat Landscape**: The advanced Zero Trust framework remains agile and adaptable to the evolving threat landscape. It integrates threat intelligence feeds, vulnerability assessments, and automated updates to stay ahead of emerging threats. This proactive approach helps organizations anticipate and defend against new attack vectors.

**Strategic Partnerships**: Advanced Zero Trust principles emphasize collaboration with security vendors, industry peers, and governmental agencies. Sharing threat intelligence and best practices is vital for collective defense against sophisticated adversaries.

**Cybersecurity Culture**: Beyond technology, advanced Zero Trust principles foster a cybersecurity culture within organizations. Employees at all levels are educated and encouraged to be vigilant, report anomalies, and actively participate in the security posture of the organization.

**User-Centric Privacy**: As advanced Zero Trust principles become more granular in user monitoring and behavior analysis, privacy concerns become paramount. Organizations must strike a balance between robust security and respecting user privacy, adhering to regulatory requirements.

In summary, advanced Zero Trust principles elevate cybersecurity practices to a dynamic, adaptive, and resilient state. They acknowledge that security is not a one-size-fits-all approach but a continuously evolving strategy that adapts to new challenges and emerging threats. By implementing these advanced principles, organizations can stay ahead of cyber adversaries and build a robust security posture capable of withstanding the complexities of the modern threat landscape.

In the ever-evolving landscape of cybersecurity, it's crucial to explore how concepts like Zero Trust are themselves evolving. Zero Trust, once a groundbreaking paradigm, has undergone significant changes and expansions in recent years, giving rise to the concept of "Zero Trust Beyond." In this chapter, we'll delve into the evolving nature of Zero Trust and its broader implications.

Zero Trust, as originally conceived, challenged the traditional perimeter-based security model. It emphasized the importance of not trusting anything or anyone, even if they were inside the corporate network. This foundational principle remains at the core of Zero Trust, but it has evolved to encompass a broader scope.

One key evolution of Zero Trust is the recognition that networks are no longer confined to physical locations or corporate boundaries. With the proliferation of cloud computing, remote work, and mobile devices, the traditional network perimeter has all but disappeared. As a result, Zero Trust has expanded its focus from network-centric security to a more holistic approach that encompasses users, devices, applications, data, and workloads, regardless of their location.

Zero Trust Beyond acknowledges that threats can originate from various sources and vectors, both internal and external. This shift in perspective means that organizations must adopt a more comprehensive and adaptive security posture. The "Beyond" in Zero Trust Beyond signifies the extension of Zero Trust principles to cover a wider array of elements in the digital ecosystem.

User-Centric Approach: One significant evolution is the emphasis on a user-centric approach. While traditional security models primarily revolved around securing devices or networks, Zero Trust Beyond recognizes that users are both the targets and the front lines of defense. Identity and access management (IAM) play a pivotal role in this evolution, ensuring that user identities are securely verified and their access is continuously monitored and controlled.

Device-Centric Security: Devices, including smartphones, tablets, laptops, and IoT devices, have become essential components of the modern workplace. Zero Trust Beyond acknowledges the need for robust device security, including ensuring the integrity of device identities, regular security assessments, and enforcement of security policies on devices.

Application-Centric Security: With the shift towards cloud-native applications, securing the applications themselves becomes paramount. Zero Trust Beyond extends its reach to secure applications and APIs, enforcing strong authentication, encryption, and access controls for these critical components.

Data Protection: Recognizing the value of data as a prime target for cyberattacks, Zero Trust Beyond emphasizes data-centric security. Data encryption, classification, and access controls are integral to safeguarding sensitive information, both at rest and in transit.

Workload Security: As organizations embrace cloud computing and microservices architecture, workloads become more distributed. Zero Trust Beyond applies its principles to securing workloads, ensuring that they are isolated, authenticated, and monitored, regardless of where they reside.

Behavioral Analytics: Evolving threat landscape demands advanced threat detection mechanisms. Behavioral analytics, powered by machine learning and AI, continuously assess user and device behavior for anomalies and potential threats, allowing for real-time response.

Threat Intelligence Integration: Zero Trust Beyond integrates threat intelligence feeds and automated threat hunting capabilities to proactively identify and mitigate emerging threats. This intelligence-driven approach ensures that security measures stay ahead of evolving attack vectors.

Automation and Orchestration: Recognizing the need for rapid response, Zero Trust Beyond leverages automation and orchestration to streamline incident response processes. Security incidents can be detected, investigated, and mitigated more efficiently, reducing the time-to-response.

Cross-Industry Applicability: Zero Trust Beyond is not limited to a specific industry or sector. Its principles are adaptable and applicable to various domains, from finance and healthcare to critical infrastructure and government agencies.

Collaborative Defense: In an interconnected digital world, collaborative defense becomes essential. Organizations and security vendors increasingly share threat intelligence and best practices to collectively defend against sophisticated threats.

Privacy and Compliance: With heightened awareness of privacy concerns and regulatory requirements like GDPR and CCPA, Zero Trust Beyond incorporates robust privacy controls and compliance measures to ensure that security practices align with legal and ethical standards.

In summary, Zero Trust has come a long way since its inception. It has evolved from a network-centric model to a comprehensive, adaptive, and user-centric security framework known as Zero Trust Beyond. This evolution is a response to the changing cybersecurity landscape, where threats are more sophisticated and diverse than ever before. Embracing Zero Trust Beyond is essential for organizations seeking to stay resilient and secure in the face of evolving challenges.

## Chapter 3: Zero Trust as a Cornerstone of Cyber Resilience

Let's explore the fundamentals of cyber resilience—an essential aspect of modern cybersecurity that goes beyond traditional security measures to ensure an organization's ability to withstand, adapt to, and recover from cyberattacks and disruptions.

At its core, cyber resilience is about building a robust and adaptable cybersecurity posture that can effectively respond to and recover from a wide range of threats and incidents. It recognizes that no system or organization is entirely immune to cyberattacks, and therefore, the focus shifts from just prevention to a holistic strategy that includes detection, response, and recovery.

One key principle of cyber resilience is redundancy and diversity in defense mechanisms. Rather than relying solely on a single security tool or strategy, organizations implement a layered security approach. This includes firewalls, intrusion detection systems, antivirus software, and security awareness training for employees. By layering these defenses, an organization increases its chances of detecting and mitigating threats effectively.

Cyber resilience also emphasizes continuous monitoring and real-time threat detection. Traditional cybersecurity models often relied on periodic security assessments, leaving gaps between assessments during which attacks could go unnoticed. In contrast, a cyber-resilient organization employs continuous monitoring systems that can identify suspicious activities and potential threats as they occur.

Another critical aspect of cyber resilience is the development of an incident response plan. This plan outlines how the organization will respond to a cyber incident, from identifying the breach to mitigating its impact and recovering affected systems. A well-designed incident response plan includes roles and responsibilities, communication protocols, and predefined steps for handling different types of incidents.

Regular testing and simulation exercises are essential components of cyber resilience. These exercises help organizations evaluate the effectiveness of their incident response plans and identify areas for improvement. By simulating various cyberattack scenarios, organizations can train their staff to respond effectively when real incidents occur.

Cyber resilience extends beyond technical measures; it also encompasses people and processes. Employee training and awareness are vital components of a cyber-resilient organization. Staff members must be educated about cybersecurity best practices and potential threats, as human error is a common entry point for cyberattacks.

Backup and recovery strategies play a central role in cyber resilience. Organizations should regularly back up critical data and systems to ensure they can be quickly restored in the event of a cyber incident or data loss. These backups should be stored securely, preferably offsite, to prevent them from being compromised during an attack.

Another key concept in cyber resilience is the principle of "assume breach." This approach recognizes that attackers may already be inside an organization's network, and the goal is to detect and respond to their activities rather than relying solely on perimeter defenses.

A cyber-resilient organization also embraces the concept of threat intelligence. Threat intelligence involves gathering information about emerging threats, vulnerabilities, and attacker tactics, techniques, and procedures. By staying informed about the evolving threat landscape, organizations can proactively adjust their security measures to counter new and emerging threats.

Cyber resilience is not a one-size-fits-all approach. It requires tailoring security measures to an organization's specific needs, risk profile, and industry. For example, financial institutions may face different threats and compliance requirements than healthcare organizations.

Moreover, the landscape of cyber threats is continually evolving, with new attack techniques and vectors emerging regularly. As such, a cyber-resilient organization must stay agile and adapt its security measures to address evolving threats effectively.

In summary, cyber resilience is a comprehensive and adaptive approach to cybersecurity. It focuses on building an organization's capacity to withstand and recover from cyberattacks by implementing layered security measures, continuous monitoring, incident response planning, employee training, and backup and recovery strategies. By embracing cyber resilience, organizations can better protect their digital assets and operations in an ever-changing threat landscape.

Zero Trust, as we've discussed in previous chapters, is a security framework that challenges the traditional notion of trust within a network. It operates on the fundamental principle of "never trust, always verify," meaning that no entity, whether inside or outside the network, is automatically trusted, and every user and device must continuously prove their identity and meet security criteria.

To strengthen resilience with Zero Trust, organizations first need to recognize that resilience goes beyond mere security measures. It encompasses the ability to not only prevent and detect cyber threats but also to effectively respond to and recover from them. Zero Trust aligns well with this broader perspective on resilience because it focuses on enhancing security at every level while enabling adaptive responses to evolving threats.

At the heart of the Zero Trust approach is robust identity and access management (IAM). In a Zero Trust environment, users and devices are granted the least privilege access required for their specific roles and functions. This means that even within the organization, employees can only access the resources necessary for their job, reducing the attack surface and limiting the potential damage that can be caused in case of a breach.

Multi-factor authentication (MFA) is a fundamental component of Zero Trust IAM. It adds an extra layer of security by requiring users to provide multiple forms of verification before gaining access to sensitive systems or data. This significantly reduces the risk of unauthorized access, even if an attacker has stolen or guessed a user's password.

Device identity verification is another critical aspect of Zero Trust. Every device seeking access to the network must be identified and verified. This ensures that only trusted and secure devices can connect. Untrusted or compromised devices are prevented from accessing critical resources, further enhancing security.

Network segmentation, a core tenet of Zero Trust, plays a pivotal role in strengthening resilience. By dividing the network into smaller, isolated segments and controlling traffic between them, an organization can contain threats, preventing lateral movement within the network. Even if one segment is compromised, the attacker's ability to move laterally is limited, reducing the overall impact of a breach.

Continuous monitoring and real-time threat detection are integral to resilience. Zero Trust emphasizes the need for constant vigilance. Suspicious activities and potential threats are detected and addressed promptly, reducing the time it takes to identify and respond to incidents. This proactive stance enhances an organization's resilience by minimizing the impact of attacks.

The Zero Trust framework also underscores the importance of maintaining an incident response plan. This plan outlines how an organization will react when a cyber incident occurs, ensuring that everyone knows their roles and responsibilities. It includes predefined steps for different types of incidents, facilitating swift and effective responses.

Regular testing and simulation exercises are essential for validating the incident response plan's effectiveness. These exercises allow organizations to practice their response to various cyberattack scenarios, uncovering weaknesses and refining their incident management procedures.

Backup and recovery strategies are critical components of resilience. Organizations must regularly back up their critical data and systems to ensure they can be quickly restored in the event of a cyber incident or data loss. These backups should be securely stored and regularly tested to ensure they can be relied upon when needed.

An emerging concept in Zero Trust is the principle of "assume breach." This mindset shift acknowledges that determined attackers may already be inside an organization's network, and the focus shifts from just preventing breaches to quickly identifying and mitigating them.

Employee training and awareness are vital to resilience. Staff members need to be educated about cybersecurity best practices and potential threats. Human error is a common entry point for cyberattacks, so well-informed employees are an organization's first line of defense.

Threat intelligence is another integral part of Zero Trust resilience. It involves collecting and analyzing information about emerging threats, vulnerabilities, and attacker tactics.

By staying informed about the evolving threat landscape, organizations can proactively adjust their security measures to counter new and emerging threats.

In summary, strengthening resilience with Zero Trust is about embracing a holistic approach to cybersecurity that combines robust identity and access management, network segmentation, continuous monitoring, incident response planning, employee training, backup and recovery, and a proactive mindset. By integrating these elements, organizations can enhance their ability to withstand, adapt to, and recover from cyber threats, ultimately becoming more resilient in the face of today's evolving cybersecurity challenges.

## Chapter 4: Advanced Identity and Device Authentication

Let's delve into the exciting world of cutting-edge authentication technologies. In our increasingly digital and interconnected world, traditional username and password combinations are no longer sufficient to protect sensitive information and systems. As cyber threats become more sophisticated, organizations are turning to innovative authentication methods to enhance security.

One of the most promising advancements in authentication technology is biometric authentication. This approach leverages unique physical and behavioral characteristics of individuals to verify their identities. Common biometric factors include fingerprints, facial recognition, iris scans, voice recognition, and even the way someone types or walks. Biometrics offer a high level of security because they are difficult to forge or steal. Moreover, they provide a convenient and user-friendly authentication experience, as users don't need to remember complex passwords.

Facial recognition technology, in particular, has gained widespread attention. It uses the unique features of a person's face to grant access. Facial recognition has become more accurate and faster with the advent of deep learning and artificial intelligence. It's now used in a variety of applications, from unlocking smartphones to securing access to buildings.

Another cutting-edge authentication method is behavioral biometrics. This technique analyzes user behavior patterns, such as typing speed and rhythm, mouse movements, and touchscreen interactions. These behavioral traits are highly individual, making it difficult for impostors to replicate them. Behavioral biometrics can continuously monitor user activity, enhancing security by detecting anomalies that might indicate a compromised account.

Additionally, wearable authentication devices are gaining popularity. These devices, like smartwatches and fitness trackers, can authenticate users based on their unique physiological traits or device-specific characteristics. For instance, a wearable might measure a user's heart rate or the unique electrical signals generated by their body to confirm their identity.

Mobile authentication methods have also evolved significantly. Mobile devices often incorporate biometrics such as fingerprint scanning and facial recognition for user authentication. Mobile apps and services can use these biometrics to ensure secure access. Moreover, smartphones can serve as authentication tokens, generating time-sensitive codes that users must enter to gain access, adding an extra layer of security.

Passwordless authentication is a trend that's gaining traction. This approach eliminates the need for traditional passwords altogether. Instead, users authenticate through methods like biometrics, smart cards, or one-time codes delivered via mobile apps or email. Passwordless authentication simplifies the user experience and reduces the risk of password-related breaches.

Multi-factor authentication (MFA) continues to evolve as well. In addition to something you know (like a password) and something you have (like a mobile device), MFA can now include something you are (biometrics) or something you do (behavioral biometrics). This layered approach significantly enhances security by requiring multiple authentication factors.

Zero Trust Architecture (ZTA) is closely aligned with these cutting-edge authentication technologies. ZTA promotes continuous authentication and access controls based on the principle of "never trust, always verify." With Zero Trust, users and devices are continuously authenticated throughout their sessions, and access is granted only if they meet the predefined security criteria.

Blockchain technology has also made inroads in authentication. Decentralized identity management systems based on blockchain offer users greater control over their personal information and authentication processes. These systems enable users to share only the necessary information for a specific transaction or interaction, enhancing privacy and security.

Quantum-resistant cryptography is an emerging field addressing the threat posed by quantum computers. Quantum computers have the potential to break traditional encryption algorithms, rendering current security measures obsolete. Researchers are developing cryptographic techniques that are resilient against quantum attacks, ensuring that authentication and data protection remain secure in the post-quantum era.

In summary, cutting-edge authentication technologies are reshaping the landscape of cybersecurity. Biometrics, behavioral biometrics, wearable devices, mobile authentication, passwordless authentication, MFA, Zero Trust Architecture, blockchain-based identity management, and quantum-resistant cryptography are all contributing to a more secure and user-friendly authentication experience. As organizations strive to protect their digital assets from ever-evolving threats, these innovative authentication methods offer robust solutions to safeguard sensitive information and systems in our increasingly connected world.

Let's dive into the fascinating world of device identity verification techniques. In today's digital landscape, where devices play a central role in our lives and work, ensuring their identities are legitimate and secure is of paramount importance.

Device identity verification involves the process of confirming that a device is what it claims to be before granting it access to systems, networks, or applications. This verification is crucial for preventing unauthorized access and protecting sensitive data from potential threats. Several advanced techniques have emerged to accomplish this task effectively.

Firstly, let's explore the realm of device fingerprinting. This technique involves collecting and analyzing unique attributes or characteristics of a device to create a distinct digital fingerprint. These attributes can include hardware specifications, software configurations, and even the device's behavior patterns. By comparing these fingerprints with known profiles, organizations can verify the identity of a device. Device fingerprinting is particularly useful for recognizing both managed and unmanaged devices within a network, helping organizations maintain strict control over their digital ecosystems.

Next up is digital certificates, which play a significant role in device identity verification. Digital certificates are cryptographic credentials that bind a device's identity to a public key. Devices use these certificates to authenticate themselves to other devices or servers during the communication process. When a device presents a valid digital certificate signed by a trusted certificate authority, it establishes its identity, ensuring secure communication. This technique is widely used in secure web browsing (HTTPS), secure email communication (S/MIME), and many other applications where device authentication is critical.

Another promising method is the use of hardware-based security modules (HSMs) or trusted platform modules (TPMs). These dedicated hardware components store cryptographic keys and perform secure cryptographic operations within a device. By leveraging HSMs or TPMs, organizations can ensure that only trusted devices with these components can access sensitive data or systems. These modules also enhance security by protecting cryptographic keys from being extracted or compromised.

Behavioral analysis is an innovative technique for device identity verification. Instead of relying solely on static attributes, this method assesses a device's behavior over time. By analyzing patterns of behavior, such as how a device communicates, the types of data it accesses, and its typical usage patterns, organizations can establish a behavioral baseline for each device. Deviations from this baseline can raise red flags, indicating potential security threats or unauthorized access. Behavioral analysis is particularly effective at identifying anomalies and zero-day attacks.

Network-based techniques are also integral to device identity verification. Network access control (NAC) systems examine devices attempting to join a network and assess their compliance with security policies. These systems check attributes like device type, operating system version, installed security patches, and the presence of specific security software. If a device meets the predefined criteria, it gains access to the network; otherwise, it is quarantined or limited to a guest network. NAC is an essential component of a comprehensive device identity verification strategy, ensuring that only secure and compliant devices can access sensitive resources.

Next, let's explore the world of token-based authentication for devices. Tokens, in this context, refer to unique identifiers or cryptographic tokens generated by a device and presented during the authentication process. These tokens can take various forms, such as time-based one-time passwords (TOTPs) or security tokens. Token-based authentication adds an extra layer of security to device identity verification, as even if an attacker gains access to the device's credentials, they would still need the physical token to complete the authentication process.

Biometric authentication is not limited to humans; it can also be used for device identity verification. Devices equipped with biometric sensors, such as fingerprint scanners or facial recognition cameras, can use these features to verify their identities. For instance, a device can use its built-in fingerprint sensor to confirm its identity before accessing sensitive data. Biometric authentication for devices enhances security and convenience, as it eliminates the need for traditional passwords.

Machine learning and artificial intelligence (AI) are revolutionizing device identity verification. These technologies can analyze vast amounts of data to establish a device's identity based on its behavior, usage patterns, and interactions. Machine learning algorithms can detect anomalies and identify unauthorized access attempts in real-time. They continuously adapt to evolving threats, making them invaluable for securing devices in dynamic environments.

Lastly, blockchain technology is making inroads into device identity verification. Blockchain provides a decentralized and tamper-proof ledger of device identities and transactions. Each device can have a unique identifier recorded on the blockchain, and any changes or interactions are transparently recorded. This immutable record ensures the integrity and authenticity of device identities, making it highly secure against fraud and manipulation.

In summary, device identity verification techniques have evolved significantly to meet the challenges posed by an increasingly connected world. These techniques encompass device fingerprinting, digital certificates, hardware-based security modules, behavioral analysis, network-based access control, token-based authentication, biometrics, machine learning, and blockchain. By leveraging these advanced methods, organizations can ensure that only trusted devices gain access to their networks, systems, and data, thereby strengthening security and mitigating potential threats.

## Chapter 5: Advanced Network Segmentation and Policy Enforcement

In the realm of cybersecurity, advanced strategies for network segmentation are essential to fortify defenses and thwart the ever-evolving threats that organizations face. Network segmentation involves dividing an organization's network into smaller, isolated segments or subnetworks to enhance security and control over network traffic. It's like creating multiple layers of protection within your digital fortress. In this chapter, we'll delve into some advanced techniques and considerations for network segmentation that go beyond the basics.

One powerful concept in advanced network segmentation is the principle of "Zero Trust." This approach assumes that no device or user, whether inside or outside the network, can be trusted by default. Zero Trust networks are designed to verify the identity of every device and user before granting them access to specific resources. This means that even if a device is inside the network perimeter, it must go through rigorous authentication and authorization processes to access critical assets. Implementing Zero Trust principles requires fine-grained segmentation and dynamic access controls, ensuring that only authorized entities can interact with sensitive data.

Micro-segmentation takes network segmentation to a more granular level. Instead of merely dividing the network into broad segments, micro-segmentation isolates individual workloads, applications, or even devices. Each micro-segment has its access controls, policies, and security measures. This level of segmentation minimizes lateral movement in the event of a breach. If an attacker gains access to one segment, they'll find it extremely challenging to navigate to other parts of the network, protecting valuable assets and data.

Software-Defined Networking (SDN) plays a crucial role in advanced network segmentation. SDN allows administrators to control and manage network traffic programmatically. This flexibility enables dynamic and on-the-fly adjustments to network policies and segmentation rules. For example, if unusual network behavior is detected, SDN can automatically isolate the affected segment, preventing the spread of a potential threat.

Dynamic segmentation is another advanced strategy that adapts to changing conditions in real-time. Instead of relying on static rules and policies, dynamic segmentation assesses the security posture of devices and users dynamically. Factors such as device health, user behavior, and threat intelligence are continuously monitored to adjust access controls accordingly. For instance, if a device starts exhibiting suspicious behavior, it can be immediately isolated until the issue is resolved.

Segmentation by application is a powerful technique for protecting critical applications and services. It involves creating segments specifically for each application or service, implementing access controls, and isolating them from the rest of the network. This approach limits the potential attack surface for each application, reducing the risk of unauthorized access or lateral movement. It's particularly useful for safeguarding essential services like databases, financial systems, or customer-facing applications.

The principle of least privilege is a cornerstone of advanced network segmentation. It stipulates that users and devices should only have access to the resources necessary to perform their specific functions. By implementing the principle of least privilege within segmented networks, organizations can minimize the potential impact of a security breach. Attackers who gain access to a segment with limited privileges will find it challenging to escalate their access and compromise critical assets.

Additionally, organizations are increasingly turning to cloud-native security controls as part of their advanced segmentation strategies. Cloud environments offer robust tools for managing and securing network traffic within and between cloud services. By leveraging cloud-native security controls, organizations can extend their segmentation strategies seamlessly into the cloud, ensuring consistent security policies across hybrid and multi-cloud environments.

Automation and orchestration are vital components of advanced network segmentation. With the growing complexity of network infrastructures and the rapid pace of cyber threats, manually managing segmentation rules and access controls is impractical. Automation enables organizations to streamline the implementation and enforcement of segmentation policies. Furthermore, orchestration ensures that all security measures, from intrusion detection to access controls, work together seamlessly to protect the network.

Behavioral analytics is an emerging field that complements advanced network segmentation. It involves monitoring and analyzing user and device behavior patterns within the network. By establishing baselines for normal behavior, organizations can detect anomalies that may indicate security threats. Behavioral analytics can identify insider threats, compromised accounts, and other suspicious activities that might otherwise go unnoticed.

Threat intelligence integration enhances advanced network segmentation by providing real-time information about emerging threats and vulnerabilities. By incorporating threat intelligence feeds and platforms into segmentation strategies, organizations can adjust their policies and access controls to respond proactively to known threats. This dynamic approach helps protect the network against the latest attack vectors and vulnerabilities.

In summary, advanced network segmentation is a multifaceted strategy that goes beyond traditional network boundaries to fortify security in today's dynamic threat landscape. Incorporating Zero Trust principles, micro-segmentation, software-defined networking, dynamic segmentation, and cloud-native security controls, among other advanced techniques, can significantly enhance an organization's ability to defend against evolving threats. The principle of least privilege, automation, orchestration, behavioral analytics, and threat intelligence integration further strengthen the network's resilience and security posture. Implementing these strategies is not just about dividing the network; it's about creating a dynamic, adaptable, and proactive defense system that keeps pace with the relentless evolution of cyber threats. Granular policy enforcement stands as a pivotal concept in the realm of Zero Trust models, serving as a linchpin in fortifying network security against modern cyber threats. It's a fundamental principle that complements the broader Zero Trust framework, emphasizing the need for fine-tuned control over access permissions, data flows, and user interactions within the network. In this chapter, we'll explore the significance of granular policy enforcement and its role in enhancing the security posture of organizations.

To comprehend the importance of granular policy enforcement, it's essential to grasp the underlying philosophy of Zero Trust. Zero Trust, as a security paradigm, challenges the conventional belief that trust should be automatically extended to devices or users within a network.

Instead, it advocates verifying and validating the identity and security posture of every entity, irrespective of their location within or outside the network perimeter. In a world where cyberattacks are becoming increasingly sophisticated, relying on perimeter defenses alone is no longer sufficient.

Granular policy enforcement takes this philosophy a step further by promoting the idea that access control should be finely tuned to the specific needs and requirements of each entity within the network. This granularity allows organizations to implement the principle of least privilege effectively. In other words, entities are granted access only to the resources and data necessary for them to perform their designated tasks, and nothing more. This approach minimizes the attack surface and reduces the potential impact of security breaches.

One of the primary benefits of granular policy enforcement is its ability to adapt to the dynamic nature of modern networks. In traditional security models, access control policies often involve broad strokes, leading to a one-size-fits-all approach that can hinder productivity and create security gaps. Granular policies, on the other hand, can be tailored to accommodate the evolving needs of an organization and its users. They can be adjusted in real-time based on factors such as user roles, device health, location, and contextual information.

User roles play a crucial role in granular policy enforcement. Organizations can define a wide range of roles, each with its specific set of permissions and access rights. For example, a human resources manager may require access to employee records, while a software developer might need access to source code repositories. Granular policies ensure that these roles are well-defined and that access control measures are aligned with the principle of least privilege.

Device health and security posture assessment are vital components of granular policy enforcement. In a world where Bring Your Own Device (BYOD) policies and remote work are prevalent, organizations must ensure that devices connecting to the network meet certain security standards. Granular policies can automatically assess the health of devices, checking for the presence of updated antivirus software, firewalls, and the absence of known vulnerabilities. Devices that fail to meet these criteria can be isolated or restricted until they are brought into compliance. Location-based policies are another facet of granular enforcement. They consider the physical location of users or devices and adjust access permissions accordingly. For example, an organization may allow full access to its internal network when users are on-site but restrict certain sensitive resources when they connect remotely from unsecured public networks. This dynamic adaptation based on location enhances security without sacrificing user convenience.

Contextual information, such as the time of day or the type of application being accessed, can further refine granular policies. For instance, access to critical financial systems may be limited to specific hours during the workday and require multi-factor authentication, while less sensitive applications can have more lenient access controls.

Granular policy enforcement also extends to data protection. Organizations can implement policies that specify who can access, modify, or transmit sensitive data. Encryption and data loss prevention measures can be applied to ensure that data remains secure, even if unauthorized access occurs. This level of control is crucial for compliance with data privacy regulations and safeguarding intellectual property.

Additionally, granular policy enforcement can be extended to third-party access. Organizations frequently collaborate with external partners, vendors, or contractors who require temporary access to specific resources. Granular policies enable organizations to grant temporary and restricted access based on predefined criteria, reducing the risk associated with third-party interactions.

To implement granular policy enforcement effectively, organizations need robust identity and access management (IAM) systems. IAM solutions are pivotal in defining and enforcing access policies, managing user roles, and integrating various authentication methods. These systems also provide auditing and reporting capabilities, ensuring compliance with security policies and regulatory requirements.

In summary, granular policy enforcement is an indispensable element of Zero Trust models, providing organizations with the flexibility and precision needed to secure their networks in an ever-changing threat landscape. By fine-tuning access control, considering user roles, device health, location, and contextual information, organizations can adhere to the principle of least privilege while accommodating the dynamic needs of their users and protecting critical data. Moreover, granular policies enable organizations to extend secure access to third parties and maintain compliance with data privacy regulations. In the journey toward robust cybersecurity, granular policy enforcement is a beacon of control and adaptability, guiding organizations through the complex landscape of modern threats.

## Chapter 6: Advanced Threat Detection and Response

Real-time threat detection techniques are a critical component of modern cybersecurity strategies, providing organizations with the ability to identify and respond to cyber threats as they occur. In an ever-evolving threat landscape, where cyberattacks are becoming more sophisticated and frequent, the need for real-time threat detection has never been more pressing.

These techniques involve the continuous monitoring of network traffic, system logs, and user behavior to identify abnormal or malicious activities. Unlike traditional security approaches that rely on predefined signatures or patterns, real-time threat detection is adaptive and data-driven, making it well-suited to combat the dynamic nature of cyber threats.

One of the fundamental elements of real-time threat detection is the use of advanced analytics and machine learning algorithms. These technologies enable organizations to analyze vast amounts of data quickly and accurately, identifying patterns and anomalies that may indicate a potential threat. Machine learning models can be trained to recognize both known and unknown threats, making them highly effective in identifying previously unseen attack vectors.

Behavioral analytics is a key technique in real-time threat detection. It focuses on monitoring the behavior of users and devices within the network. By establishing baselines of normal behavior, organizations can detect deviations that may indicate a security incident. For example, if a user who typically accesses only certain resources suddenly attempts to access sensitive data or logs in from an unusual location, this could trigger an alert.

User and entity behavior analytics (UEBA) is an advanced form of behavioral analytics that goes beyond traditional perimeter-based security measures. UEBA takes into account not only user actions but also the behavior of devices, applications, and even privileged accounts. By correlating data from various sources, UEBA can provide a more comprehensive view of the threat landscape.

Real-time threat detection techniques also incorporate the analysis of network traffic. Network traffic analysis (NTA) tools examine the flow of data within the network, looking for suspicious patterns or anomalies. This can include unusual data transfer volumes, unexpected communication between devices, or traffic to known malicious domains.

Threat intelligence feeds are another crucial component of real-time threat detection. These feeds provide organizations with up-to-date information about emerging threats, known attack indicators, and malicious IP addresses. By integrating threat intelligence feeds into their detection systems, organizations can proactively identify and block threats based on the latest information.

Intrusion detection and prevention systems (IDPS) play a significant role in real-time threat detection. These systems monitor network and system activities for signs of unauthorized access or malicious behavior. When suspicious activity is detected, IDPS can take immediate action to block the threat, such as isolating the affected device or alerting security personnel.

Endpoint detection and response (EDR) solutions are designed to protect individual devices, such as computers and mobile devices, from advanced threats. EDR solutions continuously monitor endpoints for signs of malicious activity, such as unusual file modifications or suspicious network connections. They can also provide real-time response capabilities to contain and mitigate threats.

Cloud-based security information and event management (SIEM) platforms are instrumental in aggregating and analyzing data from various sources, allowing organizations to correlate events and identify potential threats. These platforms offer real-time dashboards and alerts to keep security teams informed about ongoing security incidents.

In addition to technology-driven techniques, human expertise remains a crucial element of real-time threat detection. Security analysts play a vital role in interpreting alerts, investigating potential incidents, and making informed decisions about threat response. Collaborative threat hunting, where analysts proactively search for signs of compromise, can uncover threats that automated systems may miss.

One of the challenges organizations face with real-time threat detection is the sheer volume of data generated by their networks and systems. Managing and analyzing this data in real-time can be overwhelming without the right tools and processes in place. Scalability and automation are essential to ensure that threats are not missed due to data overload.

Privacy considerations are also paramount when implementing real-time threat detection techniques. Organizations must strike a balance between monitoring for security threats and respecting user privacy. Clear policies and transparency in data collection and analysis are essential to maintain trust with users and comply with data protection regulations.

To conclude, real-time threat detection techniques are a cornerstone of modern cybersecurity, providing organizations with the ability to identify and respond to cyber threats as they happen. By leveraging advanced analytics, machine learning, behavioral analytics, and threat intelligence, organizations can stay ahead of evolving threats and protect their networks and data. However, effective real-time threat detection requires a combination of technology, human expertise, and a commitment to privacy and data protection. In an increasingly connected and digital world, the ability to detect and mitigate threats in real-time is a critical component of a robust cybersecurity strategy.

Advanced incident response strategies are an essential aspect of modern cybersecurity, designed to help organizations effectively manage and recover from security incidents. In today's complex threat landscape, where cyberattacks are increasingly sophisticated and damaging, having a robust incident response plan is critical to minimizing the impact of breaches and ensuring business continuity.

Incident response is the process of identifying, managing, and mitigating the effects of a security incident, whether it's a data breach, a malware infection, or a network intrusion. While basic incident response focuses on containing and remediating incidents, advanced incident response goes further, incorporating proactive strategies and a more comprehensive approach.

One key element of advanced incident response is the development of a well-defined incident response plan (IRP). This plan outlines the organization's approach to handling incidents, including the roles and responsibilities of key personnel, communication protocols, and predefined steps for incident detection and response. An effective IRP is a living document that is regularly updated to reflect the evolving threat landscape and the organization's specific needs.

Advanced incident response also emphasizes the importance of threat intelligence. Threat intelligence feeds and platforms provide organizations with real-time information about emerging threats, known attack indicators, and tactics used by threat actors. By integrating threat intelligence into their incident response processes, organizations can proactively identify and respond to incidents based on the latest information, enabling faster and more accurate decision-making.

Automation plays a significant role in advanced incident response. Security orchestration, automation, and response (SOAR) platforms are used to streamline incident handling processes. These platforms can automatically collect and analyze data from various sources, such as security logs and network traffic, to identify potential incidents. They can also automate response actions, such as isolating affected systems or blocking malicious IP addresses. By reducing manual tasks, SOAR platforms help security teams respond to incidents more efficiently and consistently.

One critical aspect of advanced incident response is the establishment of an incident response team (IRT). This team consists of skilled professionals who are trained to handle security incidents effectively. The IRT may include incident responders, forensic analysts, legal and compliance experts, and communication specialists. Cross-functional collaboration is essential, as incidents often involve technical, legal, and communication challenges.

The "hunt team" is a specialized subgroup within the incident response team responsible for proactive threat hunting. Threat hunting involves actively searching for signs of compromise or suspicious activities within an organization's network. It goes beyond traditional incident response, which relies on alerts generated by security tools, by proactively seeking out hidden threats that may have gone undetected.

Advanced incident response also encompasses the use of digital forensics. Digital forensics involves the collection, preservation, and analysis of digital evidence to understand the scope and impact of a security incident. Forensic analysts use specialized tools and techniques to examine systems, logs, and data for evidence of malicious activity. This process is crucial for understanding how an incident occurred and identifying vulnerabilities that need to be addressed.

Another essential aspect of advanced incident response is the concept of continuous improvement. After an incident has been resolved, organizations conduct post-incident reviews or "lessons learned" sessions to assess the effectiveness of their response and identify areas for improvement. These findings are then used to update the incident response plan and enhance the organization's security posture.

Communication and coordination are vital components of advanced incident response. Organizations must have clear communication channels and procedures in place for both internal and external stakeholders. This includes notifying affected individuals, regulatory authorities, law enforcement (when necessary), and third-party vendors if their systems or data have been compromised.

Advanced incident response also involves the implementation of secure backup and recovery strategies. This ensures that organizations can quickly restore affected systems and data to minimize downtime and business disruption. Regularly tested backups are essential to a successful recovery process.

Legal and compliance considerations are paramount in advanced incident response. Organizations must navigate various regulatory requirements and reporting obligations, depending on their industry and geographic location. Compliance experts on the incident response team help ensure that the organization complies with relevant laws and regulations.

In summary, advanced incident response strategies are essential for organizations to effectively manage and recover from security incidents in today's complex threat landscape. These strategies involve the development of a well-defined incident response plan, the integration of threat intelligence, automation through SOAR platforms, the establishment of an incident response team, proactive threat hunting, digital forensics, continuous improvement, and clear communication and coordination. By adopting advanced incident response practices, organizations can enhance their cybersecurity posture and minimize the impact of security incidents on their operations and reputation.

## Chapter 7: Cloud-Native Security with Zero Trust

Zero Trust, a paradigm-shifting cybersecurity model, has gained significant attention and adoption in recent years. Its principles and concepts have become a fundamental framework for securing modern digital environments. One area where Zero Trust has shown particular relevance and promise is in cloud-native environments.

To understand the role of Zero Trust in cloud-native environments, it's essential first to grasp what cloud-native means. Cloud-native refers to a set of practices and technologies that leverage cloud computing and containerization to build, deploy, and manage applications. Cloud-native applications are designed to be highly scalable, resilient, and adaptable to dynamic cloud infrastructures.

Cloud-native environments present unique security challenges. These environments are characterized by their dynamic nature, with workloads shifting, scaling, and evolving rapidly. Traditional security models, which rely heavily on perimeter defenses, struggle to keep up with the dynamic and distributed nature of cloud-native architectures. This is where Zero Trust comes into play.

At its core, Zero Trust challenges the traditional "trust but verify" approach to cybersecurity. Instead of assuming trust within the network perimeter and verifying identity only at the network edge, Zero Trust asserts that trust should not be assumed anywhere, and verification should be continuous and pervasive. In cloud-native environments, this means implementing a set of practices and technologies that align with Zero Trust principles.

One of the foundational principles of Zero Trust is "Verify Explicitly." In a cloud-native context, this means that every user, device, or application, regardless of where they are located, must continuously verify their identity and adhere to security policies. Traditional network boundaries are dissolved, and access decisions are based on factors like user identity, device health, and the context of the request.

In practice, this might involve the use of Multi-Factor Authentication (MFA) to ensure that users are who they claim to be, regardless of their location. In a cloud-native environment, users may access applications and data from a variety of devices and locations, making strong authentication crucial. MFA adds an extra layer of security by requiring users to provide multiple forms of evidence to prove their identity.

Another key principle of Zero Trust, especially relevant in cloud-native environments, is "Least Privilege Access." This principle emphasizes the idea that users and applications should only have access to the resources and data they need to perform their specific tasks. In a traditional network, users often have access to broad swaths of resources, creating potential security risks. In a cloud-native context, this principle is applied by enforcing granular access controls and regularly reviewing and adjusting permissions.

In cloud-native environments, Micro-Segmentation becomes a valuable implementation of the Least Privilege Access principle. Micro-Segmentation involves dividing the network into smaller, isolated segments and applying access controls between them. This approach helps contain lateral movement in case of a breach, limiting an attacker's ability to move freely within the network.

Device Identity Verification is another critical aspect of Zero Trust in cloud-native environments. With users accessing resources from various devices, ensuring the trustworthiness of these devices is essential. Device identity verification involves assessing the security posture of devices, such as checking for the latest patches and security configurations, before granting access.

Cloud-native security controls play a pivotal role in implementing Zero Trust. These controls are designed to protect cloud-native applications and infrastructure by continuously monitoring for security threats and enforcing security policies. They provide visibility into the cloud environment, detect anomalies, and automatically respond to security incidents.

Real-time Monitoring Tools are instrumental in achieving continuous visibility into cloud-native environments. These tools collect data from various sources, including logs, network traffic, and cloud service APIs, to provide a real-time view of the environment's security posture. Security teams can use this data to identify suspicious activities and respond promptly.

Behavioral Analytics for Threat Detection is an advanced technique that leverages machine learning and artificial intelligence to detect abnormal patterns of behavior in the cloud environment. By learning what is normal and flagging deviations from it, behavioral analytics can identify potential security threats, even when traditional rule-based approaches may fall short.

Cloud-Native Security Controls are specifically designed to address the unique security challenges of cloud-native environments. They include features like container security, serverless security, and cloud workload protection platforms. These controls help organizations secure their cloud-native applications and data while aligning with Zero Trust principles.

Cloud Service Provider Integration is a crucial aspect of implementing Zero Trust in cloud-native environments. Cloud providers offer a range of security services and tools that can be integrated into an organization's Zero Trust strategy. These services often include identity and access management, security monitoring, and compliance reporting.

Secure Mobile Device Management (MDM) is essential for organizations embracing cloud-native environments. With the proliferation of mobile devices in the workplace, securing these devices becomes paramount. MDM solutions allow organizations to enforce security policies on mobile devices, ensuring they meet the organization's security standards.

Mobile App Security in a Zero Trust Model extends Zero Trust principles to mobile applications. This involves applying the same security rigor to mobile apps as to any other application. It includes measures like app containerization, app reputation scoring, and continuous monitoring for app-related security threats.

In summary, Zero Trust principles and concepts provide a robust framework for securing cloud-native environments. By verifying explicitly, implementing least privilege access, and focusing on device identity verification, organizations can enhance security in dynamic and distributed cloud-native architectures. Leveraging cloud-native security controls, real-time monitoring tools, and behavioral analytics further strengthens the security posture. Integrating with cloud service providers and implementing secure mobile device management and mobile app security ensures comprehensive coverage of cloud-native security challenges. In the ever-evolving landscape of cloud-native computing, Zero Trust remains a vital strategy for organizations committed to protecting their digital assets and data.

Securing cloud workloads in the modern digital landscape is a top priority for organizations of all sizes and industries. With the increasing reliance on cloud computing and the dynamic nature of cloud-based applications, traditional security approaches often fall short. This is where advanced Zero Trust controls come into play, providing a robust framework for protecting cloud workloads comprehensively.

When we talk about securing cloud workloads, we're referring to the protection of applications, data, and resources hosted in cloud environments, whether they are public, private, or hybrid clouds. Cloud workloads are not confined to a single location or server; they are distributed across multiple data centers and regions, making them vulnerable to a wide range of cyber threats.

At the heart of the Zero Trust model is the concept of "never trust, always verify." This means that trust is never assumed, and verification is required from every user, device, or application attempting to access cloud workloads. This approach is particularly vital in cloud environments where the traditional network perimeter is virtually nonexistent.

Multi-Factor Authentication (MFA) plays a pivotal role in the Zero Trust model for securing cloud workloads. MFA ensures that users attempting to access cloud resources provide multiple forms of evidence to verify their identities. This additional layer of security reduces the risk of unauthorized access, even if login credentials are compromised.

Cloud environments often involve remote access, with users connecting from various locations and devices. With MFA in place, even if an attacker has stolen a user's password, they would still need the second factor, which could be a fingerprint, a smart card, or a mobile app-generated code. This makes it significantly more challenging for unauthorized individuals to gain access to cloud workloads.

Least Privilege Access is another core principle of Zero Trust that applies seamlessly to securing cloud workloads. In the cloud, resources and data are no longer confined to on-premises servers or data centers. They are spread across a dynamic infrastructure that requires careful access control.

With Least Privilege Access, users and applications are granted the minimum permissions required to perform their specific tasks, and no more. In the context of cloud workloads, this means that users only have access to the data and resources necessary for their roles. For example, a marketing team member should not have access to sensitive financial data, and a developer should not have unrestricted access to production servers.

Implementing Least Privilege Access in the cloud involves robust Identity and Access Management (IAM) policies. Cloud service providers offer IAM solutions that enable organizations to define granular access permissions, ensuring that users and applications can only access what is necessary for their job functions.

Micro-Segmentation, which is a network security technique, plays a significant role in securing cloud workloads. Micro-Segmentation involves dividing a network into smaller, isolated segments and applying access controls between them. In the context of cloud workloads, this means that different parts of the cloud infrastructure are isolated from each other, limiting lateral movement in case of a breach.

For instance, a compromise in one part of the cloud should not automatically grant access to all other parts. Micro-Segmentation ensures that even if an attacker gains access to one segment, they cannot freely move to others without proper authorization.

Device Identity Verification is another advanced control that is crucial in securing cloud workloads, particularly when dealing with remote devices accessing cloud resources. Device identity verification involves assessing the security posture of devices before granting access.

This verification process ensures that devices meet specific security standards, such as having up-to-date operating systems and security patches. Only devices that meet these criteria are allowed to access cloud resources. This control is especially important given the increasing trend of Bring Your Own Device (BYOD) policies in organizations.

Real-time Monitoring Tools are essential for continuous security in cloud workloads. These tools collect and analyze data from various sources, including logs, network traffic, and cloud service APIs, to provide real-time visibility into the security posture of cloud environments.

Security teams can use real-time monitoring to detect anomalies, unauthorized access attempts, and potential security threats. By identifying and responding to these incidents promptly, organizations can minimize the risk of data breaches and service disruptions.

Behavioral Analytics for Threat Detection is an advanced technique that leverages machine learning and artificial intelligence to detect abnormal patterns of behavior in cloud workloads. By learning what is typical and flagging deviations from it, behavioral analytics can identify potential security threats, even when traditional rule-based approaches may not.

These analytics can recognize patterns like unauthorized access attempts, data exfiltration, or unusual resource usage. By continuously analyzing user and application behavior, organizations can proactively identify and respond to security incidents.

Cloud-Native Security Controls are designed explicitly for cloud environments and align with the principles of Zero Trust. These controls encompass a range of security features, such as container security, serverless security, and cloud workload protection platforms. They are essential for addressing the unique security challenges that cloud workloads present.

By implementing these advanced Zero Trust controls in cloud environments, organizations can significantly enhance the security of their cloud workloads. These controls reduce the attack surface, prevent unauthorized access, and provide continuous monitoring and threat detection capabilities.

In summary, securing cloud workloads with advanced Zero Trust controls is a critical aspect of modern cybersecurity. With the ever-increasing adoption of cloud computing, organizations must prioritize the protection of their cloud resources and data. The principles of Zero Trust, including Multi-Factor Authentication, Least Privilege Access, Micro-Segmentation, Device Identity Verification, Real-time Monitoring, and Behavioral Analytics, provide a comprehensive framework for achieving robust cloud security. By leveraging cloud-native security controls, organizations can adapt to the dynamic nature of cloud environments and stay ahead of emerging threats.

## Chapter 8: Securing IoT and Critical Infrastructure in a Zero Trust World

IoT, or the Internet of Things, has transformed the way we live and work by connecting an ever-expanding array of devices to the internet. From smart thermostats to wearable fitness trackers and industrial sensors, IoT devices have become ubiquitous in our daily lives and across various industries. However, with this increased connectivity comes a heightened need for security, and integrating IoT device security into Zero Trust architectures is a crucial step in safeguarding our digital ecosystems.

At its core, the Zero Trust security model operates on the principle of "never trust, always verify." This means that trust is never assumed, and all devices, users, and applications must continuously prove their authenticity and adhere to strict access controls. When it comes to IoT devices, the same principle applies, but the unique characteristics of these devices require special attention.

One of the fundamental challenges in IoT device security is the sheer diversity of these devices. IoT encompasses a wide range of hardware, including sensors, actuators, cameras, and more. These devices often have limited processing power, memory, and communication capabilities compared to traditional computers. Therefore, securing IoT devices requires tailored approaches that consider their specific constraints.

Multi-Factor Authentication (MFA) is a foundational security measure within Zero Trust architectures, and it plays a vital role in IoT device security as well. By requiring multiple forms of verification, such as something you know (e.g., a password), something you have (e.g., a security token), or something you are (e.g., a biometric scan), MFA ensures that only authorized users or devices can access IoT resources.

For IoT devices, MFA can involve using secure certificates or keys to authenticate the device to the network or cloud service it is communicating with. These certificates are unique to each device and are used to establish trust during the initial connection and subsequent data exchanges. This ensures that IoT devices are communicating securely and that malicious actors cannot impersonate them.

In a Zero Trust architecture, Least Privilege Access is another critical principle, and it is especially relevant for IoT devices. IoT devices often have specific functions and limited interaction requirements. For instance, a temperature sensor in a smart building only needs to transmit temperature data to a central controller. Therefore, it should be granted the minimum level of access necessary to perform this function.

By applying Least Privilege Access to IoT devices, organizations can prevent unauthorized access to critical systems or data. For example, if an IoT device were compromised, it would have minimal access, limiting the potential damage and lateral movement an attacker could execute.

Micro-Segmentation is a network security technique that is particularly valuable in the context of IoT device security. It involves dividing a network into smaller, isolated segments and applying access controls between them. This helps prevent unauthorized lateral movement within the network.

For IoT devices, Micro-Segmentation can be used to isolate them into specific network segments based on their function or security requirements. For instance, all IoT devices related to building management can be placed in one segment, while devices related to inventory tracking can be placed in another. This isolation limits the potential attack surface and reduces the risk of unauthorized access to sensitive data or systems.

Device Identity Verification is a key component of IoT security within a Zero Trust framework. Ensuring that each IoT device has a unique identity that can be verified is essential for preventing unauthorized devices from accessing the network or cloud services.

Device identity verification techniques can include the use of hardware-based unique identifiers, secure boot processes, and secure provisioning mechanisms. These methods ensure that each IoT device is recognized and authenticated before it is allowed to communicate with other devices or systems.

Real-time Monitoring Tools are crucial for maintaining the security of IoT devices in a Zero Trust architecture. These tools continuously collect and analyze data from IoT devices to detect anomalies, suspicious behavior, or potential security threats.

In the case of IoT devices, real-time monitoring can help identify unusual patterns of communication, which may indicate a compromised device or an unauthorized access attempt. By promptly detecting and responding to these incidents, organizations can mitigate potential security risks.

Behavioral Analytics for Threat Detection is an advanced technique that can be applied to IoT device security. Machine learning and artificial intelligence algorithms can analyze the behavior of IoT devices over time, establishing a baseline of normal behavior.

When deviations from this baseline occur, behavioral analytics can raise alerts, indicating potential security threats. For instance, if an IoT device suddenly starts sending data to an unknown IP address or begins transmitting unusually large amounts of data, behavioral analytics can detect these anomalies and trigger an investigation.

Cloud-Native Security Controls, specifically designed for cloud environments, are also relevant to IoT device security, as many IoT solutions leverage cloud services for data storage, processing, and management. These controls include cloud-based firewalls, encryption, and access controls that align with Zero Trust principles.

By integrating cloud-native security controls into IoT deployments, organizations can ensure that data transmitted from IoT devices to the cloud is protected and that access to cloud resources is subject to rigorous verification.

Securing IoT devices within Zero Trust architectures is not without its challenges. The diversity of IoT devices, the resource limitations of many devices, and the potential for vulnerabilities in device firmware or software all pose unique security concerns. However, by adhering to Zero Trust principles and tailoring security measures to the specific characteristics of IoT devices, organizations can build robust defenses against emerging threats in the rapidly evolving landscape of IoT security.

Critical infrastructure, which encompasses sectors like energy, transportation, telecommunications, and healthcare, serves as the backbone of modern society. These systems are vital to our daily lives and the functioning of nations, making them attractive targets for malicious actors. Protecting critical infrastructure from advanced threats is a paramount concern in today's interconnected world.

The term "critical infrastructure" refers to the essential facilities, services, and assets that a society relies on for its economic and societal well-being. Examples include power grids that provide electricity to homes and businesses, transportation networks that enable the movement of goods and people, and healthcare systems that deliver life-saving medical services. Disruptions to these systems can have far-reaching consequences, impacting not only the economy but also public safety and national security.

Advanced threats in the context of critical infrastructure encompass a broad spectrum of cyberattacks and physical threats. These threats are typically well-funded, highly sophisticated, and often state-sponsored. They include advanced persistent threats (APTs), nation-state attacks, ransomware campaigns, and coordinated cyberattacks. Protecting critical infrastructure requires a comprehensive approach that addresses both digital and physical vulnerabilities.

In recent years, the integration of critical infrastructure with digital technologies has increased efficiency and connectivity but also introduced new security challenges. The convergence of operational technology (OT) and information technology (IT) in critical infrastructure settings has created a larger attack surface for malicious actors to exploit. Consequently, safeguarding these systems demands a multi-faceted strategy.

Zero Trust principles form a fundamental framework for securing critical infrastructure. In a Zero Trust model, trust is never assumed, and verification is continually required, aligning perfectly with the need to protect critical infrastructure. In essence, Zero Trust posits that all devices, users, and applications, whether internal or external to the network, should be treated as potential threats until they can be verified.

Device Identity Verification is a cornerstone of Zero Trust security within critical infrastructure. Every device connected to critical systems, from industrial control systems (ICS) to IoT devices, should have a unique identity. This identity can be verified through secure certificates, hardware-based identifiers, or other authentication methods. Only devices with verified identities should be granted access to critical infrastructure components.

Granular Policy Enforcement plays a crucial role in controlling access to critical infrastructure assets. Access policies should be defined with precision, granting the minimum level of access required for each device, user, or application to perform its function. This approach significantly reduces the attack surface, limiting the potential damage if a breach were to occur.

Network Segmentation, especially in critical infrastructure environments, is essential for containing and isolating potential threats. Networks should be divided into smaller, isolated segments, with strict access controls applied between them. In this way, even if an attacker gains a foothold in one segment, they will face significant obstacles in moving laterally to other parts of the infrastructure.

Multi-Factor Authentication (MFA) is a robust security measure in protecting critical infrastructure. It requires users and devices to provide multiple forms of verification before gaining access. For example, an employee accessing a power grid control system may need to provide a combination of a password, a smart card, and a biometric scan. MFA adds an extra layer of security, making it more challenging for unauthorized individuals to infiltrate critical systems.

Real-time Monitoring and Threat Detection are paramount in identifying and responding to advanced threats. Advanced security tools that employ machine learning and behavioral analytics can analyze network traffic and system behavior to detect anomalies that may indicate a breach. Rapid response is critical to mitigating damage and preventing further compromise.

Incident Response plans tailored to the unique challenges of critical infrastructure are indispensable. These plans should outline how to respond to cyberattacks, physical threats, and other emergencies. They should involve coordination with relevant authorities, law enforcement, and emergency services to ensure a unified response in times of crisis.

Physical Security measures must not be overlooked when protecting critical infrastructure. Physical attacks, such as sabotage or tampering with equipment, can have devastating consequences. Implementing access controls, surveillance, and intrusion detection systems can enhance physical security.

Regular Security Audits and Penetration Testing are essential for evaluating the resilience of critical infrastructure defenses. These assessments can help identify vulnerabilities and weaknesses before malicious actors can exploit them. Furthermore, they provide an opportunity to fine-tune security measures and enhance preparedness.

Public-Private Collaboration is vital in safeguarding critical infrastructure. Governments, regulatory bodies, and private-sector organizations must work together to share threat intelligence, best practices, and resources. Public-private partnerships can strengthen the collective defense against advanced threats.

Emerging Technologies like artificial intelligence (AI) and machine learning are increasingly used to enhance security in critical infrastructure. AI can analyze massive datasets to identify potential threats more efficiently, while machine learning can adapt to evolving attack techniques. These technologies complement human efforts in defending critical systems.

The consequences of failing to protect critical infrastructure from advanced threats can be severe, ranging from widespread power outages and transportation disruptions to compromised healthcare services. In today's interconnected world, where malicious actors are becoming more sophisticated and persistent, a proactive and layered security approach is imperative. By embracing Zero Trust principles and implementing a comprehensive security strategy that combines digital and physical defenses, critical infrastructure can become more resilient against the ever-evolving landscape of advanced threats.

## Chapter 9: Cyber Resilience Strategies for a Changing Threat Landscape

In the ever-evolving landscape of cybersecurity, one thing is certain: threats will continue to emerge and adapt. As technology advances, so too do the tactics and techniques employed by cybercriminals. To effectively protect our digital assets, we must adapt our cyber resilience measures to these emerging threats.

One of the most notable trends in the realm of cybersecurity is the increasing sophistication of cyberattacks. Today's cybercriminals are well-funded, highly organized, and often backed by nation-states. They employ advanced techniques to infiltrate networks, steal sensitive data, disrupt critical services, and achieve their malicious objectives. These threats come in various forms, from ransomware attacks that encrypt and hold data hostage to supply chain attacks that compromise trusted software vendors.

One of the most significant emerging threats is the rise of ransomware attacks. Ransomware is a type of malware that encrypts a victim's data or locks them out of their systems until a ransom is paid. The attackers often demand payment in cryptocurrency, making it difficult to trace. These attacks have become increasingly targeted and destructive, with cybercriminals targeting critical infrastructure, healthcare organizations, and large corporations. Adapting to this threat requires a multi-pronged approach.

Advanced Authentication Methods are essential in defending against emerging threats. Traditional username and password combinations are no longer sufficient to protect sensitive accounts and systems. Implementing multi-factor authentication (MFA) and biometric authentication can significantly enhance security by requiring users to provide multiple forms of verification. This makes it much harder for attackers to gain unauthorized access, even if they have obtained login credentials.

Threat Intelligence Sharing is crucial in staying ahead of emerging threats. Cybersecurity professionals and organizations should actively participate in information-sharing networks to exchange threat intelligence and best practices. These networks can provide early warnings about new attack techniques and indicators of compromise, enabling proactive defenses.

Zero Trust Security, which challenges the traditional security model that trusts devices and users once they are inside the network, is gaining prominence. In a Zero Trust model, trust is never assumed, and verification is continually required. This approach aligns well with the evolving threat landscape, where attackers often operate within trusted networks using stolen credentials or compromised devices.

Continuous Monitoring and Real-time Threat Detection are vital components of modern cybersecurity. The ability to monitor network traffic, system behavior, and user activities in real-time allows organizations to identify anomalies and potential threats promptly. Advanced threat detection tools, such as those employing machine learning and behavioral analytics, can help detect emerging threats that may evade traditional signature-based defenses.

Employee Training and Awareness is an ongoing effort in building resilience against emerging threats. Phishing attacks, where attackers trick individuals into revealing sensitive information or clicking on malicious links, remain a prevalent vector for cyberattacks. Regularly training employees to recognize phishing attempts and practice safe online behaviors can prevent these attacks from succeeding.

Secure Development Practices are essential, especially for organizations that develop their software or rely on third-party vendors. Ensuring that software is developed with security in mind, following best practices, and regularly patching vulnerabilities can reduce the attack surface and minimize the risk of supply chain attacks.

Supply Chain Security is increasingly critical as attackers target trusted software vendors to compromise their products. Organizations must vet their suppliers and assess the security of the software and hardware components they rely on. Implementing robust supply chain security measures can help mitigate the risk of third-party compromise.

Incident Response Plans that account for emerging threats are essential. Organizations should develop and test incident response plans specific to the types of threats they may face. This includes scenarios for ransomware attacks, data breaches, and other emerging threats. Having a well-defined plan can minimize the impact of an incident and facilitate a coordinated response.

Evolving Regulatory Landscape is also influencing cybersecurity measures. Governments and regulatory bodies are enacting stricter data protection and cybersecurity regulations to hold organizations accountable for safeguarding sensitive information. Adapting to these regulations is not only a legal requirement but also a sound cybersecurity practice.

Cloud Security Challenges have become more pronounced as organizations increasingly rely on cloud services. Ensuring the security of cloud-based data and applications requires a shared responsibility model between cloud providers and their customers. Organizations must configure cloud services securely, apply access controls, and monitor for unauthorized access.

Threat Hunting is a proactive approach to identifying and mitigating emerging threats. Threat hunters actively search for signs of malicious activity within an organization's network, often using advanced tools and techniques. This proactive stance can help uncover threats before they cause significant damage.

Machine Learning and Artificial Intelligence (AI) are playing an increasingly significant role in cybersecurity. These technologies can analyze vast datasets and patterns of behavior to detect emerging threats more efficiently than human analysts. Machine learning models can adapt to evolving attack techniques, making them valuable tools in the fight against cybercrime.

Collaboration with Law Enforcement is crucial when dealing with advanced threats, particularly those involving nation-state actors. Coordinating with law enforcement agencies can help track down and apprehend cybercriminals, leading to their prosecution.

The challenge of adapting cyber resilience measures to emerging threats is ongoing. Cybersecurity is not a static field but an ever-changing one, and organizations must stay vigilant and proactive to protect their digital assets.

By embracing advanced security technologies, fostering a culture of security awareness, and collaborating with industry peers and law enforcement, organizations can enhance their cyber resilience and withstand the evolving threat landscape.

## Chapter 10: The Future of Zero Trust Security: Trends and Innovations

Emerging trends in Zero Trust security are shaping the future of cybersecurity, reflecting the need to adapt to an ever-evolving threat landscape. As organizations recognize the limitations of traditional security models, they are increasingly turning to Zero Trust as a foundational approach to safeguarding their digital assets. This chapter explores the latest developments and emerging trends in the field of Zero Trust security.

One of the most significant trends in Zero Trust is the growing emphasis on identity-centric security. In a Zero Trust model, trust is never assumed based on location or network. Instead, identity becomes the core element for granting access. Emerging technologies, such as continuous authentication and adaptive access controls, are gaining traction. Continuous authentication monitors user behavior in real-time, ensuring that access is granted or revoked based on the user's actions and risk profile. Adaptive access controls dynamically adjust access permissions based on contextual factors, such as the user's location, device, and behavior.

Another prominent trend is the integration of artificial intelligence (AI) and machine learning (ML) into Zero Trust architectures. These technologies enhance threat detection and response capabilities. ML algorithms can analyze vast amounts of data to identify patterns indicative of potential threats, while AI-driven automation can facilitate rapid incident response. Machine learning models can also assess the risk associated with user behavior and network activity, helping organizations make informed access decisions.

The concept of "Zero Trust Network Access" (ZTNA) is gaining momentum. ZTNA focuses on securing remote access and reducing the attack surface. It leverages technologies like Software-Defined Perimeter (SDP) to provide users with granular, role-based access to applications and resources, regardless of their location. ZTNA solutions are particularly relevant in today's remote work environment, where traditional perimeter-based security is less effective.

Cloud-native security has become a critical aspect of Zero Trust. With the widespread adoption of cloud services and the shift to hybrid and multi-cloud environments, organizations need to extend Zero Trust principles to the cloud. Cloud-native security controls, such as cloud access security brokers (CASBs) and cloud workload protection platforms (CWPPs), help organizations enforce policies and secure data in cloud environments. Integrating these controls with Zero Trust frameworks ensures a consistent security posture across on-premises and cloud assets.

The Internet of Things (IoT) introduces new challenges and opportunities for Zero Trust. As IoT devices proliferate in various industries, they create additional entry points for attackers. Zero Trust principles are being extended to IoT by implementing device identity verification, ensuring that only trusted devices can connect to the network. Behavioral analytics also play a role in identifying unusual device behavior that may indicate compromise.

Security automation and orchestration are becoming essential components of Zero Trust strategies. Automation streamlines security operations, allowing for faster threat detection and response. Orchestration ensures that security processes are well-coordinated and efficient. For example, in the event of a detected threat, automated responses can isolate affected devices, update access policies, and trigger alerts to security teams.

The convergence of Zero Trust and DevSecOps is another noteworthy trend. DevSecOps integrates security into the development and deployment pipeline, ensuring that applications are built and deployed with security in mind from the start. Zero Trust principles are applied to application access and data protection, aligning security with the rapid development and delivery cycles of modern software development.

As attackers continue to evolve their tactics, organizations are increasingly adopting threat hunting as a proactive security measure. Threat hunting involves actively searching for signs of compromise within an organization's network. It complements traditional threat detection by focusing on identifying subtle, evasive threats that may evade automated detection mechanisms. Threat hunters leverage advanced analytics and threat intelligence to uncover hidden threats.

Zero Trust is also evolving to address supply chain security. Organizations are recognizing the importance of securing the entire ecosystem of partners, suppliers, and third-party vendors. Zero Trust principles are applied to ensure that only authorized entities and devices can access critical systems and data, even when they originate from external organizations.

In summary, emerging trends in Zero Trust security reflect the ongoing evolution of cybersecurity practices. Identity-centric security, AI and ML integration, Zero Trust Network Access (ZTNA), cloud-native security, IoT security, automation, DevSecOps, threat hunting, and supply chain security are all contributing to the advancement of Zero Trust as a comprehensive and adaptive security framework. These trends are essential for organizations seeking to stay ahead of the ever-changing threat landscape and secure their digital assets effectively.

Innovations are at the forefront of shaping the future of Zero Trust, propelling this security paradigm into new frontiers of cyber defense. As the threat landscape continues to evolve, Zero Trust remains a dynamic and adaptable approach to safeguarding digital assets. This chapter explores some of the groundbreaking innovations that are shaping the future of Zero Trust security.

**1. Quantum-Safe Encryption:**
One of the most anticipated innovations in Zero Trust security is the development of quantum-safe encryption. Quantum computers have the potential to break existing encryption algorithms, posing a significant threat to data security. To address this, researchers are working on encryption methods that are resistant to quantum attacks. These quantum-safe encryption techniques will play a crucial role in the future of Zero Trust, ensuring that data remains protected even in the age of quantum computing.

**2. Zero Trust Analytics:**
Zero Trust analytics is an emerging field that leverages advanced machine learning and behavioral analytics to enhance security. By continuously monitoring user and network behavior, Zero Trust analytics can identify anomalies and potential threats in real-time. These analytics provide organizations with a proactive approach to security, allowing them to respond swiftly to emerging threats.

**3. Continuous Authentication and Biometrics:**
The future of Zero Trust will see an even greater reliance on continuous authentication and biometric technologies. Passwords are increasingly vulnerable to breaches, and multi-factor authentication (MFA) is becoming the norm. Biometric authentication methods, such as facial recognition

and fingerprint scanning, offer a more secure and convenient way to verify user identities. Continuous authentication ensures that access is continuously validated based on user behavior, reducing the risk of unauthorized access.

**4. Decentralized Identity:**

Decentralized identity is a revolutionary concept that puts individuals in control of their digital identities. Instead of relying on centralized identity providers, users can manage their digital identities using blockchain technology. This innovation aligns with Zero Trust principles by giving individuals greater control over who can access their data and under what conditions.

**5. Secure Access Service Edge (SASE):**

Secure Access Service Edge (SASE) is an emerging architecture that combines network security and wide-area networking (WAN) capabilities into a single cloud-based service. SASE is highly compatible with Zero Trust principles, as it provides secure, on-demand access to applications and resources, regardless of the user's location. This convergence of networking and security is expected to play a pivotal role in the future of Zero Trust.

**6. Immutable Infrastructure:**

Immutable infrastructure is a concept that involves building and deploying infrastructure that cannot be modified once it's in production. This approach reduces the risk of configuration errors and unauthorized changes that can lead to security vulnerabilities. Immutable infrastructure aligns with Zero Trust by ensuring that the environment remains consistent and secure throughout its lifecycle.

**7. Post-Quantum Cryptography:**

In addition to quantum-safe encryption, post-quantum cryptography is another area of innovation. Post-quantum cryptographic algorithms are designed to withstand attacks from both classical and quantum computers. These algorithms will be crucial for securing communications and data in the post-quantum era.

**8. Threat Intelligence Integration:**

The future of Zero Trust will see deeper integration of threat intelligence into security operations. Threat intelligence feeds can provide real-time information about emerging threats and vulnerabilities. By incorporating threat intelligence into their Zero Trust frameworks, organizations can make more informed access decisions and respond rapidly to evolving threats.

**9. User and Entity Behavior Analytics (UEBA):**

User and Entity Behavior Analytics (UEBA) is an advanced form of behavioral analytics that focuses on both user and entity behavior. UEBA can detect anomalous behavior not only in users but also in devices, applications, and services. This holistic approach to behavior analysis enhances threat detection and reduces the risk of insider threats.

**10. Cybersecurity Mesh:**

The concept of a cybersecurity mesh envisions a distributed security model that adapts to the dynamic nature of digital environments. This mesh architecture provides security that is woven into every interaction and connection, offering protection at the edge, in the cloud, and within applications. It aligns seamlessly with Zero Trust principles, emphasizing the need for security to be pervasive and adaptive.

**11. Autonomous Security:**

Artificial intelligence and machine learning are driving the development of autonomous security solutions. These systems can analyze vast amounts of data, detect threats, and respond autonomously in real-time. Autonomous security aligns with Zero Trust by enhancing threat detection and response capabilities while reducing the burden on security teams.

In summary, the future of Zero Trust security is marked by a series of innovations that promise to bolster its effectiveness in an increasingly complex threat landscape. Quantum-safe encryption, Zero Trust analytics, continuous authentication, decentralized identity, SASE, immutable infrastructure, post-quantum cryptography, threat intelligence integration, UEBA, cybersecurity mesh, and autonomous security are all contributing to the evolution of Zero Trust as a robust and future-proof security framework. As organizations embrace these innovations, they will be better equipped to defend against emerging cyber threats and protect their digital assets in the years to come.

## Conclusion

In the world of cybersecurity, where threats are ever-evolving and the stakes are higher than ever, the journey through the pages of "Zero Trust Security: Building Cyber Resilience & Robust Security Postures" has been both enlightening and empowering. This comprehensive bundle of books, comprising "Zero Trust Security: A Beginner's Guide to Building Cyber Resilience," "Zero Trust Security in Practice: Strategies for Building Robust Security Postures," "Advanced Zero Trust Architectures: Cyber Resilience and Expert Strategies," and "Mastering Zero Trust Security: Cyber Resilience in a Changing Landscape," has provided readers with a deep dive into the realm of Zero Trust security.

As we conclude this journey, it is clear that Zero Trust is not just a buzzword or a fleeting trend—it is a philosophy, a mindset, and a strategy that has become indispensable in safeguarding digital assets and information. This bundle of books has taken readers on a progressive expedition, starting with the fundamentals and culminating in advanced strategies that will fortify any organization's cyber resilience.

In "Zero Trust Security: A Beginner's Guide to Building Cyber Resilience," readers were introduced to the foundational principles of Zero Trust, challenging the traditional perimeter-based security model. By adopting a "never trust, always verify" approach, beginners gained insights into how to construct the initial building blocks of cyber resilience.

"Zero Trust Security in Practice: Strategies for Building Robust Security Postures" then guided readers through the practical implementation of Zero Trust. Real-world scenarios and case studies illustrated how organizations can put theory into action. It became evident that Zero Trust is not a one-size-fits-all solution; instead, it is adaptable and scalable, allowing organizations to tailor their security postures to their unique needs.

"Advanced Zero Trust Architectures: Cyber Resilience and Expert Strategies" elevated the discussion by delving into the intricacies of advanced Zero Trust architectures. Readers explored cutting-edge concepts like micro-segmentation, immutable infrastructure, and decentralized identity. The book demonstrated that the journey toward cyber resilience is an ongoing process, and innovation is the key to staying ahead of emerging threats.

Finally, "Mastering Zero Trust Security: Cyber Resilience in a Changing Landscape" addressed the evolving nature of cybersecurity. In a world where threats are constantly morphing and digital environments are ever-shifting, mastering Zero Trust is not a destination but a continuous pursuit. The book empowered readers with the knowledge and strategies to adapt and thrive in this dynamic landscape.

As we bid farewell to this bundle of books, we are reminded that cyber resilience is not just about implementing the latest tools and technologies. It is about instilling a culture of security within organizations, where trust is earned, not assumed, and where vigilance is a constant. The path to cyber resilience is a collaborative effort, involving individuals, teams, and organizations working together to protect the digital assets that have become the lifeblood of the modern world.

In closing, "Zero Trust Security: Building Cyber Resilience & Robust Security Postures" has equipped readers with the knowledge, strategies, and insights needed to navigate the complex and ever-changing landscape of cybersecurity. It is our hope that the principles and practices outlined in these books will serve as a beacon of guidance, enabling organizations to build robust security postures and strengthen their cyber resilience in the face of tomorrow's challenges. May your journey toward cyber resilience be fortified by the wisdom contained within these pages, and may your digital world remain secure and resilient in an era where trust is a precious commodity.